The Thread That Runs So True

BY

JESSE STUART

CHARLES SCRIBNER'S SONS, NEW YORK

TO THE SCHOOL TEACHERS
OF AMERICA

Charles Scribner's Sons
Macmillan Publishing Company
866 Third Avenue, New York, NY 10022

Library of Congress Catalog Card Number 58-12517

ISBN 0-684-71904-5

Macmillan books are available at special discounts for bulk purchases
for sales promotions, premiums, fund-raising, or educational use.
For details, contact:

Special Sales Director
Macmillan Publishing Company
866 Third Avenue
New York, NY 10022

34 35 36 37 38 39 40

Printed in the United States of America

ELEVEN years ago when I began writing *The Thread That Runs So True*, I said teaching was the greatest profession in the world. Not too many people agreed with me then, but, as the years have passed, many have changed their minds until they are in full accord with this statement.

When I began teaching, the schoolroom was not supposed to be a very interesting place, and this great profession was looked upon by many as being something of secondary importance. Now, the interest of all America is focused upon America's schools and their importance to our survival as a nation.

No one can ever tell me that education, rightly directed without propaganda, cannot change the individual, community, county, state, and the world for the better. It can. There must be health, science, technology, the arts, and conservation of all worthwhile things that aid humanity upon this earth. And there must, above all, be character education.

As a teacher in a one-room school, where I taught all eight grades, and then high school, as a principal of rural and city high schools and superintendent of city and county school systems, I learned by experience that teaching is the greatest profession there is, and that the classroom can be made one of the most exciting places on earth for young, middle-aged, and older people to improve themselves for more useful and richer living.

I left teaching, the profession I loved, because I thought I couldn't make enough to live. I raised sheep, lectured, wrote novels and made money, but my heart was always in the schoolroom.

The ten books I wrote before *The Thread That Runs So True* are now out of print, but this book has lived on because it is created of the things that are eternal in the destiny of the human race. Each year its sale has gradually increased. I have heard about it from parents of all strata of American life, and from youth and fellow teachers; during the regular school terms I have received on an average ten letters per day from high school and college students.

I am grateful for this great response. These letters affirm my belief that the vast majority of people are essentially the same, that we desire most of all to improve ourselves through learning, books, and contacts with others, that we strive in youth and throughout our lives for continued personal improvement.

One thing I have learned in my contacts with youth and older people as well is that when I am enthusiastic about my teaching, they are enthusiastic. When I am depressed, they seem to be that way too. Their feelings seem to rise as high as my feelings are high or as low as mine are low. Therefore I have tried to be as enthusiastic as I can about any subject I teach.

I have learned, too, to be honest with them and never to try to seem more nearly perfect than I really am. If I make a mistake and one of my students corrects me, I thank him. I know that he will ever be alert from now on to catch me in another mistake. He knows that I'm not infallible and that we are working together as a team in our living and learning. I respect him and his student rights, and he respects me and my teacher rights. I am slow to condemn him when he fails, and I commend the good he has done if and when he tries.

I know as surely as I live and breathe the positive proof of what education can do for a man. That proof is in this individual. What would I be doing without the education I have? I would not have written this book if I had not had an education. My father and mother with their good untrained minds, their sterling character, would have done greater things in their much too brief lives had they had only eighth grade educations. I wonder what they would have done had each had a high school education? Yes, with college training? But they knew the value of an education because they didn't have it, and therefore they had the good judgment to insist on their children going to school.

Yes, the struggle of a youth to amount to something worth- while is the greatest objective he can have in life. My parents and my teachers inspired me. They changed my life. And I felt I could repay them by inspiring other youth. This means more to me than all the money in the world.

I am proud that I have been a teacher and am one today. Teaching is something above and beyond teaching lessons and facts from books. It is this but more too. It is helping a youth to find a path of his own that will eventually lead him through fields of frustration and modern pitfalls of destruction until he finds himself.

It is so true that we do not live by bread alone. In any youth who has ever come to school to me I have seen something essentially good, a potential that needs to be developed. It is the teacher's duty to develop this good potential in each young individual. And teachers have done it too. Make no mistake about it. Unfortunately there is no way to measure all the good our teachers have developed in youth.

Once a young high school principal faced an assembly of teachers and administrators and his first words were, "I would not be here before you if it were not for one who is sitting back in your midst. I don't know where I would be."

It was hard for me to restrain the feeling that passed through me. My mind flashed back to his broken home, no one to help him, and how I took him to college, gave him five dollars—all I could spare. I left him stringing beans in the college dining room. He was just one of many. How can any monetary payment ever equal such compliment?

And I am firm in my belief that a teacher lives on and on through his students. I will live if my teaching is inspirational, good, and stands firm for good values and character training. Tell me how can good teaching ever die? Good teaching is forever and the teacher is immortal.

September, 1958   JESSE STUART

Contents

"*If we work upon marble, it will perish; if we work upon brass, time will efface it; if we rear temples, they will crumble into dust; but if we work upon immortal minds, if we imbue them with principles, with just fear of God and love of our fellow-men, we engrave on those tablets something which will brighten to all eternity.*"

DANIEL WEBSTER

PART I

THE NEEDLE'S EYE THAT DOES SUPPLY

1

MONDAY morning when I started on my way to school, I had with me Don Conway, a pupil twenty years of age, who had never planned to enter school again. I was the new teacher here at Lonesome Valley and I didn't know what kind of brains he had. He had left school when he was in the fourth grade. But I did know that he had two good fists and that he would be on my side. All day Sunday while I had worked at the schoolhouse, I was trying to think of a plan so I could stay at Lonesome Valley School. I knew I had to stay. I knew if one had to go it would be Guy Hawkins. I might have to use my head a little but that was why I had it.

It had taken a lot of persuasion to get Don Conway to return to school. He had planned to get married after his tobacco crop was sold. But I explained the value of an education to him in dollars and cents. I told him I would teach him how to measure a field and figure the number of acres, how to figure the number of bushels in a wagon bed, cornbin, and how many cubic yards of dirt one would have to remove to dig a cellar or a well. Don Conway was interested in this type of knowledge. I told him no man should be married and live on a farm unless he knew these simple things, for he could easily be cheated the rest of his days. I was interested in his learning these things all right, but I was interested in something else.

Don, his two small brothers, his sister Vaida, and I went to school together. I congratulated John Conway for sending all his children but one. I told him he should set the example for other farmers on the creek. It would have been hard on John to try to worm and sucker his ten acres of tobacco and care for his other crops if Flossie, his older daughter, had not volunteered to help him. And Bertha, his wife, assured him she would divide her time between the housework and work in the field.

Flossie, eighteen years old, who had left school six years ago, would gladly have started back to school if I had insisted. But I knew John and Bertha had to have someone left to help them. I insisted and almost begged Don to return to school when he and I were sitting on the porch late one Sunday afternoon and Ova Salyers and Guy Hawkins rode past on their horses. They glanced toward the porch for their first look at the new teacher, never spoke but rode silently down the road.

Don Conway looked at Guy Hawkins and Ova Salyers and then he looked at me. He didn't ask me how old I was. I didn't tell him in eighteen more days I would be seventeen. One had to be eighteen before he was old enough to teach school. Don Conway knew the fate of my sister when she was employed to teach the Lonesome Valley School. He knew how Guy Hawkins had blacked her eyes with his fists, had whipped her before the Lonesome Valley pupils. She was a fair-haired, beautiful blue-eyed girl of nineteen when she had come to Lonesome Valley. She went home a nervous wreck, long before her school was finished. After I'd seen the way my sister was beaten up, I begged to go to Lonesome Valley. My parents would have none of it. They thought if I went hunting trouble I would get more than my share.

But I made the mistake at Landsburgh High School of going to the wrong room. I'd forgotten the Greenwood County rural teachers were having "teacher's examination" in our American literature room. And when Superintendent Harley Staggers, who didn't know all his teachers, mistook me for a rural teacher an idea came to me. I knew the school I wanted if I passed the examination. I made a second-class certificate.

Then I had John Hampton, a rural teacher and friend, contact John Conway and get the school for me. Superintendent Staggers didn't want me to go to Lonesome Valley. But there wasn't anything he could do about it after John Conway, Lonesome Valley District School trustee, recommended me. That was why I was here to teach school.

When Don and I reached the schoolhouse, at least thirty-five pupils were there waiting outside. Guy Hawkins and Ova Salyers were standing together near the coalhouse with their torn-and-tattered, first-grade books. They looked out of place with the other pupils. They were larger than either Don or me. They were older too. They looked at me when I said "Good morning" to them. Many of the pupils turned shyly away and did not speak. They were waiting for the schoolhouse to be unlocked so they could rush in and select their seats. Each had his dinner basket or bucket in his hand. The majority of them carried tattered-edged and backless books.

I thought we had reached the schoolhouse very early. It wasn't eight o'clock and school didn't start until eight-thirty. The July sun hadn't dried the dew from parts of the valley yet; dew was ascending in white formless clouds from the tobacco, cane, and corn patches. But the people in Lonesome Valley went to bed early and got up early. All of the pupils in Lonesome Valley came from farms.

The girls wore pigtails down their backs tied with all colors of ribbons. They wore clean print dresses and they were barefooted. Not one pupil in my school, large or small, boy or girl, wore a pair of shoes. I'd never seen in my life so many barefooted people, young, middle-aged, and old, as I had seen in Lonesome Valley. Wearing gloves on their hands in summer was the same to them as wearing shoes on their feet. They just didn't do it.

"Well, I'm opening the door," I said, to break the silence of my pupils.

When I opened the door they laughed, screamed, and raced for the schoolhouse. Their shyness was gone now. There was a mad scramble to get inside the schoolhouse for seats. Then there was some discussion among them as to who would sit by whom. Girls had selected their seatmates. There were a few controversies and a few hurt feelings. Often two pupils wanted to sit by the same person. No trouble with Guy and Ova. They walked inside reluctantly and sat down in a seat on the boys' side farthest from my desk.

"Now let me make an announcement to you before school starts," I said, after walking up to my desk. "There will not any longer be a girls' side and a boys' side. Sit anyplace you want to."

They looked strangely at one another. Not one boy would cross to the girls' side. Not one girl would cross to the boys' side. In Lonesome Valley it was hard to break a teaching tradition more than a century old. But after I had been to high school, where there were no such things as a girls' side and a boys' side in a schoolroom, I didn't see why it wouldn't work in Lonesome Valley. Little did I dream that what I had said here would make news in Lonesome Valley, that it would be talked about by everybody, and that many would criticize me and call my school "a courting school." Boys and girls sitting together? Who had ever heard tell of it?

The schedules were not made out for the teachers at the Superintendent's office. No one had ever heard of such routine. Each teacher had to make his own schedule. And that was what I had done long before I left home for Lonesome Valley. I knew what I had to teach and I went to work, making out my schedule and dividing my time as accurately as possible for my six hours of actual work. I had to conduct fifty-four classes in this time, for I had pupils from the chart class to and including the eighth grade.

When I walked down the broad center aisle and pulled on the bell rope, the soft tones sounded over the tobacco, corn, and cane fields and the lush green valley; with the ringing of this bell, my school had begun. I knew that not half the pupils in the school census were here. There were 104 in the school census, of school age, for whom the state sent per capita money to pay for their schooling. I had thirty-five pupils. I thought the soft tones of this school bell through the rising mists and over warm cultivated fields where parents and their children were trying to eke out a bare subsistence from the soil might bring back warm memories of happy school days. For I remembered the tones of the Plum Grove school bell, and how I had longed to be back in school after I had quit at the age of nine to work for twenty-five cents a day to help support my family. If I could have, I would have returned to school when I heard the Plum Grove bell. So I rang the bell and called the Lonesome Valley pupils back to school—back to books and play. For going to school had never been work to me. It had been recreation. And I hoped it would be the same for my pupils in Lonesome Valley.

During my first day all I did was enroll my pupils in their classes, call them up front to the recitation seat and give them assignments in the few textbooks they possessed. At that time, the textbooks were not furnished by the state. Each pupil had to furnish his own. If he didn't, there was a meager allotment of cash set aside by the Greenwood County School Board of Education to buy books for those whose parents were not able to buy them. I knew that many would buy books after the tobacco crops had been sold or the cane had been made into sorghum and sold. These were the money crops in Lonesome Valley.

While enrolling my pupils, I made some temporary changes in seating arrangements. I often put a pupil without books beside a pupil with books, if they were in the same grade. As I enrolled the pupils, I tried to remember and familiarize myself with each name. I tried to get acquainted with my pupils. I found them very shy. I was a stranger among them, though I had grown up under similar circumstances with equivalent opportunities. There were approximately thirty miles separating their Lonesome Valley from my W-Hollow. But I was a stranger here.

When I dismissed my pupils for the first recess, a fifteen-minute period between the beginning of the school day and the noon hour, I was amazed to see them all jump up from their seats at the same time and try to be the first out of the house. Big pupils pushed past the little ones and there was so much confusion and disorder, I knew they would never leave the room like this again. Why were they running? I wondered. I had a few minutes' work to do before I could join them on the playground. Before I had finished this work, I heard the tenor of their uneven voices singing these familiar words:

> The needle's eye that does supply,
> The thread that runs so true,
> Many a beau, have I let go,
> Because I wanted you.
>
> Many a dark and stormy night,
> When I went home with you,
> I stumped my toe and down I go,
> Because I wanted you.

I walked to the door and watched them. They had formed a circle, hand in hand, and around and around they walked and sang these words while two pupils held their locked hands high for the circle to pass under. Suddenly the two standing— one inside the circle and one outside—let their arms drop down to take a pupil from the line. Then the circle continued to march and sing while the two took the pupil aside and asked him whether he would rather be a train or an automobile. If the pupil said he'd rather be an automobile, he stood on one side; if a train, he stood on the other of the two that held hands. And when they had finished taking everybody from the circle, the two groups faced each other, lined up behind their captains. Each put his arms around the pupil in front of him and locked his hands. The first line to break apart or to be pulled forward lost the game.

Fifteen minutes were all too short for them to play "the needle's eye." I let recess extend five minutes so they could finish their second game. It had been a long time since I had played this game at Plum Grove. These words brought back pleasant memories. They fascinated me. And my Lonesome Valley pupils played this game with all the enthusiasm and spirit they had! They put themselves into it—every pupil in school. Not one stood by to watch. Because they were having the time of their lives, I hated to ring the bell for "books." I lined them up, smaller pupils in front and larger ones behind, and had them march back into the schoolroom.

Guy Hawkins and Ova Salyers were the last on the line. When they came inside the door, Guy asked permission to go with Ova after a bucket of water. We didn't have a well or a cistern at the schoolhouse. We had to get water from some home in the district. I told them they could go but not to be gone too long, for the pupils, after running and playing, were thirsty. The July sun beat down on the galvanized tin roof. This made the pine boards so hot inside they oozed resin. We raised all the windows but still the place was hot as the room in which I slept at Conways'. My little room upstairs with a high unscreened window of only one sash didn't cool off until about midnight. Then, I could go to sleep.

I knew the reason that all the rural schools had to begin in July, though the farmers had objected because they needed their children at home to help with farm work. Rural schools began early because coal was an added expense for winter months. The county schools all over the state had barely enough funds to keep them going, and if they could have school during the hot months it sheared away a great expense from their budgets. But it was hard on the children and the teachers.

The first bucket of water Guy and Ova brought didn't last five minutes. The majority of the pupils were still thirsty. I sent Guy and Ova back for more, telling them to borrow another bucket. I sent them in a hurry. And I knew I had to do something about the dipper problem. At Plum Grove, too, we had all drunk from the same dipper, but when I went to Landsburgh High School I was taught something different.

So I made "an important announcement" to my pupils. I told them each had to bring his own drinking cup the next day. It could be a glass, teacup, gourd, dipper, just so it was his own and no one else drank from it. My pupils looked at one another and laughed as if my announcement was funny. But I had seen sweat run from their faces into the dipper, and the next in line put his mouth where the sweat had run or where the other pupil had put his lips. I noticed, too, several pupils had put the rim up near the handle to their mouths, so I knew they didn't like to drink after the others.

On Tuesday they brought their dippers, tin cups, and glasses. Only a few had forgotten, and I stopped with my busy schedule of class work long enough to teach them how to make paper drinking cups. I showed them how to take a clean sheet of paper from a tablet and fold it to hold water. I gave them a lecture about drinking water. I told them never to drink from a stream. I told them how I had gotten typhoid fever twice: once from drinking cool water from a little stream, and once from drinking in a river. I had my pupils use the dipper to dip water from the bucket into their cups. They accepted my suggestion gladly. I also borrowed another water bucket from Bertha Conway and brought it to school. The one bucket allowed me for thirty-five pupils (and there would be more as soon as the farmers were through with their summer plowing and worming and suckering tobacco, stripping their cane and boiling the juice to syrup) was not enough. They played hard at recess and noon and in the "time of books" sat in a schoolroom almost as hot as a stove oven.

Tuesday when I stood beside Guy Hawkins and showed him how to hold his book when he read, my pupils laughed until I had to stop them. I was trying to teach Guy to read as he stumbled over the simple words in the *First Grade Reader*. My pupils laughed because Guy was taller by two inches than I was and heavier. He had a bullneck almost as large as his head, and a prominent jaw. His beard was so heavy that he had to shave every day.

Wouldn't Coach Wilson like to have him! I thought. He would make the best tackle Landsburgh High School ever had.

Guy had big hands. His right hand covered the back of his *First Reader*. And he had powerful arms. The muscles rippled under his clean blue-faded shirt. I measured him as I stood beside him. I knew that if I ever had to fight him, it would be a fight. And I knew that I wasn't going to fight him unless he forced me to fight. He was more powerful physically than I was. And the outcome of our fight might depend on the one who successfully landed the first haymaker to the other's jaw.

Then I looked down at Ova Salyers sitting on the recitation seat beside me. Another tackle for Coach Wilson, I thought. This pair would be a coach's dream. Pity some coach doesn't have 'em instead of me.

If it were not for these two young men, I wouldn't have had any trouble disciplining my school. All the other pupils played hard and they were obedient. They would have been good in their class work if they had had the proper training. I had ten-year-old pupils just starting to school. Nineteen-year-olds in the first grade. Fourteen-year-olds in the second grade. I had one twelve-year-old girl in the eighth grade. They had not been promoted because they had never attended a full school term. They had taken the same grade over and over until they could stand and recite some of the beginning lessons from memory.

"Guy, how long have you been in the first grade?" I asked.

"Oh, about eight years," he laughed.

"You're not going to be in it any longer," I said.

"Why?" he asked.

"Because I'm going to promote you," I said. "Tomorrow you start in the second grade."

Then I had Ova Salyers read. He had also been in the first grade eight years. I promoted him.

When these young men sat down again I saw them look at each other and laugh as if they thought my promoting them was funny. I knew they accepted school as a joke, a place to come and see people. A place where they could join a circle of smaller children and play "the needle's eye." And I knew there wasn't much chance of reasoning with either one. But I had a feeling that time would come. I didn't believe they were coming to school for any good. I felt that Guy was waiting his chance for me. I was not going to take any chances; I was going to give him the full benefit of the doubt.

I had doubted that my second-class certificate and my three years in high school qualified me to teach school. But now, when I measured my knowledge with my pupils', I knew without a doubt that I was an educated man. I had never known that youth could be so poorly trained in school as were my Lonesome Valley pupils. But unless I was chased out of the school, as my sister had been, I was determined to give them the best I had.

2

Just across Lonesome Creek, at the other end of the foot log, was a small country store. It wasn't more than half as large as our coalhouse. All the merchandise in the store would not have filled a wagon bed. The store was not more than ten feet long and six feet wide. But Nancy Cochran, a slender, blue-eyed, fair-complexioned girl with charcoal-black hair, ran the store. She sold pencils, paper, ink, pens, and pen points, crackers, cakes, and candy to the Lonesome Valley School pupils. From my desk I could look through the window on my left during school hours. She would be sitting on the small store porch, playing her guitar and singing "Red Wing," "Red River Valley," "Listen to the Mockingbird," "Down by the Old Mill Stream," "Barbara Allen," and "The Needle's Eye." When she played and sang "The Needle's Eye," I almost had to discontinue my class periods. I always had to stop my pupils from tapping their feet. They did it unconsciously. They didn't tap their feet for any other tune, but when she played "The Needle's Eye" their dirty bare feet all over the room marked time to the music.

I loved to hear music, especially a guitar, as well as any of my pupils. But not when I was trying to teach school. Nancy's singing the words of these old songs distracted my thoughts. Every time I looked from my window toward her, she was looking toward my school, playing and singing as if directly to me. I rarely saw a customer except my pupils go inside her store. I didn't want to say anything but I knew I was going to have to if I taught Lonesome Valley School. Monday through Friday of the first week she played during school hours. And when I went to Conways' after school, Flossie played the old songs on her steel guitar and sang until we went to bed. That was too much guitar music and too much singing.

So on Friday afternoon after school was out, I dropped into the store to see Nancy Cochran. She was sitting in a com-

fortable armchair with her guitar across her lap. When I entered she arose, laid her guitar upon the small candy show-
case, and asked me very politely if there was anything I wanted.
She spoke with soft words and she was beautiful to see. Immediately I was sorry for the hard looks I had given her
from my window. Now I wondered if she had seen me frown-
ing at her and I hoped she hadn't.

"I'd like to have a bottle of ink," I said.

I bought the bottle of ink, some paper, and a pencil. I
decided that my trustee could help me here. It was not my duty
to tell her she was disturbing my school. I would tell John
Conway and he could ease a suggestion to her that would not
disturb her. For I knew she felt very kindly toward me. She,
too, was about eighteen years of age, about as old as Flossie
Conway. John Conway was the man to do it. Then there wouldn't
be any talk.

3

The following Monday I had stayed at the schoolhouse
to do some work on my school records, and Don Conway had
gone home with his sister and brothers. This was the first
afternoon I had stayed at school after all my pupils had gone.
The room was very silent and I was busy working when I heard
soft footsteps walking around the building. I looked through
the window on my left and I saw Guy Hawkins' head. His
uncombed, tousled hair was ruffled by the Lonesome Valley
wind.

I wondered why he was coming back. I wondered if he
had forgotten something.

Then I realized this was the first time he had been able
to catch me by myself. And I remembered a few other incidents
in Greenwood County's rural schools where a pupil had come
back to the school when the teacher was there alone, and had
beaten hell out of him. I could recall three or four such incidents. But I didn't have time to think about them. Not now.
Guy came in the door with his cap in his hand. I didn't want

him to see me looking up at him, but I did see him coming down the broad middle aisle, taking long steps and swinging his big arms. He looked madder than any man or animal I had ever seen. He walked up to my desk and stood silently before me.

"Did you forget something, Guy?" I asked.

"Naw, I've never forgot nothin'," he reminded me.

"Then what do you want?" I asked.

"Whip you," he said.

"Why do you want to whip me?" I asked him.

"I didn't like your sister," he said. "You know what I done to her."

"Yes, I know what you did to her," I said.

"I'm a-goin' to do the same thing to you," he threatened.

"Why do you want to fight me?" I asked him. I dropped my pencil and stood up facing him.

"I don't like you," he said. "I don't like teachers. I said never another person with your name would teach this school. Not as long as I'm here."

"It's too bad you don't like me or my name," I said, my temper rising.

"I won't be satisfied until I've whipped you," he said.

"Can you go to another school?" I asked him. "The Valley School is not too far from where you live."

"Naw, naw," he shouted, "if anybody leaves, you'll leave. I was in Lonesome Valley first. And I ain't a-goin' to no other school because of you!"

"Then there's nothing left for us to do but fight," I said. "I've come to teach this school and I'm going to teach it!"

"Maybe you will," he snarled. "I have you penned in this schoolhouse. I have you where I want you. You can't get away! You can't run! I aim to whip you right where you stand! It's the same place where I whipped your sister!"

I looked at his face. It was red as a sliced beet. Fire danced in his pale-blue, elongated eyes. I knew Guy Hawkins meant every word he said. I knew I had to face him and to fight. There was no other way around. I had to think quickly. How would I fight him?

"Will you let me take my necktie off?" I said, remembering I'd been choked by a fellow pulling my necktie once in a fight.

"Yep, take off that purty tie," he said. "You might get it dirty by the time I'm through with you."

I slowly took off my tie.

"Roll up the sleeves of your white shirt too," he said. "But they'll be dirty by the time I sweep this floor up with you."

"Sweep the floor up with me," I said.

He shot out his long arm but I ducked. I felt the wind from his thrust against my ear.

I mustn't let him clinch me, I thought.

Then he came back with another right and I ducked his second lick. I came around with my first lick—a right—and planted it on his jaw, not a good lick but just enough to jar him and make him madder. When he rushed at me, I side-stepped. He missed. By the time he had turned around, I caught him a haymaker on the chin that reeled him. Then I followed up with another lick as hard as I had ever hit a man. Yet I didn't bring him down. He came back for more. But he didn't reach me this time. He was right. I did get my shirt dirty. I dove through the air with a flying tackle. I hit him beneath the knees. I'd tackled like this in football. I'd tackled hard. And I never tackled anybody harder than Guy. His feet went from under him, and I scooted past on the pine floor. I'd tackled him so quickly when he had expected me to come back at him with my fists, that he went down so fast he couldn't catch with his hands. His face hit flat against the floor and his nose was flattened. The blood spurted as he started to get up.

I let him get to his feet. I wondered if I should. For I knew it was either him or me. One of us had to whip. When he did get to his feet after that terrible fall, I waded into him. I hit fast and I hit hard. He swung wild. His fingernail took a streak of hide from my neck and left a red mark that smarted and the blood oozed through. I pounded his chin. I caught him on the beardy jaw. I reeled him back and followed up. I gave him a left to the short ribs while my right in a split second caught his mouth. Blood spurted again. Yet he was not through. But I knew I had him.

"Had enough?" I panted.

He didn't answer. I didn't ask him a second time. I hit him hard enough to knock two men down. I reeled him back against a seat. I followed up. I caught him with a haymaker under the chin and laid him across the desk. Then he rolled to the floor. He lay there with blood running from his nose and mouth. His eyes were rolled back. I was nearly out of breath. My hands ached. My heart pounded. If this is teaching school! I thought. If this goes with it! Then I remembered vaguely I had asked for it. I'd asked for this school. I would take no other.

Guy Hawkins lay there sprawled on the unswept floor. His blood was mingled with the yellow dirt carried into the schoolroom by seventy bare feet. I went back and got the water bucket. With a clean handkerchief, I washed blood from his mouth and nose. I couldn't wash it from his shirt. I put cool water to his forehead.

I worked over a pupil—trying to bring him back to his senses—who only a few hours before I had stood beside and tried to teach how to pronounce words when he read. "Don't stumble over them like a horse stumbles over frozen ground," I told him, putting it in a language he would understand. I had promoted him. I'd sent Guy and Ova after water when other pupils had wanted to go. On their way to get water, I knew they chewed tobacco and thought they were putting something over on me. I had known I couldn't allow them to use tobacco at school. I had known the time would eventually come. But I wanted to put it off as long as I could. Now I had whipped him and I wondered as I looked at him stretched on the floor how I'd done it. He was really knocked out for the count. I knew the place where we had fought would always be marked. It was difficult to remove bloodstain from pine wood. It would always be there, this reminder, as long as I taught school at Lonesome Valley.

When Guy Hawkins came to his senses, he looked up at me. I was applying the wet cool handkerchief to his head. When he started to get up, I helped him to his feet.

"Mr. Stuart, I really got it poured on me," he admitted. "You're some fighter."

This was the first time he had ever called me "Mr. Stuart." I had heard, but had pretended not to hear, him call me "Old

Jess" every time my back was turned. He had never before, when he had spoken directly to me, called me anything.

"I'm not much of a fighter until I have to fight, Guy," I .aid. "You asked for it. There was no way around. I had to fight you."

"I know it," he said. "I've had in mind to whip you ever since I heard you's a-goin' to teach this school. But you win. You winned fair too," he honestly admitted. "I didn't think you could hit like that."

Guy was still weak. His nose and mouth kept bleeding. He didn't have a handkerchief and I gave him a clean one.

"Think you can make it home all right, Guy?"

"I think so," he said.

He walked slower from the schoolhouse than he had walked in. I was too upset to do any more work on my record-book. I stood by the window and watched him walk across the schoolyard, then across the foot log and down the Lonesome Creek Road until he went around the bend and was out of sight. Something told me to watch for Ova Salyers. He might return to attack me. I waited several minutes and Ova didn't come. Guy had come to do the job alone.

I felt better now that the fight was over, and I got the broom and swept the floor. I had quickly learned that the rural teacher was janitor as well, and that his janitor work was one of the important things in his school. I believed, after my brief experience, that the schoolhouse should be made a place of beauty, prettier and cleaner than any of the homes the pupils came from so they would love the house and the surroundings, and would think of it as a place of beauty and would want to keep it that way.

The floor was easy to sweep. But it was difficult to clean blood from the floor. I carried a coal bucket of sand and poured it on the blood and then shoveled up the sand and carried it out. I had the blood from the floor. Then I scrubbed the place but the stain was there. I could not get it from the oily, soft pine wood. I knew this was one day in my teaching career I would never forget.

4

NEWS traveled fast in Lonesome Valley. When I reached Conways' they had gathered in the living-room waiting to see me after the fight. They had waited to see if I would be disfigured. They were surprised to see me in one piece after I had fought Guy Hawkins.

"Ova started to go back with Guy," Don said, "but I wouldn't let him go. I told him I'd fight him all over the road. We waited for Guy to come back. He was in a bad shape."

Everybody knew Guy was going to fight me. And no one had ever seen him beaten up before. No one had ever seen his nose flattened, his lips busted, and his eyes blacked. And this made news. My getting Don Conway back to school had saved me.

Before sundown the news of our fight had reached the Valley. Mort Hackless knew about it and he was surprised. Mort Hackless had seen Guy Hawkins have many a fight. Guy went to the Valley on Saturdays and Sundays and if anybody wanted to fight him he was always ready. Often when one didn't want to fight him, he insisted. He was always the winner.

Guy Hawkins was respected by a certain group of people who believed that might made right, by people who loved a dog-fight, chicken-fight, man-fight, any sort of a fight. If Guy Hawkins didn't have "trouble" at the Valley, he sat around the store and told his fighting stories to young boys looking for a hero and traded his fighting stories with the old men who told fighting stories of their dead ancestors, that grew and grew with the years. This was one fighting story Guy Hawkins would be slow to tell.

Not any of the rules of cleanliness I had suggested for my pupils, not any knowledge I was trying to give them, not anything I could do at Lonesome Valley, would give me the reputation this fight gave me. I didn't know, until after Guy and I tangled, that the people talked behind my back and had said I would be a good teacher as long as I lasted but my days were numbered in Lonesome Valley. They thought when Guy Hawkins got through with me—the boy sent to teach Lonesome Valley—that I would be catching the Old Line Special in a hurry back to Landsburgh. And since there was not much excitement in Lonesome Valley, I believe to this day that many of them craved the excitement of a good fight. They loved to talk about it. And they loved the suspense. For Guy had told everybody he knew in Lonesome Valley, the Valley, Chicken Creek, and Unknown what he was going to do.

Never was any teacher more respected by everybody in his community than I was now. Men that I had met before on the Lonesome Creek Road, men that had shyly spoken or had not spoken at all, stopped and introduced themselves and thanked me for "doing the job." And before we stopped talking, nearly everyone said the same thing, that he needed his children at home to help strip cane and cut cane wood and cut tobacco, but he was going to try to do the work himself so he could send his children to school to me. And these words, coming from tall, lean, beardy-faced figures of the earth, men who when they liked and respected you would die for you, men who when they hated and despised you would kill you, made me feel good.

Narrow-gauged Lonesome Valley had made men like these. This was their small world. They had been born here. They had married here. Their children had been born here. The only ones who had seen any of the world were those who had fought in World War I. And when these men became vitally interested in sending their children to school to me instead of having them help with the work at home, I knew that I would give all to have a good school for their children, whose schooling would end with Lonesome Valley. I knew that now I was respected as a schoolteacher and that I was somebody in Lonesome Valley. And I would proceed with new ideas and with much hard work for my school.

5

I DIDN'T expect Guy Hawkins to return to Lonesome Valley School. I thought his schooling was ended. But when he left the schoolhouse he didn't take his books. I wondered if he would come back to get them, and, if he came, would he bring his father or one of his married brothers with him? Would he start another fight? The same thoughts must have troubled John Conway, more than my report about Nancy Cochran's guitar music and singing. When I went to school on Tuesday morning, John went with me.

This was John Conway's first visit to the school, for his farm work had piled up on him since all of his children but Flossie were going to school. When we got there, big Guy Hawkins with his black eyes, swollen lips, was in a circle with the other pupils, going around, and singing "The Needle's Eye." Guy greeted me: "Good morning, Mr. Stuart."

Then John Conway smiled and turned to go. I watched him cross the foot log and go into the little store. I joined in the game, "the needle's eye," with my pupils. Guy Hawkins and I were captains. I was the hard-boiled egg and he was the soft-boiled egg. When we took pupils from the line and asked them whether they would rather be a soft-boiled or a hard-boiled egg, the majority chose the soft-boiled egg. Guy Hawkins got three-fourths of the pupils. And when we formed our tug of war to pull against each other, his side toppled my side. They pulled us all over the yard, and everybody laughed, especially Guy Hawkins. It was great fun. And never did Guy Hawkins or a pupil ask me about the fight. If they talked about it, I didn't know. I did notice them observing the bloodstain on the floor. If Guy Hawkins ever said anything against me to a fellow-pupil again, I never heard of it. He had, for the first time, become a pupil like the rest. He had, for the first time, acted as if he was a part of our school.

6

THAT very day another thing happened. It was during the noon hour a big ruddy-complexioned man of perhaps fifty drove down Lonesome Valley with a mule team hitched to a wagon-load of coal. He stopped his team in the shade of a giant sycamore and climbed down from his wagon. He walked over where I was standing. I had seen this same man go down on this coal wagon toward the Valley everyday I had taught at Lonesome. This was the first time he had stopped.

"Are you Mr. Stuart? My name is Burt Eastham," he introduced himself.

"Yes, I am," I said, shaking his coal-dusty hand. "I'm glad to know you."

"You wouldn't have any drinking water, would you?" he said. "I'm a bit thirsty."

"Yes, we have water in the schoolhouse," I said. "It might be a little warm."

"Warm water will wet the throat," he said.

"Then let's go get it," I suggested.

He followed me into the school. I looked into the water bucket. It was half full. He started to lift the dipper to drink.

"Don't drink from that dipper," I snapped, and he let the dipper fall from his hand.

"Is it pizened?" he asked, startled.

"No, not that," I said. "But no one drinks from a dipper here."

He looked curiously at me.

"What do you use it for, then?" he asked.

"To dip water from the bucket into drinking cups," I said. "Wait a minute and I'll make you a cup."

I tore a sheet of paper from a tablet and made him a paper cup. He dipped the water from the bucket and poured it into the cup.

"People don't drink one another's slobbers this way, do they?" he laughed, after he had finished drinking. "But I wasn't exactly thirsty. I wanted to see the man that whipped Guy Hawkins!"

He beamed admiringly as he looked me over.

"That boy came to Upper Lonesome Church one night," he continued, "and he nearly beat my boy to death without any reason. He wanted a fight. He started it with my boy and beat him up. Whipped Les Brown's boy and Booten Tolliver's boy the same night. I wanted to see the first man to whip him. Say," he continued, as he looked me over from head to foot, "you're not such a big man. I'd a-thought you had to be a giant to whip 'im."

And when we walked out of the schoolhouse, back toward his wagon, he stopped. He stood for a minute and looked at big Guy Hawkins who was now enjoying himself playing games, and I was looking at his wagonload of coal.

"How many bushels do you have on this wagon?" I asked.

"Twenty-five bushels," he said.

"You weigh your coal?" I asked.

"Nope," he said.

"Then how do you know how many bushels you have?"

In the meantime Don Conway walked over where we were standing.

"Guess at it," he said.

"I believe you've got more than twenty-five bushels on your wagon."

"You got any way finding out?"

"Do you know the length, width, and depth of your wagon bed?" I asked.

"Nope," he answered.

"Don, run in and fetch the yardstick from my desk," I said.

Don brought the yardstick and did the measuring and I put the figures on paper. Don was very much interested as I figured the number of bushels on the wagon.

"According to my figures you have thirty-nine and a fraction bushels," I said. "Since your coal is stacked a little higher than the bed, I wouldn't be surprised if you have over forty bushels!"

"What?" he exclaimed. "I've been selling this wagon bed of coal for twenty-five bushels for the past seven years! How can I really find out how much coal I have?"

"Have it weighed down at the Valley," I said. "They have scales there."

Burt Eastham, greatly excited, climbed onto his coal wagon and drove down the road.

That afternoon, just a few minutes before it was time to dismiss school, there was a knock on the wall beside our open schoolhouse door. I went to the door. There stood Burt, his face beaming. His face was so dirty with coal dust that his not-too-white teeth looked white as dogwood blossoms in April. His smile was so broad he was showing nearly all his teeth.

"Thank you a hundred times, young man," were his first words. "I don't know how I can ever repay you! I had forty-three bushels of coal on my wagon. Here!" he exclaimed excitedly showing me the weigh bill.

I called Don Conway from the schoolroom and let him see it.

"Something told me to stop here and take a look at you," Burt Eastham said. "I'm glad I stopped. I've been swindled for seven years."

"Well, you can rest assured you've given good measure," I said. "Your conscience won't bother you. You've not cheated anyone."

"But I won't be cheated from now on," he said. "Gee, I wished I'd gone to school. Can't write my name."

"You can come here if you want to," I invited him.

"Too late to start at fifty," he admitted sadly. "Too late when a man is married and has nine children."

His words were worth more to Don than my words or any other teacher's words. Don now realized the value of a simple education.

"I've just been thinking, Mr. Stuart, whether you were married or not," Burt Eastham said. "I know you're old enough to teach school or you wouldn't be here. And when you're old enough to teach school you're old enough to be married."

"No, I'm not married," I laughed. "Haven't any prospects!"

"Then I have a prospect for you," he said rejoicingly. "See, I want to do something for you. May Woods, the teacher at Upper Lonesome, is pretty as a speckled pup. She's the right gal for you. Has long black hair, big brown eyes shaded with heavy eyelashes. If I's a young single man, I'd go for her myself!"

When Burt Eastham said these words, my pupils laughed until I had to pound on the wall for order. Guy Hawkins and Ova Salyers laughed until they shook all over. They whispered to each other and laughed out loud. For, since John Conway had visited Nancy Cochran's store, they weren't entertained with guitar music and singing during the school hours. And they had listened to every word Burt Eastham had said to me, although he had tried to whisper. Before he left he assured me that he "would fix up everything with May Woods for me."

7

MR. EASTHAM worked fast. The very next day he stopped and told me he had everything "fixed" for me to date May Woods. He said, "You know, I told her last night about you. I went over to Oscar Pennix's place, where she boards, and I told her you'd straightened that school out down where they's run off every schoolteacher. And I told her about what you did for me. I told her you even figured how many bushels of coal on my wagon bed. Oh, she was excited about it," he continued. "I was very frank with her. I put the cards on the table. I told her that she needed to go with a man like you and you needed a woman like her. I'm not a matchmaker but I think you'd make the best married pair that ever lived in these parts. We'd be glad to have a couple like you to live right here in Lonesome Valley and spend your days with us. Now I've made the date with her for you to go see her at Oscar Pennix's place tomorrow evening at eight o'clock. It's not more than two miles up there and you won't have any trouble finding the house. It's the first house on your right after you pass the schoolhouse."

"I'll be there," I said.

There was nothing left for me to say. I hadn't told him to make the date. I had never had a blind date before. I had not had many dates in my life. I knew I must keep up my end of the bargain. This was a long shot in the dark. I didn't know May Woods. But if she's a schoolteacher, I thought, and is as beautiful as he says she is, she must be all right.

At about seven that evening I was on my way to Upper Lonesome. I had waited for the dew to settle the dust before I started, because I wore white shoes and I didn't want to get them brown with dust. And I didn't want to get any dust on my white suit. I wanted to show May Woods that I was everything Burt Eastham had told her I was and more. I wanted to give her a surprise. This was a blind date and a shot in the dark for both of us. But I knew as I walked along that blind dates had developed into serious love affairs and often marriage. These thoughts raced through my mind as I walked swiftly along the brown winding road, always careful not to step too hard to stir the dust beneath the thin gossamer of dew-dampness.

I passed the Faith Healing Holiness Church. Little crowds of men, women, and children had already begun to gather. The men carried unlit lanterns and the women carried babies. They would need their lanterns for they would stay until the moon was down. Just a few steps beyond, on the opposite side of the road, was the Free Will Baptist Church, which John Conway attended. And I met the Free Will Baptists on their way to church. The men carried unlit lanterns and the women carried babies.

I had learned from my sister and from the people of Lonesome Valley that on the same night a meeting was held at one church, a meeting was held at the other. These churches were great rivals. In Lonesome Valley there were no other churches, no people of any other religious faith. If there were any, I had never heard tell of them. And, according to the conversations of these "religious people," there were two heavens.

If not two heavens, heaven was certainly divided. There was a Faith Healing Holiness heaven and a Free Will Baptist heaven. The two churches fought it out like two rival stores, across the street from each other, selling the same kind of merchandise, manufactured by the same company, yet each merchant giving a slightly different sales talk to the people ready to buy. This religious feeling divided the people more than politics. Lonesome Valley in reality was one little world to itself, but, in thought of the hereafter, it was two separate worlds. One had to believe in one of these worlds; one was high-pressured to take sides. I had steered clear of both, though I was accused of leaning toward the Free Will Baptists because I lived with John Conway, one of their hard-working members.

I chuckled to myself after I passed the crowds and couples going to the Free Will Baptist Church, about what John Conway said to me after he had gone to see Nancy Cochran: "She is one of them Sanctifiers," he said, "but I told her plainly we didn't want Lonesome Valley School disturbed by her guitar playing and singing during book hours. First time I'd ever been in her store and she was skeered to death of me when I walked in. I was skeered to death of her too."

The joltwagon-wheel of yellow moon was rolling not too high above the green hills under heaven. It was soft and mellow, with the man still in it put there for burning brush on Sunday, for I could see his shape as it had been shown to me when I was a child. He was still there for his evil deed. This devil moon, even if he did hold as prisoner this poor man, was soft and bright and beautiful. And his mellow shafts of light flooded Lonesome Valley with tainted moonlight-gold. This was the kind of night to have a date. It was the kind of night to be young and dressed in white and to be hatless with crow-wing black hair slicked back over the head. This was the kind of night for a young man to go see a beautiful girl. He felt love in his heart and brain and the air he breathed. It was the time to go see a beautiful girl he had never seen before. The whippoorwills, nightingales, and insects were inspired to sing. I couldn't blame them for singing. I sang too. Something deep within stirred me to song. And the distance seemed shorter.

The road crossed Lonesome Creek. And when I leaped the

stream to keep from soiling my white shoes, I leaped a golden stream. The moonlight had changed it to the color of the moon. What a night! What a beautiful journey! What a sentimental one, too, for I was beginning to have more dreams of May Woods, what she looked like, wondering if she were as beautiful as Burt Eastham had said. Besides falling in love with her, for I was in the mood on a night like this to fall in love, I thought we might add a little business to our first meeting. We might match our schools to spell against each other and to work arithmetic against each other and to have rival ball games and even a picnic some Friday afternoon and let our pupils play "the needle's eye" together. It would be great fun for her and me, like a father and mother, to watch over our combined large family. Such thoughts raced through my mind as I came into shadows that cut away the moonlight.

Lonesome Creek and the Lonesome Creek Road parted here like two lovers. Lonesome Creek went into the dark forest, heavy with aromatic leaf and blossom. At this point the forest closed in on both sides of the road. I followed, feeling my way with my feet, a road that was as dark and strange as time. I looked to my left and to my right for an opening of light; of golden moonlight upon the open fields, upon the patches of ripening wheat and oats, broad-leafed, lusty, green-growing tobacco, and the dark clouds of stalwart corn. I was thinking just a few yards beyond I would reach the light, and then I would be there, when a barrage of something came through the trees like a flushed covey of birds flying for their lives. One of the objects caught me square on the jaw and the juice spattered my lips. I knew by the taste and the smell it was a rotten tomato.

I stopped in the road. I couldn't think fast enough. My white suit was the same kind of target to them as a white chicken roosting in a winter-leafless tree at night is to a hoot owl. They could see me but I couldn't see them. And how many there were throwing at me, I could only guess by the way the tomatoes, rotten eggs (I knew by their smell), good eggs, apples, squashes, pumpkins, and melons were hurled at me in an avalanche like hailstones. They couldn't miss, because too many missiles were thrown from too many angles toward one white target. A rotten egg yellowed my hair. A good egg caught me on the same spot the rotten tomato had hit. A squash, melon, or pumpkin caught me on the leg above the knee, and broke into fragments. I put my hands over my eyes to protect them, and ran forward, thinking I could brave the avalanche. I couldn't push through it. Then I heard laughter and screams back in the darkness under the trees. There must have been fifty boys and men! They made more noise than all my pupils could have made at Lonesome Valley if they had screamed at the top of their voices at the same time.

In the middle of the road I did an about-face in a hurry and started back. For I was covered from head to foot with oozy and dripping stuff that didn't smell good or taste good. I was hit on the mouth several times. Now I was laying my feet down on the dusty road like a running horse. The missiles kept coming, and the wild crowd, laughing, and giving war whoops, came from the dark shadows in hot pursuit. Pistols were fired and bullets went through the leaves high over my head. I could hear them spatting the leaves and hitting the branches and bodies of trees and singing off into space.

When I came back into the light, Lonesome Creek that had been golden when I crossed it going up, was lead-colored to me. I sailed over it like a bird. Dust on my shoes meant nothing to me now. For I was running as I had never run before, with the pack on my trail; and the eggs and tomatoes were flying, for they were light and good for long-range throwing. I was afraid to look back. I was trying to outdistance this pack of screaming fury.

Just before I reached the Free Will Baptist Church, a rotten egg thrown by some strong arm, over a spur of hill where the road made a bend, came down like an artillery shell on its exact spot. It exploded on top my head. I thought once of running inside the church but something urged me on. I pushed my tired body with every ounce of energy I had. I knew if they followed much farther, I would dive into the second church. But they didn't. I heard their wild screams and roars of laughter on the wind that moved slowly down the Valley.

When I passed the Faith Healing Holiness Church, I was barely walking. I was wet with egg goo mixed with rotten tomato, melon, squash, pumpkin, and sweat. My white suit was so wet it stuck to my body and encased it like long underwear. The front door of the church was wide open on this hot night, and the house was packed with people. They were using all sorts of fans, from cardboard backs of tablets to short, leafy poplar limbs. I saw Nancy Cochran standing up front playing her guitar and singing a special number, "I'm Naturalized for Heaven." Amens were going up from all parts of the room.

I didn't linger long before the church. I moved down the road that was not as beautiful as it had been. When I reached Conways' I couldn't go inside with the clothes I was wearing— white clothes which I'd never wear again at night in Lonesome Valley. I found a bar of soap in the soapbox on the back porch. I found a hole of water in Lonesome Creek surrounded by willows. There was only one place where the moon's ray could come through. I pulled off my clothes and shoes. Even my underwear and socks were soaked with rotten eggs. I soaped and washed my body from head to toe. I washed my clothes and spread them on the brush for tomorrow's sun. Then I hurried to the house to beat Conways home from church.

8

THE news of my going to see the Upper Lonesome teacher, May Woods, spread like wildfire up and down the entire length and breadth of Lonesome Valley. Everybody was laughing. When I ate my breakfast the next morning, everybody at Conways' breakfast table wanted to laugh. Even silent Flossie thought it was funny. When she looked at me, she smiled as she had never smiled before. John Conway would break out laughing and then he would tell a joke. He tried to make me think he was laughing at something else. But I knew he wasn't. Bertha Conway smiled as she poured my coffee. Don would look across the table at me and grin like a possum. Everybody wanted to laugh and they puffed like frogs trying to hold their laughter. But not one mentioned what had happened to me. I didn't mention it either.

When I went to school my pupils smiled. All but one. Guy Hawkins didn't smile. They wanted to laugh, too, because they had heard Burt Eastham make the date for me. They whispered and smiled at one another. Often one would be looking directly at me when he whispered. But not one mentioned the affair where I could hear him. They laughed on the playground more than they had ever laughed. Something funny was in the wind. Something funny had been broadcast on the wind.

Our noon hour was over and we were back in the schoolroom when Burt Eastham drove his mule team under the sycamore shade and stopped. He jumped off the wagon and ran stiff-legged toward the schoolhouse. I met him at the door, and we walked out to the coal wagon together. We got away from my pupils' hearing.

"I'm sorry about what happened last night," he apologized. "It looks like I am the goat of all that happened."

"Plenty happened all right," I said. "And I'm the goat."

"Let me tell you what happened," he explained. "That's why I'm late with my coal today. I never heard about it until this morning. This fellow, Bill Coffee, Miss Woods has been a-sparkin', rounded back unexpectedly from the Auckland Rolling Mills. He found out she had a date with you and he went wild when she wouldn't break the date with you for him. He said he'd break it in a nice way!"

"He broke it all right," I said, "but not in a nice way. You didn't tell me she dated anybody else!"

"Yep, she's sparked Bill for a couple of years now," Burt spoke softly, "but I thought you had a good chance a-beatin' his time! He went around there among the Upper Lonesome boys, and you know they don't have much use for the Lower Lonesome boys, let alone a stranger, and they got ready for you. See, Bill Coffee is an Upper Lonesome boy hisself and he knows just about everybody up there."

"Bill can have May as far as I'm concerned," I said. "I've never seen her or him and I don't care to see them."

"I'm sorry it all happened the way it did," he said. "Did they hurt you?"

"Not exactly," I said.

"Did they run you a fur piece?"

"Just to the Faith Healing Holiness Church," I said.

"'Pon my word," he said, "ain't it awful."

He got on his coal wagon and I went back into the school-house. Right then I learned, for the first time, a joke at the other fellow's expense was funny to everybody.

9

MAN is often reminded of his past actions in the most conspicuous surroundings. I had just returned from school that day and had sat down on the porch where the Conway family was sitting, fanning themselves with long fronds of a creek willow, shooing the flies, and stirring the stuffy air, when it happened. I looked down across the yard at the Lonesome Creek Road and I saw an automobile coming down the road, larger than any car I'd ever seen in Landsburgh. It was a green convertible and the top was down. The young man behind the steering wheel was wearing a striped silk shirt and a high collar and flashy tie. He had a long cigar in his mouth, and a thin stream of smoke trailed behind the car and thinned to nothingness on the wind. He was driving the car with one hand and he had his right arm around a beautiful girl. She looked, from where I sat on the porch, like a beautiful girl. Her black hair was blown back by the wind.

"Who in the world is that?" I asked, wondering if this long automobile would manage the narrow turns in the Lonesome Valley Road.

Then everybody on Conways' porch started laughing. The pent-up laughter they had been wanting to turn loose, burst forth like water from a swimming-hole when the mud dam gives way to pressure. They laughed until they couldn't answer my question. The car turned the bend and was out of sight.

"That's Bill Coffee and May Woods," Don finally said, between spasms of laughter.

I felt a warm glow spread over my face.

"He must own the Auckland Steel Mills," I said.

"No, he just works there," Don replied. "He's a welder."

"You know Bill Coffee has done better than anybody ever expected he'd do." John admitted, after he was through laughing. "People around here never thought old Bill would amount to a hill o' beans. He never would go to school. Got to the *First Reader*. Then he quit and tried to farm. He couldn't do that. Then he went to the Auckland Steel Mills and he's made good. Makes over three hundred dollars a month so I've heard."

"He's not been at the Auckland Mills but a couple of years," Don continued. "First year he worked there he came back here with a new car and he was wearing ten-dollar shirts and fifteen-dollar shoes. Every girl on Lonesome was a-tryin' to go with 'im, but May Woods beat all their times. She makes him awful jealous by having a date with somebody else now and then."

"May Woods holds a First Class Certificate too," John bragged.

What a fool I've been! I thought. Never again will I accept a blind date. Never will I take another shot in the dark. I knew this event would be news history for the people in Lonesome Valley. I would never be able to live it down.

10

FRIDAY at noon of my third week, I dismissed the school to go home. I had to fetch much needed supplies for my school from Landsburgh. So many things needed to be done. And to get to Landsburgh, I had to walk five miles to the Valley and catch the afternoon Old Line Special. I had heard many teachers say that schoolteaching was dull and uninteresting. It was the most interesting thing I had ever done, and these three weeks had seemed like three days. I was trying to impart my scant knowledge to youth with even lesser knowledge, but I had learned more from my pupils and from the patrons of my district and Upper Lonesome than I had ever learned in three weeks before.

It took me one hour to walk through the sweltering August heat and clouds of dust to the Valley. There I caught the

Old Line Special, and, as I rode toward Landsburgh, the thoughts I had had about teaching while riding this train three weeks before came back to me. The little fears I had had no longer troubled me. There were other things, things other than discipline, that worried me. When the train reached Landsburgh, I hurried home.

Next morning, bright and early, I went to see John Hampton. I went to find out if his old car still climbed hills in reverse instead of low. But he had had it overhauled, and he promised to take me back to Lonesome Valley on Sunday. Since he had to get supplies for his school, we went together to Landsburgh in his car. Then we went to Mr. Staggers' office.

"Well, how are you getting along, Mr. Stuart?" my Superintendent asked me.

"All right, sir," I said. "Have you heard any reports?"

"No, I haven't," he said. "Not yet. But you haven't," he almost whispered, "come in to give the school up, have you?"

"Oh, no," I said. "I've come for supplies."

"What do you want in the way of supplies?" he asked, for he was pleased that I was staying with Lonesome Valley. "Coal bucket, erasers, chalk, windowpanes?"

"All of that and more too," I said, as John Hampton looked strangely at me. "I want two bags of lime, a water cooler with a faucet, enough paint to paint my schoolhouse, paintbrushes, hatchet, hammer, nails, hoe, rake, axe, and shovel."

"Just a minute," Mr. Staggers broke in, "who's goin' to paint the house?"

"I'm goin' to paint it," I said. "I'm going to clean that place up!"

"What are you goin' to do with lime?" he asked. "First call I've ever had for lime."

"Use it as an antiseptic in the vaults of the outdoor privies," I said. "Flies won't mess around lime."

After we had discussed the use of each item, he agreed to let me have all the supplies, although I was getting far beyond my allowance—because I agreed to paint the house free of cost. Mr. Staggers wrote an order for my supplies at the Lawson Hardware.

Sunday at noon, John Hampton and I started for Lonesome

Valley. As he drove along he told me of his many experiences teaching. He said I might think that I would turn the world over to see what was on the underside while I was young and a beginning teacher, but, later, I would slow down and be well contented to accept what was on top the world. I let him talk, for I was riding in his car and he had been a friend to me to help me get this school. I let him do the talking and I listened. By six o'clock we were at Conways'. We had made approximately seven and a half miles an hour, and I heard the death bells ringing in my ears after all the clatter his car engine had made climbing the steep hills.

John Hampton went back to Landsburgh, and as soon as I had eaten supper Don Conway helped me carry the lime over to the schoolhouse. We took a sack to the boys' privy, and, when we went inside, I got a surprise. Two days before, Friday, when I had dismissed school, there was not a mark on the walls. Now they were marked all over. And I was depicted in all the vulgar caricatures. There were all sorts of these. May Wood's name was written beside my name. And there were the same vulgar caricatures of her. And Don's sister Flossie's name was printed all over the walls and up overhead beside mine. She was also portrayed in obscene pictures.

"Who on earth did a thing like that?" I asked Don. "Suppose one of the pupils?"

"I don't think so," he said. "I think it's somebody that doesn't go to school."

I immediately thought, since we had dismissed at noon on Friday, that some of my pupils might have slipped back to the schoolhouse.

Don and I sprinkled lime down in the vault, and left the remainder of the bag inside for future use. Then we went to the girls' side and there was not a mark. We used our lime here and then went back to Conways', where we got a bucket of water, soap, and broom, and returned and cleaned the walls of their obscene pictures.

11

MONDAY I told my pupils that somebody had drawn obscene pictures on the walls of the boys' toilet and that, since I couldn't believe I had a pupil in my school that would do such a thing, I hoped each pupil would cooperate with me to protect our school property and help keep it clean. I told them that we planned to paint the house. I told them that this building was our home, that we were a unit same as a family and we had to work together. I told them when one pulled, the other should push. Then I explained to them we wouldn't need another dipper. And the only need we had for a water bucket was to carry water. For now we had a water cooler. I showed them this new gadget, the first one they had ever seen, and they were pleased.

That afternoon they knew we were serious about painting the house. John Conway made ladders for us. He brought our supplies to the schoolhouse. When school was over, Don and I started painting the schoolhouse. Instead of taking off soon as school was out, many of the pupils stayed to watch us work. Guy Hawkins and Ova Salyers stayed.

"Mr. Stuart, I can paint," Guy Hawkins said. "I'll help if you don't mind."

"And I can paint too," Ova said.

Guy Hawkins and I scraped off the old paint while Ova and Don started putting on the first coat.

The summer days were long, and we worked until it was late. We made considerable showing our first day. And while Guy and I removed the old paint we found a brown stain on the paint-scaled walls up about four feet from the ground. It was in blotches, big and brown as autumn oak leaves. Guy Hawkins laughed while I took my knife and scraped on one of these spots.

"Don't you know what that is?" Guy asked me.

"I'm not sure," I said.

"It's ambeer spittle," Guy laughed. "Somebody has been spittin' on the walls!"

"What do you know about this?" I said, wondering who chewed tobacco among my pupils besides Guy and Ova.

We found ambeer spittle all around the back of the schoolhouse. I knew this was something that had to stop before we got the house painted with our new white paint.

12

THE writing in the boys' privy and the spitting of ambeer on the schoolhouse walls worried me, but I had another school problem that worried me more. I knew the teachers in Landsburgh Graded School didn't have this problem, as they had a teacher for each grade from the beginners to the junior high school. The pupils in each room were almost on the same age level. Here, I had from the beginners to the eighth grade, all in one room. Their ages ran from five to twenty. This was so in every rural school in Greenwood County. I had never thought about this until I had started teaching.

The beginners were the most difficult of all to teach. I would bring my beginners up and teach them ABC's on the old dilapidated chart, used years and years before I came to Lonesome Valley. My eighth-grade pupils had been taught on this same chart. After I had gone over their ABC's with them, they went back to their seats and had nothing to do. They needed more attention than I could give them. Many of them fell asleep in the hot schoolroom. I wondered what to do about this situation.

I knew how beginners had been taught in the Greenwood County Rural Schools in the past. I knew because I had been a beginner in this same type of school. I had been taught to read on this kind of chart, and I still knew everything on it from memory. Once after I had awakened from a nap, I wandered from my seat and found a dead wasp and carried it up to the teacher while he was busy with a recitation. All the pupils laughed. I was given a sound spanking—something I had always remembered—and put back in my seat. Thereafter, I was afraid of my teacher.

When one of these little fellows I was trying to teach went to sleep, I never thought of spanking him. I let him sleep. What else was there to do? What else could I do when I was trying to hear fifty-four classes recite in six hours, give them new assignments, grade their papers? What else could I do when I had to do janitorial work, paint my house, keep the toilets sanitary, the yard cleaned of splintered glass and rubbish, and try to make our school home more beautiful and more attractive than the homes the pupils lived in?

One afternoon, after we had been painting on the house, we got to Conways' late. John Conway sat by the table while Don and I ate. The rest of the family had eaten. I told John Conway about my problem with beginners, but he didn't know about schools, and he didn't understand. He said a child should never be allowed to sleep in school. Then, I argued, the teacher should have something for the child to do interesting enough to keep him awake. I told John that if Upper Lonesome, Lonesome Valley, Unknown, and Chicken Creek Rural Schools were moved to the Valley—the approximate center of all these surrounding school districts—it could be worked out as it was in Landsburgh Graded School. It would take fewer teachers and the teachers would have pupils on an age level. One teacher could handle the beginners.

His face reddened when he asked me how the pupils could get to school as faraway as the Valley. Haul them by bus or by joltwagon, I told him. He laughed a wild laugh and told me I didn't know about the Lonesome Creek Road in winter. I told him the time would come when we would get gravel on the roads and then we could have this type of school. He said he hoped when this time came—when they took Lonesome Valley School from the people, where his children, himself, his father, and his grandfather had gone to school—he would be dead and know nothing about it. He went into as much of a tirade against this idea as if someone had walked into a field of his green-growing tobacco and started chopping it down with a hoe. He

said my thought was dangerous, and, as for me, if I wanted
to be a good teacher and stay healthy, I better stop having such
crazy talk.

I was in his house. I taught his children. I couldn't tell him
what I thought. But I thought if I ever got to a position high
enough in education, if I was ever elected any kind of legislator,
so help me God, I would abolish the abominable trustee system
if I could. If I couldn't do it singlehanded, I would help others
do it. Why should I, a teacher, be at the mercy of John Conway?
Why should John Conway have more power than the Superintendent, elected by members of the Greenwood County Board
of Education, and they, in turn, elected by the people? Why
should he have more power than the five members of the Greenwood County Board of Education, when they were elected by
the people to serve the interests of education for the people?
Why should I, a teacher, have seven bosses: John Conway,
Superintendent Staggers, and five members of the Greenwood
County Board of Education? A person didn't have to be as far
advanced in education as a Senior in Landsburgh High School
to see this. One could be an eighth-grader and reason this out.
Trustees ruled little marked-off districts like a dictator!

John Conway hadn't gone any further than the third grade.
He could see that coal was properly placed in the coalhouse,
make ladders for us to use in painting, tell Nancy Cochran to
stop playing a guitar while school was going on! He could do
these things but in all the years he had fought the Faith Healing
Holiness people to be elected trustee of his district, he had
never persuaded the Greenwood County School Board to have
a well dug for his school. He hadn't been able to get the house
painted. He hadn't offered to dig the well or paint the house
himself. I finished my supper, left the table, and sat on the
porch to enjoy the cool evening breeze and think about what I
would do with my beginners. It was a problem and I had to
think it out for myself.

13

ANNIS BEALOR, one of our neighbors with the best farm in my home community, once said to my father: If he could be alone long enough in a quiet place he could think through steel. My room was quiet enough but it was hot as an oven. I lay on my bed and thought until I heard the clock downstairs strike twelve, but I didn't have the solution.

That morning when I got up, I was still trying to think of something to do with my beginners. I wanted to start today. They were going into the fourth week already, and suffering in the hot schoolroom. Even if the room were of moderate temperature, they still would suffer for lack of something to do. I ate breakfast and got ready for school. I went early and walked slowly along by myself and tried to think of a way. Then I put the thought out of my mind. I couldn't solve the problem.

Then I started whistling. I walked along beneath the willows in the morning sun, whistling "The Needle's Eye." I watched the little pencil-stripes of shifting shadows on the sand the sun made when it found little open spaces betwixt the quivering willow fronds. Above my head the jeweled dewdrops were evaporating into thin white clouds and ascending toward the sun. It was a beautiful morning. This was the kind of morning that made me want to breathe deeply of the cool fresh wind. This was the kind of morning that made me want to be alive. It made me want to live forever. Why should I worry about the school problem that had troubled me all night? Maybe it would come to me sometime. Why not walk along on this bright and beautiful August morning and whistle "The Needle's Eye"?

The needle's eye that does supply,
The thread than runs so true . . .

What was the needle's eye? What was the thread that ran so true? The needle's eye, I finally came to the conclusion, was the schoolteacher. And the thread that ran so true could only be play. Play. The needle's eye that does supply the thread that runs so true. The teacher that supplied the play that ran so true? Play, that ran so true. Play. Play. Play that ran so true among little children, little foxes, little lambs! Yes, play, among big children and grownups! My beginners should play. Their work should be play. I should make them think they were playing while they learned to read, while they learned to count! That was it! I had it. Play.

My problem wasn't exactly solved. But, I thought, as long as my beginners could play they wouldn't want to sleep. Not during the school day when they were all together.

For on my father's farm I had seen the lambs play in the springtime on the green fields. I had seen them line up and run foot races. Many people might not believe this. But watch for yourself in the spring. Watch the young lambs on the green hills and meadows. I had seen young foxes play among the monster rocks where they denned. I'd seen them chase each other's tails, around and around on top of a sunlit rock. I'd seen the young, pretty ring-tailed coons play when they washed their food—a good lesson in sanitation—in an unpolluted mountain stream. I'd seen young ground hogs slide over the slick-worn banks on the cool summer earth on their tummies. I'd seen young rabbits play in the wheat. I'd seen young squirrels play in the green canopy of gray-barked beeches. They were learning self-protection while they played. I'd seen young chickens act as if they heard a hawk and run playfully toward the old hen for protection. That was it. Play. Play. The word was magic to my brain. I'd never thought of it in this light before. Play. Play. Play. Learn to work by play. All work should be play. Actually, teaching to me was a game. Maybe this was the reason I loved teaching. My steps quickened as the magic word *play* excited my brain.

14

WHEN time came for my first beginners' class, I tore the big sheet from the Lawson Hardware calendar. I took the scissors from my drawer and sat in a semicircle with the class. Every eye was upon me. I cut the numbers apart, told or asked what they were, and handed them to the children. Then I cut the stiff backs of tablets into squares of approximate size. Taking a jar of paste, I pasted one number to one cardboard. Then I told the class to sit four in a seat (I had eight) and paste all the numbers and cardboard squares together.

While I went on with my other classes these children were busy. When recess came they wanted more to do—rather than go out to play. Some numbers were pasted sideways, but what did that matter? They had done well with no more supervision than I had given them.

I searched my brain for an idea to tie this with reading and drawing. I drew objects on the board with which they were familiar—apples, cups, balls, and stick-figures of boys and girls—in groups of one, two, three, and four. When time came for my next beginners' class, I asked the children to identify the objects, first by name, which I wrote above the object, then by number, which I wrote beneath it. They were so excited they sat on the edge of the recitation bench, their bare feet tapping nervously on the floor. Then I reached for the stack of number cards and held them up asking the class to name the number. I was surprised they recognized so many.

The room was so quiet you could hear a pin fall. Every pupil in the room was interested. This was something they had never done—had never seen done—but they recognized it as an interesting way to learn. This was play. This was the thread that ran so true. Realizing this was enough for one time, I asked my beginners if they would like to return to their seats and try to draw the pictures as they were drawn on the board.

One idea led to another. There were dozens of ways to use the number cards. The few minutes I had to spend with each class were not nearly long enough. As days passed, the children learned to draw objects to represent a number on a card chosen by someone. They learned to add and subtract numbers and objects. They recognized the number when written. They learned the names of pictures drawn. We varied this by erasing the picture and number and reading the word. We placed a row of number cards along the board in the chalk ledge, and let the children draw pictures to represent the number on the card. There were no more little sleepy heads on desks now.

With the problem of my beginners solved, something happened to mar my happiness. That morning I had let Don, Guy, and Ova use their free periods to paint the house. After I had finished my lunch, I walked behind the house to see how the paint was drying. My face must have flushed red as a turkey's snout. There were twelve brown blotches of ambeer spittle on the last coat of our snow-white paint. They were big enough for people walking along the road to see.

When the noon hour was over I talked to my pupils. I told them that if I caught anybody chewing tobacco on the school ground, I would punish that pupil. If I caught one spitting on the paint, I would spank, and spank hard. I knew it was one of my pupils. There hadn't been anybody else in the schoolyard. And I had in mind, though I didn't accuse anybody, Guy Hawkins and Ova Salyers. I knew they chewed tobacco. I knew that Don chewed tobacco, too, but I didn't believe he would spit ambeer on the paint he had helped put on the schoolhouse. That afternoon, after school was dismissed and we started to finish the painting, we took a bucket of soapy water and a broom and scrubbed off this ambeer spittle. Then we went ahead with our painting. We worked late and finished the job.

15

FRIDAY I took my lunch, and walked outside and around in back of the schoolhouse. My pupils were sitting under the shade of the tall sycamores, eating their lunch. All but one. She was making the ambeer spittle fly against the newly painted boards. A girl! And Vaida Conway, the beautiful fourteen-year-old daughter of my trustee.

"Vaida," I said, before she saw me, "What do you have in your mouth? What are you doing?"

"Nothing," she said.

"Don't you spit it out," I warned her. "Let me see what it is."

She didn't spit the quid from her mouth. She took it out and showed it to me. Then she looked down at her bare feet.

"Why did you do this?" I asked.

She didn't answer me, and I asked her again.

"Mr. Stuart, I worked in the green tobacco," she said. "It was hot and smelly and after I quit working in it I craved a chaw."

"You mean you got the tobacco habit by working in green tobacco and smelling it?" I asked her.

"Yes," she answered.

"I've worked in it all my life and I never got the habit by smelling green-growing tobacco," I told her.

If she had ever chewed tobacco at her home, I had never seen her do so. I thought about the ideas I'd had about Ova Salyers and Guy Hawkins. I had actually thought they were the guilty ones. If I had picked over my students, trying to select the pupil that had spit ambeer spittle on this white wall, Vaida Conway would have been one of the last I would have picked. I was sorry for ever thinking it was Guy Hawkins and Ova Salyers.

"Vaida, why did you spit on this white wall?" I asked her.

"Because I liked to spit on it," she admitted. "I like to see brown against white."

"When I dismiss school this afternoon, I want you to remain," I told her.

None of the pupils had heard or seen me talking to Vaida. I don't believe any of my pupils knew who was spitting on the wall. But that afternoon when I dismissed school, Vaida Conway remained. I waited until the schoolyard was cleared of pupils. Don Conway must have known. And I think a few others suspected what was going to take place. I had to back up what

I had said. I laid big and beautiful Vaida Conway across my lap and I applied the geography book to her in stinging spanks. Not enough to make her whimper, though. She had hoed too many rows of corn and tobacco and had pulled too many green worms from the broad leaves of warm, hot tobacco, suckers from the stalks. She was beautiful but she was durable, and a little spanking didn't hurt her. It only wounded her pride. Two problems were solved. I had one more. I had to find the guilty person or persons drawing the obscene pictures in the boys' toilet.

16

AFTER I had spanked Vaida, she stopped on her way out of the schoolhouse. She stood for a minute before she went out the door and glared at me.

"I'll go straight home and tell my Daddy on you," she said, still smarting over the spanking. "He'll fix you. He doesn't like you nohow. Not after you talked about moving our school down to the Valley."

Then she ran out the door, across the schoolyard and foot log. I finished making my monthly report so I could get my much-needed pay. This was the only rule for the Greenwood County rural teachers that Superintendent Staggers enforced, so far as I knew. The monthly attendance report must be in his office before the teacher's check was sent to him.

Vaida had made her threat good. She had done what she told me she was going to do. When I got to Conways', a cold silence greeted me. John Conway had little to say. And the words he used when he said what he was almost forced to say to me were cold words. They were sharp and cold as long icicles hanging from a winter cliff. Bertha didn't bother to speak to me. I knew they regarded Vaida as a woman grown. In two more years, she would be eligible to marry. And in four more years, when she became as old as Flossie, they would regard her as one old enough to marry. If she weren't married, or about to get married, they would start worrying about her.

I sat down and ate my supper. I was paying for my board and room. I didn't know how much. Not yet. But I did know that their cold silence couldn't keep me from eating. I ate my supper, and then I walked to the Valley and mailed my attendance report so it would reach Landsburgh the following day.

I didn't hurry back. I gave my room plenty of time to get cool.

When I reached Conways', the place was silent. They had to get up early and go to the tobacco patch on Saturday morning. John Conway would plan a big day's work, since he had all of his children home from school. Vaida would smell the green-growing tobacco, and she would perhaps not require a chew. Her system would absorb enough of the intoxication of this magic plant while she pulled the suckers from behind the broad leaves and pulled the big, long, green worms from the underbellies of the leaves, and pulled them apart with her shapely fingers or laid them on the hot ground and quashed them with her brown bare feet.

17

SATURDAY morning I got up late and ate my breakfast after John Conway and all his children had gone to work. Bertha was the only one there, and she was silent. She fixed my breakfast and I ate. Then I took a volume of Kentucky School Laws and went to the Lonesome Valley School and sat down on the brace root of a giant sycamore in the shade. The hot August sun had begun to climb up the sky and the formless clouds of mist rose from the tobacco and corn up and down the valley. I began reading on the front page of the volume of School Laws while Nancy Cochran came out on her store porch and picked her guitar and sang as she had never played and sung before.

The only time she stopped singing and playing for me was when she had a customer. These times were few and far between. While Nancy entertained me I found some interesting items in

Kentucky School Laws—a document I had never bothered to read before. I discovered that the use of tobacco was not only prohibited to pupils but to patrons, and that visitors were not allowed to use this fragrant weed on school property at any time, at any school, in the state. This was the Law. I was also trying to find out whether a teacher had to board in the school district where he was teaching. I read the entire document through and I failed to find such a provision.

It was sometime in the afternoon when I finished reading these School Laws. I was just getting ready to rise from the sycamore brace root and go back to Conways' when I saw a tall young man walk down the Lonesome Creek Road. He looked first to his left, then to his right. He looked toward the little store where Nancy sat playing her guitar and singing. He slowed down when he reached the schoolhouse. He turned and looked in every direction, even toward where I was sitting, but the sycamore tree partially blocked his view. Then he took off across the schoolyard to the boys' privy. I waited minutes for him to come out, but he didn't. I walked cautiously down to the privy, eased the door open. I found him smearing the walls with vulgar pictures of me, Flossie Conway, and May Woods.

"So you're the man doin' this!" I shouted. "You're the man I've been lookin' for!"

He threw his piece of chalk down and dashed for the door. I was standing in the right position to catch him square on the chin with an uppercut. I gave the lick all I had. I know it sounds unbelievable, but it is true. I flipped this man completely over in the air and he hit on his feet running. He ran from the toilet facing the road, but, after I hit him, he was facing the toilet. He about-faced and was off like a rabbit. He didn't run toward the store but he leaped the rusted strands of barbed wire toward the cornfield. I couldn't clear the fence. I had to go between the wires. And when I got through the fence he was nearly to the tall, green-growing corn and that was a good place for me to lose him. I had never seen a man who could run like this fellow. He had a long pair of "rabbit legs," and he used them. He was off and I trailed until I lost his footprints under the tall corn.

Nancy Cochran had seen the chase. When I passed her

store on my way back to Conways', she said: "What were you tryin' to do to Alvin Purdy?"

"Who is this Alvin Purdy?" I asked her.

"Oh, he's a boy from Upper Lonesome, and he nearly worries me to death," she said proudly. "He tries to have dates with me. I won't have anything to do with him, though."

I didn't tell her what he had been doing. I had never seen him before nor had I ever heard of him until I found him fighting in his strange way. I later learned he was jealous of me. He was in love with Nancy Cochran. Nancy Cochran and Flossie Conway were old rivals. Each tried to take the other's beaus. And this was the direct reason for the ugly pictures of me in the school privy. Again, all the secret thoughts I had harbored in my brain about Guy Hawkins and Ova Salyers proved false.

18

MONDAY I got my check for my first month's teaching, exactly sixty-eight dollars. I knew then it was better that my going to see May Woods had turned out the way it had. It was better not to have a date with her. If I had had a date with her and had fallen in love with her, I could never have shown her a "good time," and could not have driven her around in an automobile.

For Bill Coffee, welder at the Auckland Steel Mills, even if he did have only a third-grade education, was four times as successful as I was, if success was measured in dollars and cents. And, believe me, success was measured that way among the young people I knew in Lonesome Valley. If Bill Coffee had wanted to switch May Woods for Flossie Conway or Nancy Cochran, he could have. And I could understand why May Woods dated Bill Coffee. She perhaps, like my sister, was teaching school to buy herself clothes. Then why shouldn't she date Bill Coffee, who could drive her up and down Lonesome Valley Road in a green convertible almost too long to make the turns in the road? Why should she refuse to date a man who smoked eight-inch aromatic cigars, who wore silk shirts, flashy ties, the best-tailored suits, and drove a big car? I didn't blame her. What could I show her on sixty-eight dollars a month? I was young, too, and wanted to date girls and show them a good time. I was also fascinated by schoolteaching. I loved my profession. I was willing to learn it from the ground up! I knew I wasn't the perfect teacher. I knew there was much for me to learn. But why should I follow this profession? It was in the twenties, and times were good. America was booming!

There had been months when I followed my trap lines and lived at home and went to Landsburgh High School, that I had more than fifty dollars a month. There had been months in the spring when I dug roots and sold them, that I had made over thirty dollars a month. After I had paid my board, how much would I have left? How much more would I make teaching school than I would make going to school, supporting myself by hunting and trapping in the autumn and digging wild roots in the spring? I didn't have long to wait to know how much I would have left. Bertha Conway charged me twenty-five dollars for a month's room and board, and I knew this was reasonable compared with "the times" in our country. But it was not reasonable compared with my salary. I had only, not counting the little things I had bought for my pupils and my school, forty-three dollars left.

19

MY HAVING to pay Bertha Conway twenty-five dollars a month for room and board was not the reason I was leaving Conways'. There were other reasons. It was all right as long as I corrected Guy Hawkins, but when I disciplined Vaida it wasn't all right. Also, my trustee was peeved at me for suggesting consolidation of rural schools.

"Remember I'm not tryin' to keep you here," John Conway said, when I was packed and ready to go, "but you do have to stay in this district."

"Who said?" I asked. "Mr. Conway, I'm leaving here a copy of the Kentucky School Laws. I've marked only one place for you to read."

Then I was off down Lonesome Creek Road to the Valley. For I had met the man and I had already seen the house where I was to stay. I had seen my room. It wasn't a "blind date" this time. I knew the people, and I knew where I was going. I was going to stay with Uncle Amos Batson, who ran the store and post office at the Valley. I would be five miles from my school and have to walk ten miles each day. But I would be away from the two factions that composed the people of my school district. The score was evened in the minds of both groups, for I had disciplined Guy Hawkins, whose father belonged to one faction, and Vaida Conway, whose father belonged to the other.

Each group knew now I didn't show partiality. I was there to teach the school. That was all. I was determined to stay until my school year was finished. I wouldn't be whipped. I'd stay until the job was done. I could do it better and not live with either faction. If I continued to live in the Lonesome Valley School District, I would have to live in a home where the people belonged to one faction. There was no middle ground. My sister had told me this, and she was right. I had learned, in my brief experience, that a schoolteacher must keep himself above the petty bickering of prejudiced groups in his school community.

There were twelve rooms in Uncle Amos Batson's two-story, white frame house. There were only three people in it. Uncle Amos and Aunt Effie had the downstairs and I had all of the upstairs I wanted. There were six large rooms upstairs, with screened windows and feather beds. The house didn't have a bathroom, but it did have running water downstairs. It was the best house in this section of Greenwood County. I wondered why I hadn't found it before. I could raise my windows. My room was cool enough so I had to sleep under cover and not naked on top of the covers. And I didn't have to fight insects all night. The place was roomy and comfortable. And the food was delicious. I had never eaten better hot biscuits, three-year-old hickory-smoked ham, and wild honey in my life. This was the place!

And I was not without music. Uncle Amos Batson, though sixty-seven years old, could draw a fiddle bow the smoothest I'd ever heard. He could make his fiddle talk, laugh, or cry. He could play music that made Aunt Effie put her long-stemmed pipe aside, and dance. The first evening I spent in their home, she danced to her husband's magic fiddle. Though she was sixty-seven, too, the mother of eleven children all married and moved away, she was as agile as a sparrow. She danced the old reels, her small feet nimbly tapping the tune that Uncle Amos played on his magic fiddle, fast as snow-melted water poured over the cliffs in an early mountain spring.

My five-mile walk to school up Lonesome Valley was a pleasant one. The morning sun in Lonesome Valley was like a golden sunflower in a deep, upturned bowl of blue. In the afternoons, the Lonesome Valley sun was a wilted sunflower in a shallow, upturned plate of blue. These were pleasant walks and gave me just enough exercise.

The first week I lived at Batsons', something happened. Uncle Amos' hired man, Bill Strickland, didn't show up to milk Uncle Amos' seven cows. For Bill Strickland had followed Bill Coffee to the Auckland Steel Mills without telling Uncle Amos he was going to quit. Uncle Amos didn't have anybody to milk his cows. Though he could play the fiddle, he couldn't milk a cow. Aunt Effie said she hadn't milked a cow in the forty-nine years she had been married and she didn't plan to start it now. Then I volunteered to go after the cows and to milk them.

Uncle Amos knew I would have to hurry if I did all this and got to school on time. He hurried to the barn lot and saddled and bridled Sundance, his large white pony, and I climbed into the saddle. I was off to get the cows up a twisting cow path that curved right and left until it reached the mountain top. There were hundreds of acres of grassy slope, gentle and rugged, dotted here and there in the deep hollows and ravines with tracts of giant trees. There were four hundred acres in this pasture. Below this mountain pasture lay the Valley. I could see the winding stream, like a silver ribbon in the early morning sun, flowing gently past the farmhouses, through the fertile level land where grew corn, cane, and tobacco. The dew was rising up in shapeless forms between the green valley and the sun, rising up and up, grotesque and beautiful. I sat for a moment in the soft saddle looking at this miracle of beauty while Sundance pranced, pawed, champed at the bridle bits. He was restless to go after the cows.

This large, intelligent, and beautiful pony, the color of an early morning sunbeam dancing on the Valley Creek waters below, knew more about finding the cows than I did. He knew what his mission was. He had been after the cows before. I gave him the rein and he found the cows. When the cows saw Sundance, they were ready to start home to be milked. All but one. She was a white cow. She wouldn't follow Sundance. But when the other six cows started to follow him, leaving this white cow alone, she began lowing mournfully and soon came running in close pursuit. I never knew a white pony could lead cows before.

It didn't take me too long to milk the seven cows for I set the big bucket under the cow and used both hands with full speed. Then I strained the milk and separated the cream for Aunt Effie to put in cans to ship on the Old Line Special. When I was through with my work, I didn't have time to walk five miles to school. I would be late and I knew there would be talk —since I had left the Lonesome Valley District—if I were late once.

"Ride Sundance to school," Uncle Amos said. "Put him in Charlie Abraham's barn durin' the day."

And that is what I did. After I had milked his cows once, strained the milk and separated the cream, Uncle Amos didn't try to get another man to do the milking and going after the cows. I loved Sundance. I loved to ride him up the Lonesome Valley Road in the morning when the dew had laid the dust and when the corn tassels and morning-glories vining up the corn were so alive with pink, blue, purple and white horn-shaped blossoms. They were good to smell and beautiful to see, for the drops of dew still clinging to them beamed like sparkling jewels in the early morning sun. The world was beautiful and I was a schoolteacher with a big white pony to ride. In the afternoon when I mounted the saddle for home, Sundance was anxious to return to his barn in the Valley and wanted to run like a fox. I had to hold a tight rein to slow him; he was fast, young, and powerful, and it was only a matter of minutes for us from school to the Valley.

20

MY SECOND month at the Lonesome Valley School, I enjoyed the cooperation of the two factions. Living in a home that didn't belong to either faction worked satisfactorily. I had never shown partiality to anyone. And my pupils understood. They went home and told their parents how fair I was with everybody, that I treated them all just the same.

Don Conway held no malice toward me. And even Vaidá soon forgot what I had done to her. She didn't chew any more tobacco, not after her father had read the section of Kentucky School Law I had marked for him. And he didn't say anything about my leaving Lonesome Valley School District. There wasn't much he could say, anyway. For I became too popular with the patrons of my school district for one man to do much against me. I had made the community news too many times for them not to know me. I had made mistakes. Small mistakes. One was the night I tried to reach Upper Lonesome. They knew I was human—that I was a man in their midst trying to do something for their children. But this was not all.

During our second month in Lonesome we started applying arithmetic to problems in the community. Burt Eastham had told almost every man in Lonesome Valley about my figuring up the bushels of coal on his wagon bed. Now they came for me to figure wagonloads of coal, bushels of corn in the bins, sizes of coalhouses, how much dirt to remove from a cellar or a well. And I never refused a request. If it was a small job, we did it after school; if it was a large one, we did it on Saturday. I took with me as many boys and girls as wanted to go along. Don Conway was always with me. Guy Hawkins became very much interested in figures and what could be done with them.

When he got interested, his bosom friend and companion, Ova Salyers, did.

One of my pupils, a large twelve-year-old boy, Denver Lykins, who was in the first grade and could count in his head with figures fast as I could, always went along. He couldn't write figures because he hadn't gone to school more than three months in his life. I gave him special attention because he was so interested. I held his hand at the blackboard and helped him make figures, starting him with figures from one to ten. Yet he went with us to figure land, cornbins, coalhouses, everywhere that we were called to figure and calculate for the patrons of our district. We started applying arithmetic, and the people loved it.

One Saturday we figured the number of acres in Tim Conley's farm. Denver Lykins carried the rod pole while Don Conway kept tally of the number of rods. Guy and Ova blazed a trail along the line fences so we could measure on the line and measure correctly. We figured the small farm to have 48.6 acres. When the County Surveyor, Don Shackleford, two weeks later ran a survey, he figured the farm to have 48.7 acres. We were that accurate. We had come that close.

But one of the funniest things to happen was in early September, when a small man by the name of Silas Higgins came to Lonesome Valley School to ask me to figure a pasture field where he had cut the sprouts. He said he was to receive six dollars per acre cutting the sprouts, and the fellow he'd cut the sprouts for, Willis Hager, had measured the land and he had measured it. He said that he had measured it for twelve and one-half acres and Willis had measured it for six. He spoke loudly so all the pupils in my school could hear. Guy Hawkins said somebody was wrong, said that was too much difference. Don Conway said he would like for all of us to measure it. We told Silas Higgins we'd be there that afternoon at four o'clock.

When we got there—Don, Guy, Ova, Denver, and I—the two men were waiting and arguing. Willis Hager must have been seven feet tall. Silas was not much over five feet. Willis would look down at Silas and laugh sarcastically and threaten to pick him up by the neck and seat of the pants and throw him from the field if he didn't accept his measurement. They had stepped the distances around the field, counting each step for three feet, five and a half steps for a rod. My pupils began laughing. Willis was so tall he could step six feet at a step and Silas so short he couldn't step three. We didn't do any stepping. We measured the land and Don Conway figured it while Ova, Guy, and Denver looked on. He figured the field for 9. 6 acres. Willis wouldn't have their figures. He wasn't satisfied at all. Silas was better satisfied. These men even threatened each other physically and with the Law. Then I went over the figures. Don had figured it correctly.

"You see, Mr. Higgins, your legs are short," Ova Salyers said, "and your steps are not long enough. Mr. Hager"—Ova laughed until he shook as he looked up at the tall man—"your steps are too long. That's why you measured this field for only six acres."

Willis Hager was going to hit me with a sassafras stick when I told him if he went to Law that he would lose and our measurement was approximately what a surveyor's measurement would be. But he didn't get very far with the stick. Four of my pupils stepped forward and little Silas Higgins picked up a rock. Willis knew the odds were against him, and he settled down and listened to reason. Before we had left, we had the dispute settled and both parties were satisfied. They shook hands and made friends. I have often thought if a little simple learning and arithmetic hadn't been applied here, one of these men would have killed the other before a lawsuit was filed in court.

My pupils were seeing the practical appliance of simple learning to everyday problems. Don Conway became so interested in school that he decided not to get married but to go through the Lonesome Valley School, then on beyond Lonesome Valley to high school, and then beyond high school to college. His brain and his heart were fired with enthusiasm for more education. His enthusiasm caught on with the other boys, who had once thought of running the teachers off. Now they were the most loyal and finely behaved pupils I had in school. Instead of wanting to tear down everything and leave a path of destruction behind them, they were constructive and wanted to build and help shape their own lives differently and that of their community.

21

ON FRIDAY afternoon of the third week of my second school month, something happened that made the pupils take more interest in schoolwork than ever. Since Burt Eastham ran a coal wagon between Upper Lonesome and the Valley, and since he was interested in a curious way in other people's affairs and in schoolteachers and schools, he had again contacted May Woods and told her that our school was a much better school than hers. He had told her that I was a better teacher than she, and this infuriated her. She challenged me to bring my pupils to her school for an arithmetic match. Challenge was all we wanted. On that Friday we all left Lonesome Valley at noon, on foot, for Upper Lonesome.

And for the first time, I came face to face with one of the most beautiful teachers I had ever seen. I could understand why Bill Coffee had bought a convertible too big for the turns in the Lonesome Creek Road for this girl. Maybe he could win her with an automobile. She was beautiful with crow-wing black hair, big, soft brown eyes shaded with heavy lashes, pretty white teeth, and lovely lips. Her schoolhouse was immaculately clean. Her pupils were well disciplined. There wasn't anything wrong with her school that I could see. Her pupils were all on one side of the big center aisle, and the other side was reserved for my pupils. The two long recitation seats were moved to the back of the schoolroom for visitors. They were filled and people were standing. There were probably over one hundred visitors to watch the match. Among them was Burt Eastham.

Before we began, Miss Woods and I agreed on a few simple rules. One was that she, Burt Eastham, and I would be the judges. We agreed that if a pupil could work the problem in his head and call out the correct answer, he didn't have to write the figures on the blackboard. And we agreed that the pupil called from his seat to the board to work against the one still standing, had his choice in addition, multiplication, subtraction, common or decimal fractions, long or short division.

We started with the beginners. She called one and I called one. We matched them at the blackboard in front so all could see. They were about evenly matched for speed and accuracy. But when my beginners were gone, she had half of hers left, for she had twice as many in the beginning. Each of my pupils had to turn down two of hers before we had an even break. Then I called Denver Lykins to the blackboard—my big first-grader. He stood there calling out the answers until he had eliminated all her beginners. Someone shouted, "Eighth-grader!" But I showed Miss Woods my record-book. Denver Lykins stood there until one of Miss Woods's pupils asked for a problem in addition. She asked for four columns of figures to add. Denver couldn't add four columns in his head, though he could add three. This girl lived near Denver and she knew his strength and his weakness. She turned down this boy that couldn't make figures on the blackboard, but this match left him with a determination to learn how.

Denver Lykins had turned down seven pupils. Then Guy Hawkins turned down five. Ova Salyers turned down three. We turned down and they turned down until we got to the fourth grade. Then I called big Don Conway and showed in my record-book that he was a fourth-grade pupil. He turned down ten—all of Miss Woods's fourth-grade pupils and six of her fifth grade. Don was pleased with himself, too, and we were pleased, for many of them were as large as Don.

In the upper grades Miss Woods had three pupils to my one. But I had one girl, Margaret Prater, who was excellent in decimal and common fractions. She was the best pupil in my school. I held her for the last pupil. The match went on, with shouts from our side if we turned down one of theirs. Shouts came from the other side when they turned down one of ours. Also, the visitors in the back of the room applauded for Upper Lonesome, for they were from this school vicinity.

I had only Margaret Prater left when Miss Woods had seven eighth-graders. Could Margaret do it? I wondered. Would she get excited and make a mistake? Miss Woods used one of her best pupils to eliminate Margaret immediately and end the match, which had taken nearly two hours. But Margaret asked for common fractions when she went to the front to work against this star pupil who had eliminated four of our pupils. Margaret turned her down. Miss Woods's pupil's decimal point was in the wrong place.

Then Miss Woods sent another star pupil to work against Margaret. He chose addition. Margaret was right and he was wrong, though he finished first. The third person she sent chose subtraction and Margaret beat her by a second. Both were right. The fourth pupil chose short division. Margaret worked the problem and checked it while her contestant stood beside her shaking and couldn't do a thing. The fifth pupil walked up with determination. She chose long division. They were trying to find one part of arithmetic that was Margaret's weakness. She turned this pupil down by a split second. Both problems were right. Their sixth pupil said, let Margaret choose the problem, for she felt she would turn her down. Margaret chose multiplication of common fractions. She won easily, almost before her contestant got started. Only one was left now. This time a tall girl, older looking than Miss Woods, and much larger. She chose decimal fractions. Margaret looked at her, then waited for the problem. Miss Woods's pupil put the problem down so fast that she mistook a seven for a three. She worked what she had on the board correctly, but Margaret had beaten her by a split second. Margaret was right again. We had won the match against odds. Then we had to hurry home. Everybody had his evening chores at home to do. We were late too. I had to ride to the Valley, fetch my cows from the pasture, and milk them.

22

THIS arithmetic match with Upper Loresome made news the entire length of Lonesome Valley and beyond. Burt Eastham was our publicity man. He reported the match to anyone willing to listen. He knew the pupils on both sides, and he remembered how many were turned down and who turned them down. This match created a school spirit at Lonesome Valley.

Though it was late, we organized a baseball team. Good clean play, good clean fun, in the form of competition, was the thing. The last week in August my pupils met pupils of the Chicken Creek School and defeated them. The first week in September we met the Unknown School and defeated them. We had only the Valley, largest of all the rural schools, left. When this match came off we had visitors that had to stand in the yard and look through the windows. People could hardly believe that we defeated the Valley and that we never used Margaret Prater, our best pupil. Guy Hawkins turned down fifteen. This was a new kind of fighting for Guy, and the people around the Valley got the surprise of their lives when this happened. Guy had found out about a new kind of fighting that he liked much better. We had spelling matches against these same schools, and we lost two and won two. They organized ball teams, too, and we played them. We lost two and won seven games. Denver Lykins, Don Conway, Guy Hawkins, and Ova Salyers were good baseball players.

Play for my pupils! Play for myself! I was the needle's eye! Play was the thread that ran so true! Teaching was not work as it had been. Teaching was play! Teaching was play-work! It was the spirit of something. It was great! It was fun! I had never in my life, much as I loved to go to school, enjoyed myself more. My teaching school was a great game of play.

Perhaps someone else thought we were doing too much play. I will never know who reported my school to County School Superintendent Harley Staggers. I was afraid to accuse anyone. But John Conway made a trip to Landsburgh to pay his taxes and get winter supplies. And it was shortly after his trip to Landsburgh that the County School Superintendent "slipped in" to my schoolhouse and was sitting there before I knew it. It was the first time he had ever been to Lonesome Valley in the five years he had been Superintendent. But his presence didn't bother me. I went ahead teaching. I let Margaret Prater teach my numbers game to the beginners outside the schoolhouse. Superintendent Staggers followed her outside and listened. My school was not too noisy but it did have a working noise, as I explained to Superintendent Staggers later. Bees made noise in the hive when they made honey. It was a working noise. If bees were extremely quiet they wouldn't make any honey!

"You're doin' a wonderful job here," Superintendent Staggers admitted. "One of the most wide-awake schools I have seen in this county."

Then I talked to Superintendent Staggers and told him about the substitute of play for work in my school. I told him about the spirit of competitive play in our arithmetic matches, spelling bees, ball games; and how my pupils were interested, how patrons were interested enough to come and watch these matches, and how the school spirit had stimulated the pupils and their parents alike. I told him how we had applied arithmetic in the community. I told him everything, and then I answered every question he asked me. He didn't ask me why I had moved from the community. I would have told him if he had asked. But he knew, after I had talked to him and he had questioned me, that my school and its community was as alive as a beehive when the bees are gathering their summer sweets from the blossoms.

When I drew my second check and started to pay Uncle Amos and Aunt Effie, they would take only twelve dollars because I had milked their cows. By a little work, I had cut my living expenses to less than half. This left me fifty-six dollars clear money from teaching. In addition to getting my expenses cut to less than half for this excellent place to live, I got the use of the most intelligent and one of the prettiest ponies that ever carried a saddle. I rode Sundance when and where I wanted to. One week end I rode him thirty miles home on Friday evening, and on Sunday rode him back.

23

SELDOM if ever did one of my Lonesome Valley pupils stay out of school because he wanted to. He stayed out of school usually for one of three reasons: he was sick; he had to help harvest the crops; he didn't have sufficient clothes, shoes, or books. In September the tobacco ripened and many of my pupils had to stay home and help with tobacco cutting and hauling to the barn. The cane ripened, too, in September and it had to be stripped, topped, cut, hauled to the mill, and the juice pressed from it and boiled into sorghum molasses. It was better to do this before frost so the sorghum would keep its delicious flavor and its golden color. Potatoes had to be dug. Corn had to be cut. September was a busy time in Lonesome Valley, where the men of this rugged American earth eked a bare subsistence for themselves and their families.

My attendance was down considerably in September. There wasn't an attendance officer to see why they didn't come to school. If the pupil went, it was all right. If he didn't, it was all right too. It was a land of freedom and work. But we had made our school so attractive in appearance that the pupils loved the place. They had had a hand in helping to make it beautiful—to make their school their home during school days, their workshop, their beehive. This was their place and my place. It was the liveliest spot in our community. It was the only place they could go, and many would never go beyond this school. Their education ended when they finished at Lonesome Valley. These were their happy days. Beyond these days, for those that remained in Lonesome Valley, it was eternal work, work, work, and the sameness of life. It was marriage, children, death, and burial in Lonesome Valley.

I thought of these things when I taught my pupils all the practical things I could teach them. How to write letters, measure land, be clean with drinking water, about personal sanitation, screens for their windows, and so many things aside from the dry-as-powder, uninteresting textbooks I was forced to teach because they were *standard*, selected by someone in the state department who didn't teach, perhaps never had, and if he had taught once upon a time was far-removed from it now. When I gave them assignments to write themes, I never gave them the topics listed in their books. I told them to write about the things they knew about: people, places, things, and adventures in Lonesome Valley.

In October my attendance grew. And to show you that my pupils loved to come to school, many came thinly clad and barefooted, after the white frosts had fallen and had blanketed the frozen land. For the farmers hadn't sold their tobacco crops yet. They usually sold them about Christmas time, and this was their "money crop." Many times I saw the red spots on the white frost from the bleeding little bare feet of those who came to school regardless of shoes. I couldn't buy shoes for them. Not on my salary and in my circumstances.

But for one little boy and girl, whose father was serving a sentence in the federal penitentiary for converting his corn into moonshine whiskey, I did buy shoes. No one knew I bought them. Their mother, with another child on the way, was fighting a brave battle to keep her children and home together. I had lived all my life in a community where these things happened. When I saw blood on the snow from this moonshiner's children coming to my school, it did something to me. I wanted to fight for them harder than I had ever fought Guy Hawkins.

24

THE sea of multicolored leaves were whipped from the Lonesome Valley trees by the raw and biting November winds. The two great furrows, turned in opposite directions by some great mythical plow in the beginning of time to make narrow-gauged Lonesome Valley, were naked, grotesque, and ugly now. Great, gray scaly rocks slept like monsters high on the rugged slopes undisturbed by winter's icy blasts. Lonesome Valley had lost the beauty of summer bloom, bud, and leaf that had clothed its scars with many shades of green. Autumn had passed. Winter was on us. And if there was ever a cold icy funnel anywhere on the earth's surface, it was Lonesome Valley.

We crowded close to the potbellied stove. We fired it until it was red-hot. The heat from it hurt our eyes. And now we wished for the evenness of the July heat. We knew we could bear the July heat more easily than we could the screaming fury of icy wind that continued to smite Lonesome Valley. The corners of our schoolroom were cold even when our stove was dangerously overheated. But my thinly clad pupils braved the smiting winter wind. My attendance grew in this weather because the farm work was done, and the pupils were free of home labors for the first time. This was the time to get learning. This was the time for everybody in the school census to attend Lonesome Valley, attend school in the dead of winter, and sit by the potbellied stove. Seats had to be pulled up and placed in circles around the stove like an amphitheater. The teacher couldn't stand in the middle either. Weather had drawn the seat-circles around the potbellied stove but had left the teacher outside the circle.

Suddenly we would have sunshine that would thaw the frozen earth, and Lonesome Valley would be a sea of mud. Sundance would sink to his knees as he carried me five miles through the mud on these short winter days. The whole valley would be dark and hauntingly ugly. Hungry birds would fly hither and thither, looking for weed seeds, chirruping their mournful winter notes. The narrow-gauged valley looked hungry and barren as the wind lifted the carcasses of old leaves from the bottom of the funnel and swept them away to unknown places. And when I saw this barren, hungry, desolate land, where there was not food for crow, beast, ŏr fowl in winter, I knew why everybody worked in the fields while the season was here and it was time for work. It was the fable of the ant and the grasshopper. And the Lonesome Valley people were ants. They were not the idle dancing grasshoppers. They worked while the season for growth was with them. And they laid away, but not too much, for the horrible, monstrous winter weather we now knew.

25

DECEMBER came. We had a Christmas tree and my pupils drew numbers from a hat and exchanged gifts. We had a Christmas program and I bought candy, apples, oranges, and bananas. We lost only one day for Christmas holiday. My pupils hardly knew the meaning of letting out school a week for Christmas. For these were the days when they could go to school. These were the days when they couldn't plow and till 'the earth and harvest the crops. These were the days to get an education. Our six-months' school couldn't go too far into the late winter. For they had to start burning tobacco beds and getting ready for another crop year.

January came. My attendance leaped to sixty, though I had never seen more snow, more icy winds, more unbearable weather. But this was our last month of school. Time was running out for them. Time to get their education, time for their play, relaxation, the fun of association, was coming to a close. Our good school year, our good time together, ended on February 4th. And now was the time for pupils to get their promotions. Guy Hawkins had received the highest number. He had gone from the first to the fifth grade. Ova Salyers was promoted to the fourth. Don Conway leaped to the seventh. Not one had failed. Six eight-graders had finished school. They would not go any more. Their "good years" had ended.

Last day of school, we had a program. Members of the community were invited. They came until the house was packed. We had readings, and then Guy Hawkins and Don Conway "chose up" and we had an arithmetic match. Finally I shook hands with my pupils, their mothers and fathers, and thanked them for their cooperation, for their sending me such rugged, fine young Americans. I told them that I would soon be a pupil again, and expressed my heartfelt joy for this chance to teach their children. I made them laugh when I told them I had learned more in six months of teaching than I had learned in my three years of high school. And that I would return to school a much smarter pupil. And I would.

At 1:00 P.M. I was in the saddle for the last time. My pupils watched me ride away, around the bend and out of sight. They waved to me and shouted their good-byes and I waved to them and shouted my good-byes. The ground was frozen and I made good time, giving Sundance the rein. I looked to my right and to my left, for the last time, at Lonesome Valley. I was leaving a familiar land where I had lived six of the most exciting months of my life. At one forty-five I was home. I put Sundance in the barn, and patted his nose. My clothes were packed, and I said good-bye to Aunt Effie and Uncle Amos.

"I won't say good-bye to you," Uncle Amos said. "I aim to play you a little fiddle piece so you'll remember us."

He played "Chicken Reel," and Aunt Effie danced.

"You know, Stuart," Uncle Amos laughed, "Effie and I have thought of taking out adoption papers for you! We always wanted a dozen and we just got eleven. You'd make the dozen."

Latin and plane geometry, and "got by" algebra by the skin of my teeth.

"What subjects will I have to teach at Winston High School?" I asked.

"Algebra, Latin, plane geometry, history, and English," he said.

"I'm afraid I can't teach algebra," I said.

"You've got mighty good college marks in algebra," he reminded me. "I have a transcript of your credits here! That's one reason I'm holding this high school for you. You fit the schedule. We don't have to warp the schedule to fit you."

I couldn't tell Superintendent Larry Anderson I had for my roommate at Lincoln Memorial, Mason Dorsey Gardner, who had won the coveted award of twenty-five dollars for being the best math student. I couldn't tell him Gardner had worked my algebra and I had written his themes.

"I'll take Winston High School," I said. "I'll be the faculty."

3

SATURDAY afternoon in early September I caught the Reo Speed Wagon that carried mail and passengers. I was on my way to Winston High School. I had a suitcase with my belongings. I had with me school supplies allotted a rural school. The Speed Wagon was packed with passengers. Women were sitting on men's laps, and children were sitting on the floor and the mailbags. There was a roof over us to keep the sun from blazing down upon our heads. There wasn't anything around us to keep away the wind and dust. Clouds of dust rose up behind us. When the Speed Wagon slowed down, the dust clouds swirled in behind and nearly choked us. We rode over the winding trail like a stagecoach in an earlier day. But we went much faster. This was the only communication line between Landsburgh and Winston.

We followed the Sandy River and then we went up Raccoon and over a mountain and down into Hinton Valley. Then we climbed another mountain, and, when we reached the top I saw before me, deep down, one of the prettiest valleys I had ever seen. The Tiber River wound slowly through the fertile farm lands like a silver ribbon in the sunlight. We went down this east wall of the valley, around the curves and up until we came to a store and post office. This was Winston. This was where I got off the Speed Wagon. I saw only one schoolhouse. This was the Winston Rural School. But I was not looking for the schoolhouse now. I was going to Baylors'—the big white house overlooking the Tiber River. I saw the house in the distance. This was the place where I would room and board.

That afternoon after Lucretia Baylor had shown me to my room, Snookie and Robin Baylor, two pupils whom I would have in Winston High School, went with me to show me the high-school building. Though I had seen this dilapidated little building when I passed by on the Speed Wagon, I didn't dream it was the high school. This squat, ugly little structure had once been used as a lodge hall. The lodge had been dissolved twenty years ago, but the hall still stood though tumbling to decay. When I walked inside a bat barely missed my head in its flight to escape. There were wasps' nests, mud-daubers' nests, and birds' nests above the window. A mavis flew from the nest through a broken windowpane in her escape to freedom.

I walked outside. I wanted to inspect the outdoor privies and the playground. Of all the thousands of acres of land there were in this spacious broad valley, I had less than one sixteenth of an acre for my high-school pupils. There was an outdoor privy in each corner of this tiny lot. Houseweeds grew as tall as the lodgehouse roof. The community's obscene artists had found these privies. I sent Snookie back to the Baylors' to get water, broom, scrub brush, soap, and a scythe.

That afternoon I went to work with two good helpers. We cleaned the lodge hall. We scrubbed ceiling, walls, and floor. We washed the walls of the privies. I scythed the small yard and raked the horseweeds from the lot. Then I hacked down the sharp stubble with a hoe. Snookie, Robin, and I put the schoolhouse, the privies, and the yard in order. We were ready for school on Monday morning.

While we were working on the yard, a tall boy swaggered up the road and stopped. He stood there silently watching us. His hair was long. His face was pimpled. He had elongated blue eyes that squinted brightly when he looked at us. His loose-fitting clothes looked as if they would fall from his body.

"Hiya, Budge." Snookie spoke as soon as he saw him standing watching us.

"Hi are you, Snook?" Budge said.

"Comin' to school Monday, Budge?" Robin asked.

"Yep, I wouldn't miss it," he said.

"Here's your teacher," Snookie introduced us. "Mr. Stuart, this is Budge Waters."

"Glad to know you, Budge," I said. I'd never seen a youth in my life that looked anything like him. I'd never seen one with his peculiar actions when he walked. He used his hands to pull against the wind. This strange youth stood silently watching us work a few minutes. Then he walked away, swaggering as he walked and pulling the air with his hands.

"Are you kidding me about this fellow?" I asked Snookie. "Is he really a high-school pupil?"

"I'm telling you the truth," Snookie said. "He'll be the first one here Monday morning. He'll be here by daylight."

"How faraway does he live?" I asked.

"About seven miles," Snookie said.

"Doesn't he have any work to do at home?" I asked.

"Plenty of work," Snookie said. "They grow about ten acres of tobacco every year. They raise corn and cane too. Old Budge is a good worker."

"He might be a good worker," I agreed, "but he's going to find it hard to get through high school!"

"Don't you worry, Mr. Stuart," Snookie warned me. "If you're not awfully smart, he'll be teaching you!"

4

MONDAY morning when Snookie, Robin, and I got to school—an hour before time to start—twelve pupils were waiting, and I got the surprise of my life. Not one was barefooted. They were well dressed too. All but Budge Waters. His clothes were new and clean but they didn't fit his angular body too well. There was one new automobile parked near the school. There were two handsome saddle horses tied in the shade of an elm tree. And there was one pony almost as pretty as Sundance tied to the schoolyard fence. The pupils came up and introduced themselves before we started school. There were six girls and eight boys. Before time for school to begin, I was acquainted with them and knew their names.

Their schedule was already written on the small blackboard. During my first day I gave them assignments, and we discussed briefly the beginning lessons. With fourteen pupils and five classes, each forty-five minutes long, I had a little time on my hands. It was not like teaching at Lonesome Valley, where I had fifty-four classes each day. During our brief discussions I realized these Tiber Valley pupils would not be as easy to teach as my pupils in Lonesome Valley had been. When I taught at Lonesome Valley, I had completed my third year of high school and was only three years ahead of my eighth-graders. But in training and general knowledge, there was a wide gap between us. I was eight years ahead of my Winston High School pupils, and I had thought, when I took this school, there would be a wide gap between us.

When I started teaching ancient history I found one pupil who knew more facts about this subject than I did. He was Budge Waters. He went back to the beginning of the Pharoah kings of Egypt; he named the kings, gave the dates in history when each served, and told what each did for his country. I asked Budge if he had taken this subject before. He told me he hadn't but he had read all of his textbooks except algebra that summer. He said algebra was hard for him, the other subjects were easy. Then I asked him to read two paragraphs in his history book and when he had finished I asked to hold his book. Then I asked him to tell me what he had read in these paragraphs. While he told what he had read I followed him in the paragraphs. He quoted the book almost verbatim. Now I knew Snookie Baylor had told me the truth! I asked Budge to read three more pages of history aloud to the class and then tell how much he had gotten from three pages. Again, he almost quoted three pages. I had heard of photographic memories. This was it. This boy didn't forget, either. He had a retentive memory.

During my first week at Winston High School I knew my problem was keeping ahead of these pupils, teaching them the subjects that had been hard for me in high school. I had to go home and work long hours in the evenings. I had to know my lessons. If I didn't, my pupils taught me. They did their assignments, no matter how much I gave them. The amount of work I gave them depended upon how much I wanted to study ahead. I had to study ahead in algebra, Latin, and plane geometry. I had to review my history and English too. I had to prepare five subjects.

I had accepted Winston High School, thinking it was a little place among the hills where my pupils would be the products of rural districts like Lonesome Valley. I had brought along a number of books to read so I wouldn't get lonesome. I wanted to have something to do. I found that I had plenty to do. I had to work to keep ahead of Budge Waters. He remembered dates better than I. When we had disagreed on dates, we looked them up in the encyclopedia, and Budge Waters was always right. Where did this boy get all his knowledge? Where did the other thirteen get their information too? Who were these pupils? What was their background? I was faced with one of the strangest problems I had ever known a teacher to have. And here was the place I would least expect to find such a problem.

5

NINE of my fourteen pupils came from farms. The sales of farm products were their total earnings. Billie Leonard, who rode the pony nine miles to school, was the son of a coal miner. Another was the son of a rural teacher, who supplemented his salary by farming during the summer. And I had the son and daughter of a deputy county sheriff. He had farmed before he was appointed deputy sheriff. Not one of the parents of my pupils was a college graduate. Not one had ever been to college. Not one was a high-school graduate. The rural teacher had only a few credits in high school. The majority of them hadn't finished grade work in the rural schools. But these parents had another kind of education. They knew the soil they farmed. They knew what to plant, where to plant, and when to plant. They knew how to cultivate their land. They had learned these things by experience. And they knew when and how to harvest.

While the men worked with the soil and the seasons, their thrifty wives ran their homes. There was some contrast to the homes in Tiber Valley and in Lonesome Valley. The reason for these differences perhaps was the soil. The Tiber River soil was better than the Lonesome Valley soil. And the Tiber Valley farmers used newer methods of farming, better machinery, and they cared for their land. This land to them was something like their own flesh and blood. Their forefathers, approximately a century and a half before, had settled in this valley. The same names, same families, same blood streams were here. With the passing of the years, the farms had grown smaller. They had been divided by the children when their elders died, divided again and again until the farms had not great boundaries they once had. Each cliff, forest, stream, and large roadside tree had some affectionate meaning to them.

During crop season if one man got behind with his work, or if he had sickness in his family and couldn't work, his neighbors helped him. It was the same in autumn harvest. The people worked in unison. They helped each other. There were no feuds. They were good neighbors. There were four different religious denominations. There were as many churches. Not anyone was particularly interested in what church you attended. That was your business. If you didn't attend a church at all, you weren't criticized. And everybody, in the different churches, aimed at the same heaven. This was hard for me to believe after my experience at Lonesome Valley, which was less than thirty miles away.

Of the thirty-two voting precincts in Greenwood County, Winston was the only precinct where neither of the two major political parties could use money. They didn't even attempt to buy votes at Winston. Each political party could almost count the Winston vote before it was cast. Usually there was a tie vote. At least, neither party ever carried the precinct with more than seven votes. Often the majority either way would be one or two votes. These people were the parents of the pupils I was teaching in Winston High School. These were the old landlocked Americans for whom Superintendent Larry Anderson had established a high school to give their children more educational opportunities. Their children were willing to take advantage of any opportunities.

At the end of my first two weeks I knew I was learning algebra, Latin, and plane geometry. I didn't worry about my pupils. All I worried about was keeping ahead of them. I thought I might ease the situation and not have to work so hard myself if I brought them more books to read. We didn't have a library. We had only a dictionary and an encyclopedia. The books I had brought to read myself, my pupils read in the first two weeks. And they were asking for more books. Budge Waters didn't read by sentence. He read by paragraph.

That was the reason on the Saturday morning of my second week I caught the Speed Wagon for Landsburgh. From Landsburgh, I walked five miles home. I didn't have any way to get back to Winston on Sunday. The Speed Wagon didn't carry mail on Sunday. I might be lucky enough to catch a ride after I walked from W-Hollow to the Sandy River Turnpike. I would have a heavy load of books to carry a long distance. But I didn't mind carrying books to pupils as eager to read as my Winston High School pupils.

I didn't know the kind of books to select for these pupils. There was an "age level of books" recommended for high-school Freshmen, but I didn't know about it. I filled my suitcase with books I loved. Books, I thought, that would keep them reading for some time. I chose books by Tolstoy, Melville, Chekhov, Victor Hugo, De Maupassant, Balzac, Thomas Hardy, Sinclair Lewis, Emerson, Whittier, Hamlin Garland, Dreiser, Whitman, Poe, Edgar Lee Masters, Bret Harte, and Jack London. With my suitcase full, I followed a fox path across the Seaton Ridge to the Sandy River Turnpike, which was three miles closer than if I had gone by Landsburgh. I walked up the dusty turnpike along the river, then up Raccoon Valley and over the mountain. I walked down into the Hinton Valley and up to the top of the east wall overlooking the Tiber Valley. I put my suitcase down and was resting under the shade of a roadside tree. I had walked about eleven miles with a forty-pound load. I was sweaty and tired. Then a stranger with an Ohio license on his car drove up, stopped, and asked me to ride. He took me all the way to Winston.

Monday I introduced my pupils to these new authors. I told them to take the books, read them, and exchange them until everybody had read them. I told them they were my books. All I wanted them to do was to take care of them and return them when they were through. Budge Waters selected *War and Peace*.

My getting novels, books of poetry, essays, and short stories didn't keep my pupils from crowding me. How I wished that I had worked harder in high school and college! How I wished that I had learned everything in my assignments! I had thought I would never use this subject matter again. All I hadn't learned, I was having to learn. All I had learned and had tried to forget, I was having to review. And this kept me busy. This was the first time in my life I had ever heard of high-school pupils crowding their teacher. It had always been the other way around. This made me wonder if I had been a good forgetter of all I had learned, or if I hadn't learned at all.

Since I had had only two years of Latin and was now trying to teach first-year Latin, I had to spend considerable time on this subject. And by doing this, I neglected to work

ahead of my pupils in algebra. One day in the third week,
Billie Leonard came up to me, and said, "Mr. Stuart, will you
show me how to work this algebra problem?"

I looked at the problem. It was a problem about trains
starting at given points and running toward each other so many
miles per hour and how long would it be before they met. I had
never solved this problem in my first-year algebra.

"Billie, I can't work this problem," I laughed, telling
him the truth.

"Mr. Stuart, I understand," he answered. "You want your
pupils to work these problems, don't you?"

"Yes, if they can," I said.

In less than thirty minutes Billie Leonard was back with
the problem solved. He showed it to me.

"Your theory is right, Billie," I said. "You've solved this
problem."

I knew he was right after I had seen it worked. But Billie
Leonard never knew that I couldn't actually work this problem.
Often my pupils solved algebra problems before I could. I
threw the responsibility of plane geometry, algebra, and Latin
directly upon them. I was just a little-better pupil in plane
geometry and Latin working along with them. In the subject
of algebra, I doubt that I was as good as half the members of
my class. But the way we covered algebra and the way my
pupils learned it gave me another thought. I wondered if many
teachers weren't too good in the subjects they taught and if
they didn't teach over their pupils' heads. This experience
made me wonder if it wasn't better when the teacher didn't
know his subject too well and had to work with his pupils
closer. Then he had more sympathy and understanding.

Budge Waters had a strange sense of humor. He never
laughed unless one of his classmates made a mistake. And
they made mistakes. When he laughed he laughed all over.
His whole body shook. And when his teacher made a mistake,
he would laugh until tears came from his elongated eyes and
ran down his pimpled cheeks. He would laugh until all his
classmates and his teacher would start laughing at him. His
teacher did considerable laughing too.

6

WHEN I had first come to Winston, I wondered what my pupils did for recreation. I wondered what I would do for recreation. I had thought reading was about the only kind of recreation. It didn't take me long to learn differently. One evening in September I was invited to Bill Madden's home. He was one of my pupils. His father had invited six or seven of the local musicians in to play for us. We sat in the yard where the grass was dying and the peach-tree leaves had turned golden and the moon was high in the sky above us. We listened to this local band play with their banjos, fiddles, guitar, mandolin, and accordion from seven until eleven. They never played the same tune twice, and often when they played a fast breakdown, one of the listeners would dance. I had never heard old-time music sound as beautiful as this, in the moonlight of the mild September evening.

There was hardly a family in this big vicinity who didn't have a musician. This was part of their recreation. People had learned to play musical instruments to furnish their own music just as they had learned to plant, cultivate, and harvest crops for their food supply. They depended upon themselves for practically. everything.

I went with my pupils, their parents, and neighbors to cornhuskings, apple-peelings, bean-stringings, square dances, and to the belling of the bride when there was a wedding. Often we rode mules many miles through darkness or moonlight to these community events. I never missed a party at the mill when they made sorghum molasses in this great cane country. We went to the sorghum mill, shoved each other in the skimmings-hole and ate the soft sweet foam from the boiling cane juice with long paddles whittled from willow wood. I went to all of the churches. I went with my pupils to the churches of their choice. I went to parties where we played post office and where we danced Skip to my Lou. . . . I didn't worry about recreation. I found plenty of recreation. It was the kind of recrea-

tion in which the old, middle-aged, and young took part. There
were not a few having fun and a whole crowd around them to
watch. This was the most democratic recreation I had ever seen.

Not one of my pupils had ever seen a stage play. If one
had ever seen a movie, I'd never heard of it. They didn't have
to leave landlocked Winston to find recreation. They had it at
home. They created it just as they created most of their necessities of life. As the autumn days wore on they popped corn
over the blazing wood fires and made molasses-and-popcorn
balls. There was somewhere to go every night. I couldn't accept
all the invitations. Each pupil invited me to his home to spend
the night. This was an old custom, for in the past years the
teacher had boarded with his pupils since his salary wasn't
enough to enable him to pay his board and have anything left.

When the hunting season came I hunted quail with my
pupils. I hunted rabbits with them in the Tiber weed fields.
My pupils were good marksmen. But I gave them a few sur-
prises at some of the shots I made. I had never told them about
my years of hunting experience. I went to the autumn-coloring
hills to hunt possums. And I taught them—as I had tried to
teach them high-school subjects—a little about possum hunting: that on the still and misty, warm nights when not a leaf
stirred was the time to catch possums and coons. When I
learned more about the terrain of the east and west walls,
where the persimmons and pawpaws grew, I showed them
where to find the possums. They—as I had once done—hunted
for animal pelts, shipped them, and bought books and clothes
with the money. I showed them how to take better care of their
pelts.

Many nights I climbed with them to the top of the east or
west wall with a pack of hounds. Often there were twenty-five
or thirty men with us and we'd have from thirty to fifty hounds
to chase the fox. We'd build a fire on the highest peak of stone
or earth and listen to the music of the running hounds. We
could hear the music of their barking, for we were high enough
to listen to them circle the fox around us. We braved all sorts
of weather to listen to the magic barking and running of the
hounds. On many a moonlit night we saw the fox not more
than a hundred yards ahead of the speckled, black, white,

brown-and-tan hounds as they came pouring from the autumn woods into an open field with their heads high in the air. The fox was hot and left much scent on the wind. The hounds didn't have to put their noses to the earth. They could smell the fox ahead instead of nosing the earth for his track.

Then came the autumn rains when the Speed Wagon no longer made the mail run to Landsburgh. The only road that connected the valley with the county-seat town was impassable. Anybody wanting to go to Landsburgh had to provide his own means of transportation. He had to walk, ride muleback or horseback, or take two teams hitched to one wagon. For the valley—after the autumn rains, after the freezes and thaws—became a sea of mud. The slender, winding road was a ribbon of mud. I saw loads of tobacco leaving Winston with as many as three mule teams hitched to one wagon. I never saw a wagon loaded with barrels of sorghum or tobacco have less than two mule teams. It took one good mule team to pull an empty wagon; the wheels sank in mud to their hubs. Winston was isolated. This was why the people depended upon themselves for everything. When the Speed Wagon stopped making the run to Landsburgh, people knew the long winter months of isolation had begun.

The mail was carried by horseback. Wid Maddox put his Speed Wagon away to use again next May or June, depending on the condition of the roads. The people in Winston knew spring had returned when the Speed Wagon started hauling mail. Now Wid used from four to six horses. He rode one and led a pack horse. When the mail was heavy, he often led two pack horses. He rode part of the thirty-odd-mile mail route to where he put these horses in a barn at "midway." There he got fresh horses and continued his journey to Landsburgh. He spent the night in Landsburgh. Next morning he rode to midway, where he exchanged his tired horses for fresh ones so he could continue his journey over the ribbon of sloppy mud.

7

WHEN the leaves changed color in the valley and the sun was bright as a brush-pile flame, I went on long hikes with my pupils. We'd take a hike to the autumn-colored hills soon as the school day was over. We'd take food to cook over an open fire on the summit of one of the walls that enclosed the valley. Sometimes the girls would go with us. The hike to the highest summits was often a strenuous climb. We would see the valley below in its autumn colors while we ate and talked.

The Tiber Valley walls grew mostly one type of tree. That was the tough-butted white oak. This tree choked almost all other types of growth on these infertile slopes. It would root well into the hard, bony earth and into the rock crevices, and in autumn when these leaves colored they were beautiful to see. On each side of the valley, these leaf-clouds rose toward the sky until they reached the pine groves on the walls' crests. These leaf-clouds were brilliant when they rippled in the sun. The pine groves made green clouds between the golden leaf-clouds and the blue of the sky.

Down in the valley we could see every splash of color. Green leaves were there still, for the Tiber mists had protected them against the biting frost. There were blood-red shoe-make leaves, golden sycamore and poplar leaves, slate-colored water-birch leaves, and the dull- and bright-gold willow leaves. And down in the valley the corn shocks stood like wigwams in an Indian village. We could see the bright knee-high corn stubble glittering in the autumn sun. We could see the brown meadow stubble, too, where the hay had been mown and piled in high mounds with poles through the center.

Often I walked alone beside the Tiber in autumn. For there was a somberness that put me in a mood that was akin to poetry. I'd watch the big sycamore leaves zigzag from the interlocking branches above to the clear blue Tiber water and drift away like tiny golden ships. I'd find the farewell-to-summer in bloom along this river. Then a great idea occurred to me. It wasn't about poetry. It was about schools.

I thought if every teacher in every school in America— rural, village, city, township, church, public, or private—could inspire his pupils with all the power he had, if he could teach them as they had never been taught before to live, to work, to play, and to share, if he could put ambition into their brains and hearts, that would be a great way to make a generation of the greatest citizenry America had ever had. All of this had to begin with the little unit. Each teacher had to do his share. Each teacher was responsible for the destiny of America, because the pupils came under his influence. The teacher held the destiny of a great country in his hand as no member of any other profession could hold it. All other professions stemmed from the products of his profession.

Within this great profession, I thought, lay the solution of most of the cities', counties', states', and the nation's troubles. It was within the teacher's province to solve most of these things. He could put inspiration in the hearts and brains of his pupils to do greater things upon this earth. The school-room was the gateway to all the problems of humanity. It was the gateway to the correcting of evils. It was the gateway to inspire the nation's succeeding generations to greater and more beautiful living with each other; to happiness, to health, to brotherhood, to everything!

I thought these things as I walked in the somber autumn beside this river and watched the leaves fall from the tall bank-side trees to the blue swirling water. And I believed deep in my heart that I was a member of the greatest profession of mankind, even if I couldn't make as much salary shaping the destinies of fourteen future citizens of America as I could if I were a blacksmith with little education at the Auckland Steel Mills.

8

NOBODY could keep me from starting home. I was determined to go. I needed more novels, books of short stories, books of poems and essays for my pupils to read. I wanted to see Superintendent Larry Anderson. When Lucretia Baylor learned I was determined to go, she prepared a quick hot lunch for me. She did this while I packed my clothes and got ready. For my teaching day ended at 3:30 p. m., and I had walked the three-fourths mile to Baylors' in a hurry. It was early in the afternoon, but the dark December skies hung low over the valley, and there were six inches of snow on the ground. I had seventeen miles ahead of me. The only way I could get to my destination was to walk.

"If you were a boy of mine," Ottis Baylor said, "I wouldn't let you go. Not on a seventeen-mile journey on a night like this! I advise you against going. I know the road to Landsburgh better than you do. I've walked it enough to know. It's a treacherous road when you leave the Tiber Valley Road and try the short cut around Laurel Ridge."

I knew that I wasn't listening to Ottis Baylor. I was going, anyway. I knew that I was fast on foot. I had walked thirty-five miles in a day. That hadn't even made my legs or feet sore. If I could walk this far on a short day, then I was as positive as death, by steady walking, I could cover a mile every twelve minutes. I thought: If I had luck, I could make the journey in three and a half hours. I allowed myself four hours and that was plenty of time. And I was leaving Baylors' at four.

The massive black cloud rested on the east and west walls of the valley like a roof. The east wall was the one I had to climb. When I reached the top I would be on Laurel Ridge. By going this way, I could cut three miles from my walking distance. I knew the path to Laurel Ridge. I'd been over it many times before. Whether the snow was broken over this path or not, I did not know. I did not care. I said good-bye to Baylors', and I was on my way.

The December wind whistled in the barren shoe-make tops, where the red birds hopped from limb to limb and chirruped plaintive notes. Snowbirds stood by the clumps of dead ragweed the snow hadn't covered. They were searching for a scanty supper of the frozen seeds. Though time was early on this short winter day, I thought darkness might come soon. Going up the mountain, I made excellent time. I followed the path all right. I had to break the snow, for no one had traveled this path. I knew how to follow the path by the clumps of trees, rock cliffs, and fences. These were the landmarks to follow. When the path was covered in snow these landmarks still looked the same.

When I reached the big opening—a cleared cove where tobacco had been farmed—I knew I was halfway to Laurel Ridge. And from Baylors' to Laurel Ridge was approximately three miles. I looked at my watch and it had taken me thirty minutes. This was slower time than I had expected. The snow was even deeper high on the mountain. The path was harder to break. Ottis and Lucretia Baylor might have been right when they warned me against going but I would not turn back. I was going on even if I didn't get home before midnight. I was halfway to Laurel Ridge now. I saw a rabbit hop across my path, and when he saw me he took long hops for a saw-brier thicket. The rabbit thought night was here, for rabbits sleep on winter days and stir at night.

Before I reached the second small opening near Laurel Ridge, I lost my path. I walked into a forest of tough-butted white oaks. They grew close together shutting out the diminishing winter light. I had never seen these trees before. I turned quickly, retracing my steps until I found the path. I knew I had been in too much of a hurry. I'd have to be more careful. I'd not walked more than a hundred yards when a red fox, almost as big as a collie, crossed my path. When he saw me he took off with full speed and disappeared in the wintry dusk that was getting thicker on the mountain. I wondered now if I had reached the black cloud that seemed to rest there. I wondered if that was why the dusk was suddenly turning to darkness. But why should I worry now? I had at least reached Laurel Ridge, for there was a five-strand, rusty barbed-wire fence nailed to the trees. I knew this fence. It followed Laurel Ridge some distance before it turned back down the mountain. When I held my arm up to look at my watch, I couldn't see the figures on the dial. I didn't know what time it was, but I knew it was early. I knew I was in the snow cloud. For the big snowflakes were falling around me. I could see them dimly, these white flakes about the size of dimes, falling just in front of my eyes. I could feel them hitting my overcoat.

All I had to do was turn to my left after I reached Laurel Ridge. That was the right direction. I could follow the wire fence even if I had to follow it with my hand as I walked. I had one free hand. I carried my suitcase with my right hand. My left hand was free. But I didn't touch the fence. Not yet. I was following Laurel Ridge Road. I was following it with my feet. I had hunted much at night in my lifetime. Darkness had never bothered me too much. But now I couldn't see the woods and I knew it couldn't possibly be six o'clock. I was in a snowstorm. I could hear the snowflakes falling through the barren oak tops whose branches interlocked above the road.

Then I heard voices, and the sound was sweet to hear. I had barely time to side-step for two mule teams. I almost walked into a mule before I saw him. Yet there was a lighted lantern on the joltwagon the mules were pulling. When I recognized Eif Potters, he stopped his mule team in great surprise. He asked me where I was going on a night like this. Then I knew what he was talking about.

The fury of the storm almost blotted out the lantern light. It didn't give light more than six feet away. The snowflakes were larger than nickels. They were almost as large as quarters. I was in the cloud I'd seen before I left Baylors'.

I told Eif Potters and his son Zeke, who was sitting on the wagon beside him, I was on my way home. That snow wasn't falling down in Tiber Valley when I left, not more than two hours ago. He told me they hadn't been in the snowstorm until they reached the top of Raccoon Hill. Then he invited me to get on the wagon and go home with them, but I refused. When I refused he said he would loan me his lantern, but that they couldn't get around Laurel Ridge without it. Said he had five more miles to go, that he had taken a load of tobacco to

Landsburgh and was getting back the same day, that he and his mules were very tired to push through five more miles of darkness and storm.

On this lonely ridge, high up in a snow cloud, I said good night to Eif and Zeke and was on my way, for I had lost about five minutes talking to them. I hadn't walked but a few steps when I looked back. The mule teams, wagon, riders, and lantern had disappeared in the storm. Yet I heard the jingling of the mules' harness, and I heard the men's voices as they talked to each other. Then I plunged on, alone, taking in both sides of the road. I hunted for the fence with an outstretched hand in the darkness, but I couldn't find it.

Eif had warned me about one place. He told me if I bore too far to my left I would go into a vast tract of timber that lay on the east wall of Tiber Valley. And for this reason, I bore to my right, feeling with my feet while the snow came down as I had never felt it fall before. One thing I had forgotten to ask Eif for was matches. He was a pipe-smoker too. He had smoked his pipe all the time he sat on his wagon and talked to me. If only I had a match! I was stumbling over the road. Once I went in water to my knee. Then I knew I must be on the Laurel Ridge Road. This was a deep wagon-wheel rut, and Eif had driven over it and had broken the thin ice down to the water. My foot was wet. Water squashed in my shoe. One of my galoshes was filled with water.

Then I stepped into a hole of water with my dry foot. I went in to my knee. Both pant legs were wet to my knees. Again and again I stepped into water, but my feet were already wet and it didn't make any difference if I did get them wet again. I kept moving. I followed the road the best I could. I knew I was on the Laurel Ridge Road. That was the main thing. I would soon reach the turnpike at the top of Raccoon Hill. That was where the Laurel Ridge Road ended. And this distance was approximately three miles from where my path from Baylors' had gone through the barbed-wire fence onto the Laurel Ridge. If I could only see my watch! I had surely walked three more miles!

Time in the night, I thought, when one was walking alone, might seem longer than it actually was. I kept on going. I waded water, and I waded snow. The snow was almost as deep as my galoshes were high. I walked on and on and on. Then I knew I'd gone far enough to reach the turnpike on Raccoon Hill . . . the turnpike that would take me straight to Landsburgh. While I thought about the fast time I would be able to make on the turnpike when I reached it, I suddenly walked into a cornfield. I thought it was a cornfield. I thought I was standing beside a fodder shock. It stood like a white wigwam before me. I pushed my hand through the snow and felt the dry fodder stalks. I knew now that I was lost.

I couldn't even retrace my steps. I couldn't see them. If it had been light enough for me to see them, I couldn't have followed them far because they would have been snowed under. I was lost, that was all. I was in this cornfield and I would have to make the best of it. I stood beside the fodder shock—this tiny thing of security—while I screamed at the top of my voice. I knew that in this part of Greenwood County there was much wasteland. There were miles and miles where there wasn't a house. But I screamed, anyway. I thought somebody might hear me and come to my rescue. The only answer I got was the faraway barking of a fox. When I screamed he mocked me with his barking.

When I had reached this fodder shock, my feet were still warm and my face was wet with perspiration. But in this open space where corn had grown on the mountaintop there was an incessant sweep of wind. The wind carried the snow directly at me. I could measure the speed of the wind by the way the soft flakes hit my face. The soft flakes felt like grains of corn. I had to start walking to keep warm. I had to do something in a hurry. Then a thought came to me. If there was one fodder shock here, there were others. The cornfield must be fairly large to give the wind such great velocity. I was almost afraid to leave the fodder shock I had already found. Even when I did, I held to my suitcase. I walked a few paces and found another fodder shock. I put my arm around the top of the shock and dragged it back to the first one. I carried eight fodder shocks to one place. The fodder shocks were not large. The shocks were not as tall as I was. I used one hand to carry them; I held to my suitcase with the other. I was afraid I'd lose it and that it would soon be snowed under. Besides, I had other ideas.

After I'd pulled these fodder shocks together, I laid the heavy ends of the fodder to the windward side of the mountain. I bedded three shocks down on the snow. Then I put a shock on each side of the floor I'd made. I stood two shocks up on the windward side, to pull down on me as soon as I was ready to lie down. The last shock I stood up, to use where the fodder would be thinnest above me. Then I stood on the fodder and pulled off my shoes. The wind-driven snow was cold to my wet feet and legs. I pulled off my overcoat and wet pants. I took a dry soiled shirt from my suitcase and dried the water from my feet and legs. I tied dry dirty shirts around my feet. I put on a pair of soiled trousers I was taking to have dry-cleaned. I bundled myself with all the clothes I had in my suitcase. I lay down and spread my overcoat over me. Now I reached up and pulled the fodder shocks down upon me. The fodder quilt was thick but not too heavy. I lay there and listened to the mice in the fodder around me and the ticking of my watch while over me the wind moaned and the snow fell.

I knew that I should not go to sleep. For if I did the wind might blow the fodder from over me. I would freeze to death and I would not be found in this cornfield until the farmer came to haul his fodder home. I must have been half-asleep when I heard the hoot owls start calling to one another from the timber all around this cornfield. I didn't know exactly where they were. But I knew they frequented the less-populated places. From their calls, coming from all directions, I knew this must be their meeting place. I no longer heard the wind nor felt it seeping through the fodder. I parted the fodder stalks to see what had happened. There were a million bright stars high in the clear blue sky, and in a short distance all around me—for there was not more than two acres of this cornfield—I could see the dark outlines of trees. Among these trees were the hoot owls. They were on every side. They cried jubilantly to each other, asking always the same: "Who, who are you?"

I pulled the fodder quilt back over me and lay there listening to the hoots of the owls, to the mice over me, around me and through the fodder, and to the ticking of my watch. I thought that I could stay awake until morning. Since the skies had cleared, I knew the weather before morning would be sub- zero on this mountaintop. I went to sleep dreaming that I would not go to sleep.

9

WHEN I awoke there were fewer stars in the sky. Day- light didn't come on these short December days until nearly eight. I tried to see what time it was, but I couldn't see the hands of my watch. The owls had flown away, and all was silent save for the ticking of my watch and the mice that had never slept the whole night through. I had slept warm on this cold night. I had warmed the fodder for the mice. The place was comfortable for all of us. But now I sat up and placed the fodder around me like a wigwam. I wanted the day to break so I could put on my clothes and be on my way. I had never been so hungry in my life.

Just as soon as it was light enough to see what I was doing, I started dressing. The legs of the pants I'd pulled off were frozen stiff and hard. My shoes had frozen so that I couldn't get them on. I didn't have a match to build a fire to thaw them. It was impossible to put them on. I wrapped a soiled shirt around each foot. I put my feet into my frozen galoshes. I put my frozen shoes and pants into my suitcase. It was light enough for me to see dim footprints in the snow. I could retrace myself. I wanted to see where I had made my mistake.

I followed my tracks, dim little prints in the crusted snow, for more than a mile. Then I came to Laurel Ridge. Far, far, down below, I could see Hinton Valley, now a great white silence except for the dark, leafless, sleeping trees. And to my right, if I had gone just fifty feet to my left, I would have found the turnpike on Raccoon Hill. I had borne too far to my right after Eif Potters had warned me about turning left. I had gone somewhere on the mountain between the headwaters of

North Fork and Raccoon, where I had found the cornfield and slept in the fodder.

Though it was Saturday morning when farmers would be on their way to Landsburgh, I was the first person on the turnpike. The white silence of snow that was even with the tops of my galoshes remained unbroken until I made a path. I walked down Raccoon Hill, and in the distance, somewhere far down the road, I heard voices. They were coming toward me. I was going toward them. Their shouts at their teams grew louder. I saw three teams hitched to a snowplow and the county roadworkers were breaking the road. I walked past them, and they looked at me. I hadn't noticed the fodder blades still hanging to my overcoat, and I brushed them off before I stopped at Gullet's gristmill.

I knew Ephraim Gullet. When I went inside the gristmill he asked me if I wasn't traveling early. I told him I had been lost and had slept on the mountain. He put more coal in the potbellied stove. He made a pot of coffee. I thawed my shoes and my pant legs while I drank hot coffee and warmed myself in front of the red-hot stove. Ephraim told me that his thermometer was twelve below at six that morning. He couldn't understand how I had stripped my clothes and dried the water from my legs and feet there on the mountaintop facing the great sweeps of snow-laden wind. He couldn't understand how I had managed to survive the rigor of the raw elements on the mountaintop when it was twelve below in the valley.

10

WHEN Superintendent Larry Anderson unlocked his office door at nine that Saturday morning, I was there waiting for him. I had caught a ride in on a coal truck from Gullet's gristmill to Landsburgh.

"Well, well, how did you get here so early?" Superintendent Anderson asked. "You didn't come all the way from Winston this morning?"

"Just part of the way," I said.

He didn't ask me where I stayed. And I didn't tell him. I had something else I wanted to talk to him about.

"How are you getting along with your school out there?" he asked me.

"I think I'm getting along all right," I said. "What reports have you heard?"

"Good reports," he said.

"I'm glad to hear the reports about my teaching have been favorable," I said. "I am learning myself. My pupils are working me as hard as I am working them!"

My Superintendent thought I was joking. He started laughing. He laughed until he couldn't talk.

"I'm telling you the truth," I said. "I'm not telling you a joke. I've worked harder than I did in high school or in college!"

Superintendent Larry Anderson laughed harder than before. He laughed so loud anybody in the corridors of the courthouse could have heard him.

"You know there's not anything as good for a man as a good laugh early in the morning," he said.

I knew that he still thought I was joking.

"Superintendent Anderson," I said seriously, "I'm up against teaching those fourteen pupils. I've not got a slow one among them. I've got a couple of average pupils, and they can do every bit of work I give them. And," I explained, with a gesture of my hand for emphasis, "I've got one pupil that's a genius. He knows more facts than I do. He's only a Freshman in high school. I tell you, Budge Waters is a genius! If he isn't, I'm terribly dumb. I've got six or seven A pupils and he's above them!"

"Do you grade by the curve system?" he asked.

"Certainly not," I said.

"Why not?" he asked.

"I didn't make a bad record in high school," I said. "I made better than B average in college. I have first-year high-school pupils crowding me. They ask me intelligent questions I cannot answer. Why should I string pupils like these over a curve system? Not any more than I should take a poor pupil from a group of poor ones and give him an A because he is a fraction better than the others!"

Superintendent Larry Anderson sat silently looking at me for a minute. We were in his office alone. No other rural teachers had reached Landsburgh. Then he spoke thoughtfully: "Well, what is your problem?"

"I haven't any," I said. "I've not had to discipline a pupil. They work hard. They play hard."

I knew he was wondering why I had come to his office.

"But there is one thing I'd like to do," I said. "That's why I've called on you this morning. I'd like to test my own judgment to see if I am wrong or right in my opinion of my pupils. I'd like to know how to go about entering them in the state scholastic contest. The contest is held each spring, isn't it?"

"Oh, yes," he said, "but there is an elimination process. Your pupils will have to take an examination against the pupils in Landsburgh High School! Then, if you are successful there," he explained, "they'll go to Auckland to enter the district contest. If they are successful there, they'll go on to the state contests!"

I knew that to get past Landsburgh, now a joint city-and-county high school, we'd have to compete with the best from nearly four hundred pupils. To get past the regional, we'd have to compete with the best, selected from thousands. Yet, it took only one brain to win a contest. I knew Budge Waters had that brain if it was properly trained. I thought he was capable of competing state-wide. I thought Billie Leonard could take the district in algebra. And I was willing to challenge big Landsburgh High School in all the five subjects I was teaching my pupils.

"If it's all right with you, Superintendent," I said, "you make arrangements and set a date for us to meet Landsburgh High School in algebra, Latin, English, plane geometry, and history!"

"I'll do it," he smiled. "Would sometime in January suit you?"

"Any time's all right with me," I said. "Make it convenient for the Landsburgh High School!"

"That's fair enough," he said.
"This is all I wanted to see you about," I said.
With these words, I left him alone in his office.

11

SUNDAY morning at nine o'clock I left W-Hollow for Winston. I walked briskly over the frozen snow that crunched beneath my feet. I faced the unmerciful December wind. It whipped my clothes. It stung my face. But I knew I would not get cold. For I was carrying a load of twenty books I had borrowed for my pupils. They had already read all of my books. I was also carrying a limited supply of clothes. I couldn't bring all the clothes I wanted to bring because the books occupied most of the space in my suitcase. I was on my way over the frozen snow, beneath a sunless sky, facing a ter-rific wind . . . and I would go all the way this time in day-light. I wouldn't make the mistake I'd made before. Despite the frigid wind, the sunless sky, the crunching, frozen snow, I was carrying a load that would keep me warm.

I took the near cut across the Seaton Ridge. This would save me three miles. And when I reached the Seaton Ridge, I had never faced such a biting wind as blew from the north. I was glad to get over the ridge and down to the Sandy River Turnpike. It was much warmer down in the Sandy River Valley. Here I had hopes of catching a ride. But I walked on and on along the slick turnpike. The road plows hadn't scooped away the ice on the road. It was still there. I never met a person on the Sandy River Turnpike. Then I reached Raccoon. I walked all the way, hoping against hope that I would catch a ride. Though perspiration stood on my face, my body was chilled by the wind, and if I stopped thirty seconds the per-spiration dried on my face.

When I reached the top of Raccoon Hill, I looked at my watch. It was twelve noon. I had six more miles to go. I had walked eleven miles in three hours. If I hadn't been loaded and the turnpike hadn't been ice-coated, I could have walked faster. This was slow time. I took a sandwich from my coat pocket Mom had made me bring along. I was surprised to find it frozen. But I was hungrier than I thought. The frozen sand-wich tasted good. I ate it as I walked on the Laurel Ridge Road. If ever in my life I had felt a velocity of frigid wind, it was on this road. It went through my overcoat and through my clothes. I thought the terrific force of this wind would lift me from the road over into the Tiber Valley.

I felt the cold as I had never felt it before. My hands and feet ached. Water ran from my eyes. Before I had walked three miles along Laurel Ridge, I would get behind a big tree here and there to serve as a windbreak so I could warm. Often I stood behind a rock cliff for a windbreak. The cold was doing something to my body and my senses. Friday night's sleeping in a fodder shock was warm in comparison. Finally I reached the path where I left the ridge. I was almost too stiff to bend over to get between the fence wires. I wondered if I could go on to Baylors'. Once, I sat down on the snow. I thought of leaving my suitcase and trying to run to warm my body.

As I walked and ran slowly down the mountain, stepping in my own dim footprints I had made Friday, my senses came to me enough to make me realize I had to go on. I couldn't stop now. If I did, I'd soon be a goner. The thought of sitting down again scared me. I hadn't any feeling in my feet. I felt as if I was stepping with wooden feet. My numb, lifeless hand felt chained to my suitcase. I reached Baylors' at two-thirty. It had taken me two and a half hours to cover the last six miles. If it hadn't been for Ottis Baylor, I believe to this day my hands and feet would have been frozen. The first thing he did was take the suitcase from my hand, and then he pulled off my gloves and shoes. I couldn't.

He poured ice-cold water into a tub and had me put my feet in the water. I couldn't feel the water with my feet. He had me put my hands in a pan of ice-cold water. I couldn't feel the water with my hands. In a few minutes Lucretia brought hot water and Ottis tempered the water gradually until a little feeling came back to my hands and feet. He tempered the water more and more. And more feeling came to my hands and feet. He continued this process until the water was approximately body temperature. The normal feeling to my hands and feet was restored.

"I don't know why you had to go to Landsburgh on a day like last Friday," Ottis Baylor said, when I started putting on my socks. "Then you come back here on the coldest day I have ever seen in my life. I wouldn't have slept out on a night like last Friday night, when it was twelve below in the valley; nor have walked back here from Landsburgh on a day like this, for this farm! Why did you do it?"

"Then you know about my getting lost last Friday," I said.

"Everybody knows about it around Winston," he answered. "Everybody's talking about it. Not anybody can understand why you did it," he added thoughtfully, as I slipped my feet back into my shoes.

"You must have a girl in Landsburgh," Lucretia laughed.

"Here is why I did it," I said, as I opened my suitcase. "I'll show you! See these books! I went after these for your boys and for the pupils in my high school. Smartest pupils I've ever taught."

Then Ottis looked at Lucretia, and Lucretia looked at Ottis.

"I did something else, too, you'll hear about in a month from now," I added. "I went to see Superintendent Anderson about a little matter."

"You're not resigning from Winston High School, are you?" Ottis asked.

"Oh, no," I answered. "I wouldn't think of it."

12

WHEN I told my pupils about a scholastic contest with Landsburgh High School, I watched their expressions. They were willing and ready for the challenge. The competitive spirit was in them.

"We must review everything we have covered in our textbooks," I told them. "We must cover more territory in our textbooks too. Hold up your right hands if you are willing!"

Every pupil raised his hand.

Right then we started to work. In addition to regular assignments, my pupils began reviewing all of the old assignments we had covered.

Despite the challenge ahead and all the reviewing and study we planned to do, we never stopped play. The Tiber River was frozen over. The ring of skates and merry laughter broke the stillness of the winter nights. We skated on the white winding ribbon of ice beneath the high, cold winter moon. Often we'd skate until midnight. We'd hear the wind blow mournfully over the great white silence that surrounded us and sing lonesome songs without words in the barren branches of the bankside trees. And we'd hear the foxes' barking, high upon the walls of sheltering cliffs, mocking the music of our ringing skates.

Over the week ends we'd go to Tiber where we'd cut holes in the ice and gig fish. The boys and I would rabbit-hunt up and down the Tiber Valley in the old stubble fields now covered with snow and swept by wind. We'd track minks, possums, raccoons, weasels, and foxes to their dens. We'd climb the mountains and get spills over the rocks into the deep snow. This took our minds from books and taught us another kind of education. It was as much fun as reading books. Now that a big contest was before us, we needed diversion. And we got it. Our state was not usually cold enough for winter sports. This winter was an exception, and we took full advantage of it.

When we hunted the girls didn't go with us, but when we skated, fished, and rode sleighs they went along. There was a long gentle slope not far from the schoolhouse, we found ideal for our sleighs. It was almost a mile to the end of our sleigh run. We went over the riverbank and downstream for many yards on the Tiber ice. We rode sleighs during the noon hour, before and after school.

On winter days when the snow had melted, leaving the dark earth a sea of sloppy mud, we designed floor games for our little one-room school. They were simple games such as throwing bolts in small boxes. And we played darts. We also played a game called "fox and goose." We made our fox-and-

goose boards and we played with white, yellow, and red grains
of corn. We had to make our own recreation. I never saw a
distracted look on a pupil's face. I never heard one complain
that the short, dark winter days were boresome because there
wasn't anything to do. I think each pupil silently prayed for
the days to be longer. We were a united little group. We were
small but we were powerful. We played hard, and we studied
hard. We studied and played while the December days passed.

13

THAT day in early January, we dismissed school. This
was the first time we had dismissed for anything. We had
never lost an hour. I had actually taught more hours than was
required. This was the big day for us. It was too bad that
another blizzard had swept our rugged land and that a stinging
wind was smiting the valleys and the hills. But this didn't stop
the boys and me from going. Leona Maddox, my best Latin
pupil, couldn't go along. Her father, Alex Maddox, wouldn't
let her ride a mule seventeen miles to Landsburgh to compete
in a contest on a day like this. I couldn't persuade him to let
her go.

On that cold blizzardy morning, Budge Waters rode his
mule to school very early and built a fire in the potbellied
stove. When the rest of us arrived on our mules at approximately seven o'clock, Budge had the schoolroom warm. We
tied our mules to the fence, stood before the fire, and warmed
ourselves before we started on our journey. Then we unhitched
our mules from the fence and climbed into the saddles. Little
clouds of frozen snow in powdery puffs arose from the mules'
hoofs as six pupils and their teacher rode down the road.

Though the force of wind in the Tiber Valley was powerful, it was at our backs. The wind was strong enough to give
our mules more momentum. We made good time until we left
the valley and climbed the big hill. Here, we faced the wind.
It was a whipping wind—stinging, biting wind on this mountain—that made the water run from our eyes and our mules'

eyes, but for us there was no turning back. We were going to Landsburgh High School. That was that. We were determined to meet this big school; big to us, for they outnumbered us twenty-six to one. Soon we were down in Hinton Valley. Then we rode to the top of the Raccoon Hill, where we faced the stinging wind again.

"Mr. Stuart, I have been thinking," Budge Waters said, as we rode along together, "if you can sleep in a fodder shock when it's twelve degrees below zero, we can take this contest from Landsburgh High School! I've not forgotten how you walked seventeen miles to carry us books. All of your pupils remember. We'll never let you down!"

Budge Waters thought of this because we were riding down the mountain where I had slept that night. Then we rode down into the Raccoon Valley, and Billie Leonard, only thirteen years old, complained of numbness in his hands, feet, and lips. He said he felt as if he was going to sleep. I knew what he was talking about. I had had the same feeling the day Ottis Baylor had put my hands and feet in cold water. We stopped at a home, tied our mules to the fence, and went in and asked to warm. Bert Patton, a stranger to us, piled more wood on the open fire until we were as warm as when we had left the schoolhouse. We told him who we were and where we were going.

"On a day like this!" he said, shaking his head sadly.

We climbed into the saddles again. We were over halfway now. The second hitch would put us at Landsburgh High School. We had valley all the way to Landsburgh, with walls of rugged hills on each side for windbreaks.

14

AT ELEVEN o'clock we rode across the Landsburgh High School yard, and hitched our mules to the fence around the athletic field. There were faces against the windowpanes watching us. Then we walked inside the high school, where Principal Ernest Charters met and welcomed us. He told us that he was surprised we had come on a day like this and that we had been able to arrive so soon.

In the Principal's office my pupils and I huddled around the gas stove while we heard much laughter in the high-school corridors. The Landsburgh High School pupils thought we were a strange-looking lot. Many came inside their Principal's office to take a look at us. We were regarded with curiosity, strangeness, and wonder. Never before had these pupils seen seven mules hitched to their schoolyard fence. Never before had they competed scholastically with so few in number—competitors who had reached them by muleback. The Landsburgh High School Principal didn't feel about the contest the way we felt. To him, this was just a "setup" to test his pupils for the district contest which would soon be held. He told me this when he went after the sealed envelopes that held the questions. We warmed before the gas stove while he made arrangements for the contest.

"These questions were made out by the state department of education," he said when he returned. "I don't know how hard they are."

My pupils stood silently by the stove and looked at each other. We were asked to go to one of the largest classrooms. A Landsburgh High School teacher had charge of giving the tests. When the Landsburgh High School pupils came through the door to compete against my pupils, we knew why Principal Charters had selected this large classroom. My pupils looked at each other, then at their competitors.

I entered redheaded Jesse Jarvis to compete with ten of their plane-geometry pupils. I entered Billie Leonard against twenty-one of their selected algebra pupils.

"Budge, you'll have to represent us in grammar, English literature, and history," I said. "And I believe I'll put you in civil government. Is that all right?"

"Yes," he agreed. Budge had never had a course in civil government. All he knew about it was what he had read in connection with history.

"Robert Batson, you enter in history and grammar.

"Robin Baylor, you enter in algebra.

"Snookie Baylor, you enter in algebra and plane geometry.

"Sorry, Mr. Charters," I said, "we don't have anyone to enter in Latin. My best Latin pupil, Leona Maddox, couldn't make this trip."

After the contest had begun, I left the room. Miss Bertha Madden was in charge. I took our mules to Walter Scott's barn on the east end of Landsburgh, where I fed and watered them.

With the exception of an interval when the contestants ate a quick lunch, the contest lasted until 2:30 P. M. I had one pupil, Budge Waters, in four contests. I had planned to enter him in two. Just as soon as Budge had finished with civil government, we started grading the papers. All the pupils were requested to leave the room.

We graded the papers with keys. Mr. Charters, Miss Madden, and two other teachers, and I did the grading. Mr. Charters read the answers on the keys, and we checked the answers. Once or twice we stopped long enough to discuss what stiff questions these were. We wondered how far we would have gotten if we—all of us, college graduates—had taken the same test. One of the teachers asked me, while we graded these papers, if Budge Waters had ever seen these questions before.

When we were through grading the papers, Mr. Charters called the contestants into the classroom.

"I want to read you the scores of this contest," Principal Charters said. His voice was nervous.

"Budge Waters, winner in English literature.

"Budge Waters, winner in grammar.

"Budge Waters, winner in history with almost a perfect score.

"Budge Waters, winner in civil government.

"Why didn't you bring just this one boy?" Principal Charters asked me.

"Because I've got other good pupils," I quickly retorted.

"Billie Leonard, winner in algebra, with plenty of points to spare.

"Jesse Jarvis, second in plane geometry, lost by one point.

"Snookie Baylor and Robin Baylor tied for second place in algebra.

"Congratulations," said Principal Charters, "to your pupils and to you, on your success. It looks as though Winston High will represent this county in the district scholastic contest. I've never heard of such a remarkable thing."

When we left the Landsburgh High School we heard defeated pupils crying because "a little mudhole in the road like Winston beat us."

In a few minutes our mule cavalcade passed the Landsburgh High School. Faces were against the windowpanes and many pupils waved jubilantly to us as we rode by, our coattails riding the wind behind our saddles, and the ends of our scarfs bright banners on the wind. We rode victoriously down the main street of Landsburgh on our way home.

15

THE news of our victory over Landsburgh High School spread like wildfire in dry autumn leaves. It was talked about in every home up and down the Tiber Valley. Alex Maddox told his neighbors he regretted now he hadn't let Leona go with us. The victory of our little school over Landsburgh High School was not only talked about up and down the Tiber Valley, but the length and breadth of Greenwood County. Superintendent Anderson told his rural teachers, and the rural teachers told their pupils, and their pupils told their parents; and in this way the news reached the entire county. Everybody was proud of us because we were the smallest of the rural high schools and the only one that had ever thought to challenge the scholastic standing of the large Landsburgh High School.

Soon we gave our Superintendent Anderson, his rural teachers, and the people of Greenwood County additional pleasant news. Billie Leonard and Budge Waters entered the district scholastic contest. Budge Waters won three contests: grammar, history, and civil government. Billie Leonard won first place in algebra. Then Billie Leonard took pneumonia fever and couldn't go to the state contest. Budge Waters went alone and captured two first places: history and grammar. I knew my judgment of my pupils wasn't wrong.

I thought about the normal curve system! I was convinced a good teacher recognized ability of his pupils without the help of cataloguing their grades by some theory.

I had to whip Guy Hawkins to give me a reputation in Lonesome Valley. That was the greatest thing I had done in a community where might made right. In Tiber Valley, my pupils had to win scholastic contests. That was the difference. Now I had a reputation as a teacher in Tiber Valley.

16

SPRING brought a new life to all of us. We went back to the field to play ball. We played ball while the girls played croquet. Then we went to the river and dropped our nets. We set our troutlines. It was great fun to get back to the Tiber in the spring. This clear blue water from the limestone country was beautiful, flowing under the fronds of the large willows. Like the Tiber River people, I had come to know this river and to love it. I even tried to write poems about it. This river whose lullabies of rippling waters sang me to sleep every night. . . . This river where I had fished, hunted, and skated; where I had walked in the autumn and had seen the golden leaves float like so many ships sailing to a far-off destiny beyond this valley and these hills. . . . The banks of this river where the trees first leafed and bloomed in spring, I had learned to love. It had become a part of me.

Our school year was coming to a close. We had covered the entire contents of each textbook. We had started over these books again, for the last review. I did not have a pupil fail a course. I had two pupils make average grades. The other twelve ranged from good to superior. The only B's Budge Waters made in his life in school were two in algebra. I had never had a discipline problem. Pupils had gotten along better than if they had been brothers and sisters. They respected me as much as if I had been their father. I had taught them, had hunted and fished with them. I had accepted and loved the recreation they had made for themselves and for me. I had been one of them even though I was their teacher.

One day after school while I sat on the bank of the Tiber fishing, I heard the green sycamore leaves swish behind me. I was getting a bite on my hook when it happened, but the fish suddenly stopped biting. He must have heard the noise too. A big man wearing a gray suit, cap, white shirt, and bow tie came through the brush.

"Here I find this great teacher fishing!" he laughed. "I'd like to be doing the same thing this time a year, but business," he sighed, "keeps me tied down. I'm Larry Kenwood," he introduced himself, gripping my hand. "I'm Chairman of the Landsburgh City School Board."

"I'm glad to know you," I said.

"Well, to come to the point," he said, "the Landsburgh City Board members have decided to hire you for Principal of Landsburgh High School for this coming school year. It's a big school and your main problem will be discipline, but you have a good reputation and we've decided you're the man. Mr. Charters resigned to take another job."

I was so stunned I couldn't speak for a minute.

"Will you be interested?" he asked.

"Of course," I finally said.

"Then meet with us second Tuesday of next month in the Landsburgh High School office," he said.

"I'll be there," I said.

And the Chairman of the Landsburgh City School Board, was off as suddenly as he had come.

After he had disappeared beyond the cloud of tender sycamore leaves, it was hard for me to believe he had approached me to take this big position. It was big to me. Only five years ago I had graduated from Landsburgh High School. I had entered Landsburgh High School by taking an examination. I had passed the examination, making an average of seventy-eight, after having an approximate thirty months of rural school training. I had been perhaps the poorest-trained pupil ever to enter the high school. And now I had been invited back to become Principal. I had been called "polecat" at high school because I had hunted in the autumn and was scarcely ever without a little of the scent. I won't be called "polecat" now! I thought, as I caught the fish that had been biting before Mr. Kenwood had come. Nine years from the time I entered, I go back to take over!

Why do they ask me back? I wondered.

Because Winston High School had defeated Landsburgh High School in the scholastic contests. That was the only reason. That was why they had heard of me. That was why they had come for me instead of my going to them. It was the reputation of my pupils that had brought me this unexpected advancement. It wasn't that I was a good teacher. I had good timber to work with. I had taught the ambitious descendants of a landlocked people, who for the first time in their lives had the advantage of high-school training. They had made the best of it. They had repaid me for everything I had done for them. They had given me their best. I had given them my best. They would return soon to their plowing and planting, to their work beneath the sun, wind, and stars in their valley of mists and tender voices of spring. And I would return to college to take courses in education, to prepare myself for the greater school task ahead.

PART III

I STUMPED MY TOE AND DOWN I GO

1

NOW you see who was right," Dad reminded me that September morning. "You'll never regret the advice your Ma and me gave you. Remember when you bummed your way home with a college education in your head and you planned to go back to the Auckland Steel Mills! See, my son," Dad explained, with a sweeping gesture of his hand, "you're on the ground floor of the Greenwood County Schools. It's not been six years since you followed your trap lines to and from the school, and sold animal pelts to buy your books and clothes. Now you go back and take over this big school. I'm proud of you, Jess! The boys I work with on the railroad section are proud of you! Old Daddy Melvin talks about you all the time. Pert Snyder, our Boss, is nicer to me than he's ever been. He doesn't put me down under the fills any more to carry big crossties up the steeps to the track. Jess, you keep on and you'll amount to something!"

"He's already amounted to something, Mitch," Mom said, as she fixed Dad's lunch. "He's already made his mark in life. He's done more than any of your people or any of mine but Everett Hilton. Everett's finished college and he's a school-teacher too!"

"You'll never have to make your livin', Jess, like I've made mine," Dad said, as he put his heavy leather gloves with holes worn in the palms into his hip pocket. "You'll make your livin' with a pencil behind your ear. Five miles to and from my work and ten hours a day on a railroad section will get the best of the strongest men. Takes a strong back and a weak mind to stand it. Hurry, Sall, fix my dinner! I'll be late if you don't. I've not been late in twelve years!"

Dad picked up his battered old dinner bucket from the table.

"This is a great day for me, Jess," he said. "You handle the school. Don't let it handle you. Stick to your thirty hours a week like I stick to my sixty and you'll make a go of it!"

Dad closed the kitchen door behind him and he was off in a hurry with his lighted lantern in one hand and his dinner bucket in the other. I could see him in the dim halo of yellow lantern light, move through the September dawn across the pasture valley and up the orchard hill to the ridge road.

I could remember he had advanced from digging coal in a mine, where he had to crawl back on his belly like a snake. The roof was brittle, and the coal vein was thin. After coal digging, he tried farming. He moved from one farm to another. We rented eight different farms in W-Hollow. Then he got the railroad section job, which was the best he ever had. I knew it wasn't the person who had an education that knew the value of one. It was a man like my father who couldn't read and write. It was a woman like my mother who had gone only to the second grade. And this was the reason they were so proud of me. That was why my mother had thought, when I was made Principal of Landsburgh High School, that I had made my mark in life.

I didn't tell my father that he had made more money working on the railroad section than I did when I taught at the Winston High School. My father could average $75 a month straight time, working on the section. If he worked overtime, as he often did during the winter months sweeping snow from the switches, he got time and a half. And often when there was a train wreck on his division and his section crew was called out on Sunday, he got double time. He averaged better than $75 a month for twelve months a year. At Winston High School I got $100 a month for eight months; averaging my salary over twelve months, I made $50 a month. After I paid my board I had $75 left. But I had other expenses, and I bought many little things for my school.

I had never told my father and mother that when I went to Peabody College to do a summer of graduate work in courses I thought would help me with the principalship of Landsburgh High School, I had to borrow money from the Landsburgh National Bank. I had saved approximately $200 after I had paid Lincoln Memorial University the $100 I owed for college expenses. I hadn't been able to work out all my expenses in my Senior year, when I was busy with many school activities. And with a little less than $300 I had gone to Peabody College for the summer, since this college for teachers had been recommended to me as the "Columbia University of the South." I took courses in English, philosophy of education, extracurricula activity period program, and education. There were teachers, principals, city, and county school superintendents in my classes. I met many of these educators and sat under the famous "tree of education" (whose branches were drying at the top and whose green leaves were then curling in the sun) and discussed high-school management and high-school problems.

After I had hitchhiked home from Peabody College, I had my first teachers' meeting. It was on the Saturday before the Monday when Landsburgh High School would commence. For the first time, I met the teachers I would work with. I hadn't recommended one of them. I had been told at Peabody College by a famous teacher and educator that a principal should recommend his teachers, since he had to work with them. Then his superintendent and the members of his board of education should hold him responsible for the outcome and growth of his school.

But while I was away at Peabody College, my teachers had been hired. Not one was a native of my county, for we still had less than ten native college graduates. One was from an adjoining county; one from New York City; one from Lexington, Kentucky; and four were from near Louisville, Kentucky. Larry Anderson, Superintendent of Greenwood County Schools and the joint Greenwood County Board of Education and the Landsburgh City Board of Education, had done the hiring. When I was a pupil in Landsburgh High School, it was an independent city school system. Now it had joined with Greenwood County and Larry Anderson was Superintendent of both city and county schools; however, they still had two school boards. After I met my teachers, I thought Larry Anderson and his boards of education had made good selections. It was certainly a young faculty.

Coach Watson, the oldest of our faculty and the only married one, was twenty-six. The ages ranged down to my age, which was twenty-three. Only three of our faculty had high school teaching experience. My seven teachers and I had approximately 280 pupils to teach. I had to carry a full teacher's load to keep my teachers from being overloaded, for the state had passed a law that limited the number of pupils to each teacher. Yet it loaded the teacher with a fourth more pupils than he should teach if he was to do a good and thorough job. I thought: When I knew the number of teachers on the faculty and the number of pupils we would have to teach, that only the very young teachers could stand the load. Perhaps even they couldn't. I didn't know. Not even about my own load. I wondered if I could do it. There was definitely a point in their hiring a young faculty. We worked in unison when we made our schedule. We laughed and joked about our work to come.

I didn't laugh when I went to see about my pay. When I had been hired Principal of Landsburgh High School, I asked how much I would be paid. I was told my salary could not be determined until the Superintendent had some idea about the per capita money from the state, and an estimate of county school taxes had been made. Then, I was told, a schedule for paying teachers would be worked out and I would be paid accordingly. I had thought that I would receive approximately $1,500 for nine months. But when my Superintendent told me I would receive $111 per month, I was dumbfounded. I was on the same salary schedule as the teachers. One of my teachers made more than I did because she had had more experience. If this sort of thing was just, then all the teaching at Peabody College was wrong. I couldn't very well back out now. Not when my coach, with a wife and two children, was teaching a full schedule and coaching after school for $100 a month. I got up from the Superintendent's office and walked silently away.

I knew how I could cut living expenses. I could stay home, where I would pay less for room and board. I could walk over the same path and climb the same high hills that my father had climbed for twelve years going to and from his work. I could walk over the old path that I had followed four years to Landsburgh High School. Dad had made this path when he had started working on the railroad section. I never told my mother and father how much Landsburgh High School paid me. I told them I wanted to stay home and pay them board. They laughed when I told them I would pay them board. They were glad to have me home again.

2

MY FATHER had gone in a hurry toward Landsburgh at five that morning. That gave him an hour to walk to his work. I was ready and on my way at seven. My day didn't begin until eight-thirty. That gave me an hour and a half. I didn't want to walk fast enough to raise a sweat and wilt the collar of my white shirt in the mild September weather. Because I knew from high-school experience that walking five miles over a country road I would have to watch my clothes. I knew my pupils would see each defect in my clothing, each speck of dirt on my shirt, or spot of mud on my shoes. I was careful where I stepped, and how fast I walked. I was careful as could be about touching the fringe of ragweed, Queen Anne's lace, smartweed, and sprouts that bordered my path. My father had knocked part of the dew from their leaves, stems, and blooms with his overall legs, but there was still enough left to wet my pant legs. I had to walk directly in the center of the path until I reached the wagon road in Academy Hollow.

When I reached Landsburgh High School, three big busses were unloading county pupils. Many of these pupils had come from farms fifteen miles away. They, too, had to rise early, and often had to walk long distances before they reached the highways to catch the busses. The majority of these pupils had their morning chores to do on farms before they could start to school. Many had to rise as early as four in the morning. All of the teachers were there, but the Landsburgh pupils who lived the closest—only a few blocks away—were the last to reach school. To my surprise, eight of my fourteen Winston High School pupils were there. Budge Waters had walked to Landsburgh to follow me. The first thing I did was greet my Winston High School pupils. I asked Budge where he was staying. He didn't have a place to stay or money to pay for board and lodging. I told him to go home with me. Others had secured boardinghouses in Landsburgh. Redheaded Jesse Jarvis, 180 pounds of energy, had come from his father's farm in Tiber Valley to go to Landsburgh High School and play football. Coach Watson was talking to him.

While the new pupils met each other and their teachers, we let time run over. We began school a few minutes late. There were three times as many pupils in Landsburgh High School now as when I was a pupil here. The schoolhouse was the same size as when I had graduated. When all the pupils were inside, we didn't have room to seat them. We had to use my office for a classroom. We had to mark off the west section of the upstairs' corridor for another classroom. We had to borrow chairs and tables from a local church to give our pupils a place to sit and work. Four pupils were assigned to each locker.

My first half-day at Landsburgh High School was interrupted by pupils who had been expelled the year before. They asked in good faith to be reinstated. Many asked if they could make up last year's work, since they had been expelled just a few weeks before the school year was over. They were intelligent-looking youths with good steady eyes. My brother, James Stuart, was one of these. One of the first things I had done was to reinstate him; now I reinstated them. I didn't even ask why they had been expelled.

At the noon hour of my first day at Landsburgh High School, I noticed a last year's sign beside the walk that read:

KEEP OFF THE GRASS. Beneath these words, in smaller print, the sign read: *If you don't, you will be punished. This means YOU!* I didn't like that. It made me want to step on the grass. I made a new sign and put it back on the same spot: PLEASE, PROTECT THE GRASS.

My pupils reacted well to the new sign. They knew that we were working for and not against them. They understood the difference between threatening and leading. We had two acres of back yard where our pupils didn't have to watch the grass. I later learned that one of the pupils I had reinstated had been suspended the year before for walking on the grass.

3

ALL of my teachers but Miss Welch carried maximum teaching loads. My teaching load equaled that of my teachers' until I switched one of my classes to Miss Welch. She divided my Freshman algebra class, taking part of it in her morning, and part in her afternoon class. This gave me one free period so that I could deal with the attendance problems of our Landsburgh pupils. County pupils didn't give us this problem since they came to school by bus, remained at the schoolhouse during the noon hour, and went home by bus in the afternoon.

Landsburgh pupils went home for lunch. Often they forgot to return in the afternoon. At this time, an attendance officer was unheard-of. The principal had to be attendance officer. If pupils were out of school—loafing on the Landsburgh streets—we heard about it. The parents criticized the school if their sons and daughters were not there. They assumed the attitude that it was the teachers' responsibility to keep all pupils, including their own, in school. I thought it was the responsibility of the parents as much as it was of the teachers. I thought there should be cooperation between the two. I had never been up against this problem at Winston High School and Lonesome Valley.

At a special teachers' meeting during our first week of school, we discussed this attendance problem and came to some very definite conclusions. We decided each morning to check pupils in their homerooms first. We would also have a home-room checkup after noon hour. At each period, the pupil left in my office would go to each room and each study hall to check the attendance. If there was a telephone in the home of an absent pupil, we called the parent. If there was not, we asked the pupil to bring a note from the parent explaining why he was absent. If the absence was not excusable, we deducted 5 per cent from his grades in all his subjects, since there were twenty days in a month and our grading system was based on 100 per cent. If the absences were excused, we let the pupil make up his work. Three unexcused tardies we considered an absence. We announced our conclusions and explained them in each homeroom. We made sure each pupil understood that the responsibility of his being in school, and being there on time, rested squarely upon his own shoulders. We explained to our pupils that we filed each written excuse they brought us. We told them their parents would have access to the files. Yet this system did not end our attendance problems. Unexcused absences and tardies cluttered our files.

4

BEFORE I started teaching at Landsburgh High, I thought one of my problems would be the association of the county and city pupils. I wondered how they would get along. I remembered that when I was a pupil in Landsburgh High School, the rural pupil was not always respected. There were only a few county pupils then—not more than a dozen. Now we had more pupils from Greenwood County than we had from Landsburgh. I thought when these different groups were put together, each pupil would hold to his own group. I had missed my guess. They got along together.

But there was trouble among the pupils. It popped up in the most unexpected place. There was a feud among the players on our football team. Jack Alexander came to my office one day after school. He told me he wanted to discuss a prob-lem. I wanted to hear his problem. He said he had starred three years for the Landsburgh Wildcats and Rodger Sutherland was jealous of him. He had always played in the backfield while Rodger had always played on the line. This was their fourth year on the same football team, and for the past three years Rodger had failed to block for him when he carried the ball. He said Rodger would block for any other ball carrier from the backfield. So he said that he was going to hurt Rodger.

I asked him if they had ever had any trouble before they played football. He told me this story. Each family had kept cows in the same pasture on the steep rim of hills on the south side of the town. He told me he and Rodger used to fight every time they met in the pasture. They had fought in pawpaw patches with peeled pawpaw clubs, beating each other over the head and shoulders. Then he went back further than this. He told me their families had fought each other politically down through the years. He said they went to different churches. They didn't have but one thing in common: that the children from each clan went to the public school.

When he had finished I told him no generation should inherit the quarrels of an older generation. I stayed in my office and talked with Jack Alexander long after the school busses had reached their destination and the Landsburgh students had reached home. This was important to him, for he was keeping away from football practice since he thought Coach Watson was siding with Rodger Sutherland. The problem was so long and so involved, I couldn't solve it.

Next day I talked to Coach Watson. He told me this feud had divided his football team into two camps. Jack Alexander had his following, and Rodger Sutherland had his. Each had about the same number and every man on the squad took sides with one or the other. The only unprejudiced men he had were his untrained county men. Coach Watson told me Alexander and Sutherland were the best men he had. But he couldn't have both on the team, for practice, at the same time. I told him to take Alexander back and to have a heart-to-heart talk with both men.

That day after school, Rodger Sutherland came running into my office. He told me that Coach Watson, due to my influence, had taken Jack Alexander back for practice, and when

Jack came onto the field he walked off. He said the athletic field was not big enough for both of them and that he planned to hurt Jack Alexander. I asked him to tell me why. He told me a story of the two families very similar to the story Jack had told me. As I listened to Rodger's story I knew feuding was not confined to people who inhabited the high hills, valleys, and hollows.

The following day Jack came to me and threatened Rodger. Then Rodger came to me and threatened Jack. Each came to me twice during the day and told me what he was going to do to the other. I told them to meet me in the office after school. There we would see if the trouble could be ironed out. I told Coach Watson to postpone football practice and to meet with us.

Jack and Rodger quarreled and threatened each other in my office. When I suggested that I might suspend both of them, they said that wouldn't solve their differences. Each confessed to their coach and to me that he hated the other. They would have fought in my office if the Coach and I hadn't preserved order.

"You fellows come with me," I said.

Rodger, Jack, Coach Watson, and I walked out behind the schoolhouse. Only a few football players—eight or ten—remained to see what we did with Jack and Rodger. They didn't have long to wait.

Rodger and Jack turned their pockets wrong side out so we could see that nothing was left in them. I took a stick and drew a big circle on the athletic field.

"Since there is no other way to solve your differences," I said, "I want you to get in this circle and fight it out. After the fight don't either of you ever come to me and tell me what you're going to do to the other. If you do, you'll leave this school forever."

"This suits me fine, Mr. Stuart," Jack said.

"It suits me, too, Mr. Stuart," Rodger said.

They went into the ring. I had seen fights in my day. But I never saw one like this. They pounded each other with terrific blows. Each man was a good boxer, but gloves for them made the fight too easy. We let them back up their threats now.

The football players came around to watch the fight.

Jack Alexander was nineteen years old. He was six feet four and weighed 190 pounds. Rodger Sutherland was five ten and weighed 195. He was nineteen years old. He was the best-muscled man I had ever seen. He was the only man I had ever seen muscle above his head, with one hand, the heavy, steel-based, highway road signs. When these men struck each other it was like mules kicking. They followed up short and fast. There were no bells in this fight. It was stay in the ring without rest periods until the fight was finished.

The fight lasted approximately five minutes. Blood spurted. Faces were smeared with blood. Shoulders were red with blood. Then suddenly, Rodger Sutherland reached for a stick that lay outside the ring. We knew the fight was finished. And we stepped in. We took hold of Rodger and wouldn't let him have the stick. He was glad to stop fighting. Jack was glad too.

"If any more football players have any grievances," I said to those who had remained to see what was going to happen, "this is the way you will settle them."

It was a strange thing for us to see. Jack Alexander walked over to Rodger Sutherland and laid his arm around his shoulders.

Rodger and Jack went to the showers together as if they had finished a hard football game. They washed the blood off each other. From this time on, Rodger blocked for Jack when he carried the ball. And Jack carried the ball for many touchdowns. The feuding Alexander and Sutherland clans of our Landsburgh Wildcats were solidified.

5

ONE afternoon when we were in the fourth week of school, I got a telephone call from Jason Hinton, member of the Landsburgh City School Board. "Jesse, I can't discuss this problem with you over the telephone," he said in his soft voice. "I'd like to see you when you're not too busy."

"I'll have to see you after school," I said.

"That'll be all right," he said. "It's very important."

After school I worked in my office while I waited to see Jason Hinton. I wondered what he wanted to see me about. I knew it was something that concerned me personally or the high school. For Jason Hinton had always been very kind to me. When I graduated from the Landsburgh High School, he was the only person to give me a graduation present. He and Mrs. Hinton sent me a five-dollar bill sealed in an envelope. There was a note with the money, scribbled in Jason's almost illegible longhand, saying that he had seen me day after day walk to high school through the winter mud, rain, snow, and sleet, without an overcoat; and that he and Mrs. Hinton were glad that I had stuck with the grind until I had finished my task. Once he had told me personally that if he and Mrs. Hinton had ever been able to have children, they would have loved to have a son as ambitious as I was. When he had a problem to present to me, I knew it must be one that concerned my personal interest.

"You know, Jesse, my wife and I have always been your friends." Jason spoke softly when he entered my office. "I thought it best that I come personally to inform you about a few little things."

"Something gone wrong about the school?" I asked, for I was worried.

"Not exactly that," he said. For a second I felt relieved. "It's about you!"

"What about me?" I asked.

"I talked it over with Nettie before I came," he said, as he sat down in a chair opposite my desk. "We thought we'd better let you know the facts. It's a personal matter that concerns you. I hate to be the one that tells you, but you've always seemed as close to me as if you were my own son."

"I'm very curious to know what this is," I said.

"Two things," Jason admitted, getting his face closer to mine and whispering softly, as if someone were trying to listen. "It's about your clothes!"

"About my clothes?" I broke in. "What's wrong with my clothes?"

"Look at your pant cuffs," he said.

I pulled my legs from under the desk. I looked at my pant cuffs.

"I don't see anything wrong with them," I said.

"Maybe the room's not well-enough lighted for you to see," Jason said.

"What's all this about?" I asked. "Am I awake or am I dreaming?"

"We're here together, Jesse," Jason said. "You and I— Jason Hinton—in your office in this schoolhouse, and I'm trying to tell you something that is the talk of the town. Listen to me," he advised me seriously, as he got up from his chair and walked over to the window and upped the blind until the rays of the afternoon sun slanted through the panes. "Now, look at your pant legs," he said. "Don't they have a funny color? Aren't they sulphur-colored? Haven't you dyed them?"

"Dyed them!" I repeated. "I've never dyed a pair of pants in my life. What are you talking about? I don't understand!"

"Well, you can see for yourself the legs of your pants are not the same color below the knees as they are above the knees!"

"I believe you are right," I confessed, as I observed the different shades of color. "I'd not noticed it before. The sun has to shine on my pant legs before it's noticeable. And I don't know what it is. I know it's not dye!"

"It's talked all over Landsburgh that you have dyed your pant legs where they have lost their original color, and that you have dyed them a color that doesn't match the rest of your suit. You know, Jesse, how particular the people in this town are about clothes! You know what they expect of their high-school Principal!

"Good reports," he said. "Every report I've heard is good. People are saying it's the best-disciplined school we've ever had here. But getting back to your pants——"

"I know what this is on my pant legs," I almost shouted. "It's the sulphur from the ragweed stems! I get it on them as I walk along the path of a morning and the dew dampens my pant cuffs and holds it there. That's it! But you have to look close before you can see it," I said, as I looked at my pant legs again in the mellow sunlight.

"Then you haven't dyed your pants," Jason said softly. "I didn't think you'd done a thing like that. But you know how high-school pupils will see little things and go home and tell their parents!"

"I'm beginning to learn," I admitted. "First time anything like this has ever happened to me."

"We have a rule here I must tell you about," he said. "I've been explaining to members of the board you didn't understand when you accepted the position. We have a rule here that you're to live in Landsburgh when you teach here!"

I sat silently while thoughts raced through my mind.

"Come to think about it," Jason said, breaking our silence, "if you stay in Landsburgh you'll solve your first problem. There's not any ragweed along our streets," he smiled. "Your pant legs won't look like they're dyed. You can keep your clothes in good shape."

"Is it compulsory I stay in Landsburgh?" I asked.

"Yes, Jesse, it is," he said.

"If Will Hadden can stay at the hotel and pay forty dollars a month for board and room from his eighty-nine dollar check, I can too," I said. "After all, I make more than he does!"

"Jesse, I hate to bring these criticisms to you," Jason apologized. "But the other board members know that I know you well."

"You're a member of the school board," I said. "It's your duty. I'll move to Landsburgh Monday."

"That's better, Jesse," Jason smiled. "Everything will be all right now." He picked up his hat from the table and quietly walked from my office.

6

MY ROOM in the Landsburgh Hotel was directly above Main Street. From my window I could see almost from the east to the west end of the town. And my room was high enough for me to look down upon the section of Landsburgh toward the rugged rim of hills that fenced the town on the south. I could see almost every street and intersection except along the river front toward the north. This was the quiet residential section of Landsburgh.

Perhaps I was lucky to get this room in the Landsburgh Hotel. I could not have gotten any other place where I could learn more about the town. I had selected it because it was a nicely furnished room and it was empty. I didn't know that it was a key to the night activities of the town. My first night in this room I shall never forget.

After dinner at the hotel I had taken a walk from one end of the town to the other. It was just like any other small town. People walked along the street laughing and talking on this mild autumn evening. They greeted me and I greeted them. Many were parents of the pupils I had in school, and I greeted many of my pupils who were enjoying a walk on Main Street same as I. After my walk I went back to my room and made preparations for my next day's teaching. Then I switched off my lights to go to bed.

After I got in bed I couldn't sleep for the noise. It was not that I had come from the quietness of a farmhouse in W-Hollow, for I had spent my summer in Nashville, Tennessee, not far from the Peabody College campus where the streetcars screeched nightlong around the curves and where the automobiles zoomed by like bullets at all hours of night. This was a different noise. Landsburgh didn't have streetcars, and the cars didn't zoom down Main Street like bullets through the night. The noise I was hearing was loud voices and hilarious laughter. Many of the voices were familiar to me. The laughter was familiar too. I got up from my bed and sat by the window. It was midnight now and the town was just coming to life under the bright moons of dry electric lights up and down Main Street and out into the shadowy bystreets, where the small street lights were few and far between.

At this late hour I saw my Landsburgh pupils walking the streets. I saw a few girls and many boys on the streets. My guess was: There were 30 per cent of the Landsburgh High School pupils. These were the pupils that were tardy in the mornings. These were the pupils that made low grades in high school. And these were the pupils whose parents criticized the teachers for giving their sons and daughters low marks. Several of the parents of these pupils had even said that I should be removed as Principal and that half the teachers should be "fired." We—Principal and teachers—had been blamed because these pupils had not made as good marks in school as other pupils whose parents accepted the responsibility of their children after school hours.

The Landsburgh High School Principal and faculty had received much criticism about the high-school teenagers' drinking at night and over the week ends, in this section of Kentucky that had long been dry. I wondered now about the parents of these boys. I thought they must know or have pretty good ideas where they got it. For where did the judge get his? Where did many of the businessmen in the town get theirs? Everybody in the town, I was quite sure, knew where they got it. I was now finding out.

I had heard about Landsburgh's favorite bootlegger who sold a good brand of illegal whiskey. He had bootlegged for a living all the time he had lived in Landsburgh. And never once had the law of either political faction in power arrested this man. From my window I saw him on the street, walking slowly here and there, talking to this one and that one. Though the weather was mild, he wore his topcoat. In this topcoat, I was later told, he had large pockets in the lining where he carried his half-pints and pints, each one in a separate pocket so the bottles wouldn't clank together when he walked. I saw this going on night after night.

I knew this was one problem I couldn't solve alone. It didn't matter how much I loved to face a school problem and try to figure a way to solve it. I loved to meet one, face it and fight it. But this problem was too big. It was a problem for the town, county, and state to handle. Yet it affected our school. I couldn't go meddling in the town's business. Yet the town's business was my business as long as it affected Landsburgh High School pupils.

And these things were affecting our school. Teenage young men would stay out late at night and oversleep during the morning hours. They would get to school late after a bad night. Many of them were failing their classroom work. Unexcused absence and tardy marks were piling up on them. I had heard the old saying: "An ounce of prevention is worth a pound of cure." Why should we have these things before them for temptation? Why shouldn't the parents help do something about them? How would I get these problems over to the people without making everybody mad at me? I wanted to use tact. I didn't want to be a young crusader. But I knew the life, morals, spirit, and progress of Landsburgh High School depended upon everybody in the community. I had to have cooperation. I had to work these problems through Landsburgh organizations. I couldn't meet them alone.

7

THE parent-teacher organization was the best organization we had, to present the Landsburgh problems that affected our high school. It was not a large organization. Not half the parents whose sons and daughters attended Landsburgh High School belonged to the P.T.A. None of the parents of our county pupils attended since they lived miles away and were without, for the most part, convenient methods of travel. Our P.T.A. was, and had been, more or less a social function where parents and teachers got together and drank tea and ate cakes at the end of each meeting. I thought it time to do something besides drink and eat. It was time we did something constructive for the high school and community. But I didn't know how to go about presenting my problem to these mothers, for seldom did a father attend one of the P.T.A. meetings, and the husbands of these women were, in many cases, involved in the vices we had to eliminate.

Then something happened that gave me the chance. I had been going to the hotel for lunch. We had arranged a schedule whereby two teachers remained at the high school during noon hour while the others went downtown for their lunches. We rotated this schedule. My turn came to be at the high school during the noon hour. I had heard gambling had been going on beyond the high board fence that surrounded the athletic field. I made it a point to start walking leisurely around this fence. Autumn was in the air and the sycamores, birches, and willows between the schoolhouse and the river were flaunting their bright-colored leaves to the autumn wind. The air was crisp and fine to breathe. It was a beautiful day.

When I walked around the corner of the high board fence, I came upon the young cardplayers. A topcoat was spread on the ground. Cards, silver, and folding money were lying on the coat. Four young men were sitting on the ground around the coat, with cards in their hands. Fifteen or twenty young men were standing around watching this poker game. I had walked around the fence corner and was standing in their midst unnoticed, for everybody was watching the cards and money.

"Who's winning and who's losing, fellows?" I asked.

One of the young men playing poker was the son of a Landsburgh minister. One was the son of a rural schoolteacher. Two were the sons of a Landsburgh merchant. When they saw me, their faces turned sliced-beet red. They couldn't speak. They looked at each other. The young men who had gathered to watch the poker game began to scatter. I didn't bother the cards or the money, or tell them to take them up or to quit playing poker. I walked on. I left this problem in the pupils' hands—for them to worry about. I walked on around the board fence, where the sycamore, birch, and willow leaves were drifting like golden birds with every gust of autumn wind. When I reached the far corner of the fence, I looked back, and the gamblers, money, and coat had disappeared.

That afternoon these young men expected me to have

them in my office. But I was going further than just to repri-
mand them for a temptation placed before them. We had to
have the ounce of prevention to effect the pound of cure. I
knew my catching these young men playing poker would be
news in Landsburgh. I knew that everybody would know it,
for there were too many young men standing around not to tell
it, and I knew it was not good publicity for our school.

The first person to ask me about her son's gambling was
Mrs. Hunter, wife of the Methodist Minister. She asked me
what punishment I was going to inflict. I replied I hadn't made
up my mind. I told her, on second thought, I probably wouldn't
punish any of them. She couldn't believe me.

"Do you believe in letting your pupils gamble?" she
asked, staring at me wildly.

"No, I don't believe in letting pupils gamble," I told her.

"Then why don't you do something about it?" she asked
me.

I didn't say anything more. I wanted her to talk. I wanted
her to tell other women, and I knew she would. I wanted them
all to talk.

The mother of each son caught in this act came to ask me
what I was going to do about the gambling at Landsburgh
High School. I didn't give one of them a satisfactory answer.
I let them talk and tell others.

Finally these women must have decided I approved of
gambling, for the members of the P.T.A. took the responsibility
upon themselves to bring it up at our next meeting. I had not
punished any offender. Each one of these young men was worried, too, for he had come to me more than once and apologized
and wanted to know what his punishment was going to be. He
was getting his punishment, but he didn't know it. Suspense is
a great punishment.

At our first P.T.A. meeting after the gambling incident,
I noticed that the members of the P.T.A. were very somber.
They didn't laugh and talk as they had done at each of our
former social meetings. The Methodist Minister, Reverend
Hunter, was among the P.T.A. members. Several fathers had
come to this meeting. After the meeting had come to order,
Mrs. Albert Davis, president of the P.T.A., soon finished with

the organization's business. Then she said: "Something has been going on at the high school I would like to bring up. It is a sad reflection but a true one, and it is the talk of the town. It is the gambling that has been going on here. Pupils were caught in the act and have never been punished. We would like to hear from Mr. Stuart if he has anything to say regarding this situation."

"I have a lot to say," I said, rising to my feet. "First, I want to tell you why I haven't punished these young men. I don't see any use in punishing them until a few temptations are removed. I happen to know about these temptations."

Then I told them how my clothes had been criticized and how I had moved to the Landsburgh Hotel. I told them their criticising my clothes was the reason for my knowing all about the town. That in my room in the Landsburgh Hotel, I could see over the town in all directions but one. And that if anyone didn't believe me, he should come to my room and switch off the lights and look over the town at night. I told them I had the room the town's police ought to have. Then I said to the mothers and fathers in the P.T.A., that I had seen their sons and daughters walking the streets until midnight. I asked them if they knew where they were at night. If they knew what time they got in off the streets.

Women whispered to each other. Their faces reddened and they looked down at their desks. I told them their sons were able to buy illegal whiskey, and there was not one among them that didn't know where they could get it. That to stop the sale of whiskey to their sons was their business. It was the town's business and not the teachers'. Yet it did concern the high school, for our young men had gotten drunk on river-boat excursions and the school had been blamed for it. Now it was their duty to eliminate the temptations.

"And another thing—" I said. "Gambling is carried on in many of the homes in this town. Poker for money is played before your sons and daughters. You know who these people are. Fathers of the young men on our football team, wearing derby hats, with long cigars in their mouths, walk up and down the side lines with a bank roll in their hands and bet as much as fifty dollars on one of our football games! You know this is true! It is said that the men in this town will gamble over who can spit the closest to a knothole on the wall or a crack in the floor. The parents in this town must have a change of heart if we are to break up gambling in this school. I'm certainly glad, Mrs. Davis, you brought this up.

"And another thing—" I continued. "Somebody had better pass the word to the town's favorite bootlegger to be careful to whom he sells his whiskey. Remember, he has five pupils in this school! If you want to watch him sell some evening, come up to my room. If you want to know his customers, be sure to come to my room.

"One thing more and this is all I have to say," I concluded. "Landsburgh High School is not a separate unit from you. We are part of you. Every man, woman, and child in this community is a part of Landsburgh High School. Your ways of life in your homes and in the town reflect here in the school. You can help us or you can hurt us. Our success here depends largely on you. I used to think when I first started teaching school that it was all up to the teachers and the pupils. I have changed my mind. The little island of humanity that is each one of you must unite with other islands and become a mainland if we are to have a successful school."

The results of this P.T.A. meeting solved the problems in Landsburgh. I never again saw any parents betting on football games. Something suddenly happened to the little race-horse slot machine. The jukebox dancing ended gracefully at nine o'clock, for the city's board of aldermen imposed a curfew to ring at nine, and every pupil enrolled in school had to be in off the streets. Drinking suddenly ended among our young men. Not one person was arrested. Our school had caused a moral reformation among the citizens of Landsburgh. Gambling never occurred again, at our high school. And the only punishment I gave the four young men caught in the act was suspense. They waited and waited for something to happen but it never did.

In six weeks we gladly showed members of our P.T.A. what their cooperation had done in their sons' and daughters' grades. Many of their sons and daughters who had been failing were now making passing grades. Many pupils who had been passing with low marks had lifted their average a letter higher. The unexcused tardy and absence marks had diminished approximately 70 per cent. Schoolwork had been made easier for us. The pupils were happier and loved school more. This was the result of cooperation between parents, citizens, teachers, and pupils. "This P.TA. has taught us something," Bill Hadden remarked later at a teachers' meeting. "All you have to do to solve a town problem that hurts your school is to get the women on your side. Show 'em what's wrong, and they'll clean it up."

8

HELEN KIRSTEN was our only faculty member not from Kentucky. She was from New York City. She was born, educated, and had lived all her life, in New York City; and when she came to the small town of Landsburgh in faraway Kentucky she had many adjustments to make. We didn't know this. Not one of us had ever been in New York City. Teachers and pupils in Landsburgh High School were more interested in Miss Kirsten's dialect. And she was very much interested in our dialect and in our idioms of speech. She was interested in everything. Especially in work. We didn't have a faculty member that worked harder than this tall, slender, black-haired, blue-eyed young teacher from New York City.

After our first faculty meeting she never complained about the work given her. When she learned the number of pupils we had in school and the too-few teachers to do the work, she didn't complain about her load. She was hired for the position of part-time librarian and part-time teacher, but after we had our first teachers' meeting, Miss Kirsten was made almost a full-time teacher. She assumed also responsibility for the library.

"I think I can work this situation out, Mr. Stuart," she said. "Don't you worry too much about it. Don't expect too much for about two weeks."

In two weeks Miss Kirsten had selected girls from the high school and had trained them in simple library rules. She selected two girls to stay in the library for each period during the day, and at intermission between class bells Miss Kirsten would hurry to the library to see if any problem had arisen the girls couldn't handle. She had one free period in the afternoon, when she could remain in the library. But she worked out a library system with the help of our pupils and her supervision, which operated smoothly. We didn't lose a single book during the year. A few were mislaid, but Miss Kirsten found and returned them.

At first, we regarded Miss Kirsten as very different from us. Her speech was different. Her training was different. She had different ideas about teaching school. She was an exacting person. She didn't give, and she didn't take. If a pupil lacked 1 per cent of making a passing grade, that pupil failed in Miss Kirsten's Freshman English. She was the first teacher at school each morning, and she was the last to leave in the afternoon. At faculty meetings she was very quiet unless she was asked for an opinion. And she was never without opinions on school problems. She had her own ideas how to solve them. Her ideas were very different from ours.

Soon we faculty members learned to know and to understand Miss Kirsten. She learned to know and to understand us. Once she came to me and said: "Mr. Stuart, now I am teaching English and composition for you, I want you to tell me exactly how you want me to teach. I want to do it your way, so you will be perfectly satisfied."

"Miss Kirsten, when I have a teacher with your originality," I said, "I would like to put the responsibility of teaching English directly into your own hands. Original English teachers are hard to find. You are one of the few. All I ask you to do is to teach English your way. I'll give you all the freedom you want."

This pleased Helen Kirsten more than anything I ever said to her. One day she came to me with a smile.

"Here, Mr. Stuart," she said, giving me a sheaf of theme papers. "I know you are interested in creative writing and I want you to see these themes from my classes."

When I read these themes, I got a great surprise. In them was the beauty of simple English language where many common nouns, simple verbs, and few adjectives were used. There was something in these Freshmen high-school themes that was akin to early English and Irish poetry. There was something in the mood of them that left in me a feeling such as I had had when I first read *Riders to the Sea* and *Playboy of the Western World*. I had regarded these plays as poetry. And I regarded these themes as poetry. They sang themselves. They were as natural in their singing as little streams of melted snow water, pouring over the rocks on a steep Kentucky hill in March. They were as natural in their choice of simple common nouns, verbs used as nouns, and nouns used as verbs, as red sails of redbud blossoms and white sails of dogwood blossoms are to the bright April winds in Kentucky.

I try to write, why don't I write like this? I thought, as I returned these themes to Helen Kirsten.

"How did you get work like this from pupils who have never written themes before?" I inquired. "I know many of your pupils have never been required to write a theme. I think this is excellent work. I've never read better creative work from high-school pupils. These themes are poetry."

"Yes, Mr. Stuart," Miss Kirsten smiled, "poetry is in these people from your hills. Your hills, rivers, trees, log shacks, crying waters, wild flowers, and little fields of grain— green in spring, ripening in summer, and harvested in autumn —have put this poetry in them. But the language," she sighed, "ah, the language! I've never heard anything like it. It's not too soft. It's not harsh. For the first time in my life, I've heard people talk with rhythm. It's poetry. You never pronounce *g* at the end of a word. And you supplement the prefix *a*. I've noticed that in all my pupils. Their language is poetry. Poetry is in them. Why don't they write it? They are crying for creative expression."

"Tell me more of your observation of the people here, Miss Kirsten," I said. "I've never thought of these things before."

"No, you live in them," she said. "You grew up here. You are a part of all this. That is why you don't see it. You live poetry instead of writing it. All of you do. Your pupils do."

"But tell me, how do you get your pupils to express themselves like this?" I asked.

"I let them write their own thoughts any way they see fit," she said. "I give them all the freedom they want to express themselves, and on any subject they choose to write. I let them put it in any form they choose. After they have written their themes," she explained, "we read them in class. Anybody has the right to offer any suggestion he may have on his class-mate's theme. We don't always correct all the mistakes. You've noticed that."

"Yes, I have."

"We don't correct a mistake when it gives color and orig-inality to a theme," she said.

Though Helen Kirsten had come to Kentucky a stranger, she was not a stranger very long. Soon the pupils and teachers began to know her better. The pupils from the Greenwood County hills were especially fond of her. They invited her to their homes over the week end. Often on Friday afternoons, I saw her climb onto one of the crowded school busses with a suitcase in her hand. She went into the valleys and hollows, to the land of log shacks and lonesome waters. She went to shacks where there had never been an electric light, a bathroom, or a telephone. And surely, Miss Kirsten, from New York City, had been used to these conveniences all her life.

Helen Kirsten had never seen men cut corn, dig potatoes, make sorghum at a cane mill in a bright gold-leafed autumn. She had never seen men chop down trees and draw the logs on the ground with cattle and mules to a woodyard, and saw these logs into sticks with a crosscut saw, and burn the sticks on the big open fireplaces. She had never seen cellars and smoke-houses filled with provisions for winter the way the Greenwood County people, who were often isolated during the winter, had provided for the hard winters ahead. And she had not been among people who had to make their own entertainment, such as dances, games, and old-time music. It was these pupils, who played the old-time music without knowing a note of music, who had written the good themes for her.

Our having Helen Kirsten, with an entirely different background, added to our school. It gave me this idea: That there should be an exchange of teachers in the schools of America. That teachers from different parts of America gave pupils a broader outlook on life, gave them better background and preparation for the future. That each school needed a variety of faculty members. That to select all teachers from the home town would eventually mean intellectual inbreeding and that soon the results would begin to show in the community. That the whole of America was greater than any of its parts, and, therefore, we should have a cross section of thought and stimulation from different parts of America to give us originality, to make us vigorous and strong. Each of America's regions complemented the other materially and made the wealthy whole! Then why wouldn't each of America's parts complement the other intellectually in our school systems, to give us greater understanding of each other and to give wisdom to the whole? I knew that Helen Kirsten was one teacher who would be on my faculty as long as she wanted to stay.

9

NO LONGER did we hear criticisms from anybody in Landsburgh of our faculty, Principal, or Superintendent. Not after we had the cooperation of the people in Landsburgh. Not after we had the largest P.T.A. in the history of Landsburgh squarely behind us.

In the early spring we took a number of our best pupils and entered them in the district scholastic contest, held at Auckland, Kentucky. In this competition we were up against schools four times our size. And we were up against many high schools. But we had Budge Waters, thanks to my mother and father, who kept him without cost. My mother laundered his clothes. Every time she bought clothes for my brother James, she bought the same for Budge. Also we had other excellent pupils. Budge Waters won all three contests he entered. This gave us the advantage in points. We won two other first places; and we won many second, third, fourth, and fifth places. We took first place in the district scholastic contest, and we won it with points to spare. The newspaper publicity we received on this achievement gave us a scholastic reputation among the high schools in our section of Kentucky. We rated high in athletics, but we rated first scholastically. Landsburgh was given A rating by the state. For our school music, we had brought a bandmaster from Ohio. Parents, instead of the school board, paid him. For the first time, Landsburgh High School had a band. We had put ourselves into our work. And we had done the work. Everybody had worked.

But there was one thing we couldn't do. When we were asked to give to a "good cause," we could do little about it. We didn't have the money. Not on our small salaries. Each teacher gave what he could. That was very little. In our school we had one young man who also worked an eight-hour shift for the C. & O. Railway Company, in the railroad yards. He played football and made good grades. When people came for donations, he always doubled what I gave. He gave often as much as the combined total of the teachers. He was a generous young man, and we appreciated seeing him give. But it did hurt his Principal and his teachers more than he ever knew—because he showed us up. Pupils didn't know the low salaries their teachers made. For them to see one of their student body give more than Principal or teacher, and sometimes as much as their combined total, made them believe we were very tight with our money or else that we didn't support worthy causes.

Coach Watson supplemented his salary by refereeing football and basketball games. Not one of our teachers owned the roof over his head, and not one that I knew had a checking account in the local bank. It was all that I could do to make ends meet and to save enough to pay back the money I had borrowed to go to Peabody College.

Helen Kirsten, Martha Welch, Barbara Carter, and Edith Nolan lived on their salaries, which ranged from $98 to $117 a month. Lonnie Maxwell, who taught science and agriculture, was a Smith-Hughes man; and his salary was a little more, since it was supplemented by the state. However, he bought himself a car because he had to visit the farms in Greenwood County. He often had to borrow money to pay his living expenses and make payments on his car. On three different occasions I signed his note when he borrowed money at the local bank during his first year at Landsburgh High School.

10

MAY DAY was the great holiday for our schools. The meeting was held at Landsburgh High School, since we were almost in the center of Greenwood County and all the Greenwood County roads led to Landsburgh. Teachers and pupils from every rural school in Greenwood County were invited. Many didn't come because of impossible roads. School busses hauled teachers and pupils. They came by automobile. And those from the rural schools close to Landsburgh walked to this great celebration, for it was something they didn't want to miss.

The schoolhouse was filled. The sign was removed from the schoolyard grass and the pupils ran helter-skelter and played unless they were participating in some program. We had Maypole dances. We had athletic events supervised by Coach Watson. We had school displays in the high-school auditorium. We had "4-H" club displays. The food was prepared by members of Landsburgh P.T.A. Classroom work was forgotten, for this was a great day for everybody's getting together, for recreation, play, and fun.

When I was walking from the athletic field to the schoolhouse to help arrange the displays, I met face to face a person who looked familiar. She stopped suddenly when she saw me. She was going through the gate to the athletic field and I was coming out. In each hand she held the hand of a small girl.

"You're Jesse Stuart, aren't you?" she asked, looking me over as though she wasn't quite sure.

"Yes," I answered, "and you . . . I ought to know you. I've seen you some place."

"You've grown a lot since I knew you," she laughed.

"You're not Nancy Cochran, are you?" I asked, wondering if it were possible for a woman to change so much in a few years.

"That's who I used to be," she said. "I'm Mrs. Ova Salyers now. Remember Ova, don't you?"

"I certainly do," I said. "Are these your daughters?"

"We have three girls and two boys," she said. "These ones are the oldest. Bertha is six and Loamie is five. Bertha is goin' to Lonesome Valley School. I heard about this fair and I brought them here today."

"Didn't Ova come with you?" I asked.

"No, I left him home paintin' the house and takin' care of the babies," she laughed.

"Where do you live now?" I asked.

"Ova bought the old Lon Turner farm on Lonesome Creek," she said. "You know that farm, don't you?"

"Don Conway, Guy Hawkins, Denver Lykins, Ova, and I measured that farm once," I said.

"Yes, Ova told me you did," she said.

"Tell me, what's happened to Guy Hawkins?" I said, as we moved over to let the people going and coming pass through the gate.

"Oh, he's away at school," she said. "He and Don Conway are over at Morehead, Kentucky. Since there was no high school close for them, they went down there to school. Don is in Morehead College. Guy is in the Morehead Training School. Don plans to make a teacher of himself. Guy does too."

"Is John still trustee out there?"

"Oh, no," she said. "John lost the election by one vote."

"What has happened to Flossie Conway?" I asked.

"She's married and has six children," Nancy smiled. "Married the same time I did, but she's got twins. She married Ennis Cooper from Chicken Creek. Flossie's not nigh as pretty as she used to be when you knew her."

"I'd like to know if May Woods married Bill Coffee."

"She certainly did," Nancy answered quickly. "Hear they're not gettin' along so well. Everybody said May married the big green convertible instead of Bill. They had a wreck and smashed the car. Then Bill lost his job. They've had their troubles. I hear news about them all the time in Lonesome Valley."

"Is Vaida Conway still going to school?"

"No, she's married to Tom Abrahams you used to teach in Lonesome Valley, and they have two children."

"She married young," I remarked.

"No, she was nearly seventeen when she got married."

"Come, Mama," Bertha said, pulling at her mother's hand. "Let's go see the races!"

"Wait a minute longer," Nancy said. "Then I'll take you."

"Some day I'm going out there for a visit," I said. "I'd like to see Lonesome Valley again. I'd like to spend a night with Uncle Amos and Aunt Effie Batson. I'd love to hear him play his fiddle and watch her dance."

"He won't play his fiddle any more unless he does it in another world," Nancy told me. "He died in his sleep. Aunt Effie went to stay with one of her sons. Their big house, farm, and store were sold to Alec Prater."

"Then everything has changed at the Valley," I said.

"It's not the same as it was when you were there," she said.

"What happened to my pony?" I inquired. "Is Sundance still alive?"

"Oh, that pony!" she laughed. "He's still alive but he's too old to run like a white ghost up and down the Lonesome Valley Road. I remember how you used to ride him past my store morning and afternoon. Alec Prater owns him now."

Then Nancy's girls started pulling at her again. They wanted to see the events at the fair.

11

IN MIDDLE May I sat beside Big River and threw round gravel into the moonlit water while I waited for a decision of the Landsburgh City School Board and my Superintendent, Larry Anderson. Our school year was over. The schoolhouse was silent now and the grades had been recorded. They were locked in steel files. County pupils had gone back to the farms. City pupils were free for the summer. Miss Welch and Miss Kirsten had gone home. Miss Kirsten didn't reapply for her position. It was rumored over Landsburgh that she left, hitch-hiking for New York City. One rumor was she hadn't made enough to pay her way home. Another rumor: She was hitch-hiking home for the experience.

Miss Carter, Lonnie Maxwell, Coach Watson, and I reapplied for our positions. My application was with reservations. I asked for my salary to be upped to $1,500 for nine months. In the letter with my application I stated that unless my salary was upped to $1,500 I didn't want to be rehired for Principal of Landsburgh High School.

I sat beside the river and waited for the school board and the Superintendent's decision, without a dollar in my pocket. I had kept myself during the year. I had paid a hundred-dollar note at the bank. I hadn't bought myself a new suit of clothes. I had bought only the bare necessities of life. The dates I'd had with Naomi Deane Norris had been inexpensive. She had paid her own expenses while attending Morehead College to prepare herself for the teaching profession. She was now a teacher and making less than I. She understood what it was for a teacher to have dates on the wages he received.

Once I walked to Larry Anderson's office door and knocked. He came to the door and I asked him if a decision had been reached on my application. He told me they had been attending to other business matters and hadn't considered the teachers' applications yet. I went back to the river and sat in the stillness of the evening where the long arms of the willows bent down to finger the bright water tenderly. Again, I grew restless and went back to ask Larry Anderson what had been done about my application. I got the same answer as before.

I waited outside the office door until the board meeting adjourned. When they came outside, I asked Larry Anderson about the board's decision.

"We didn't hire you," he said. "You asked too much."

"That's all I want to know," I said.

I put on my hat and walked down the corridor of the old courthouse. I knew that schoolteaching was a great profession, and that I loved it. But I would not teach again. I knew that I had joined with the four teachers of my faculty who had not reapplied for their positions. They were excellent teachers but they were leaving the profession. I went back to the hotel, packed my clothes and walked home in the moonlight over the old path fringed with a new growth of ragweed. I was not particular about the sulphur-colored stains on my pant legs now.

PART IV

MANY A DARK AND STORMY NIGHT

1

AFTER the Landsburgh Board of Education refused to rehire me, I spent the summer working on my father's farm. My brother James and I raised a crop of tobacco. He planned for his part of the tobacco crop to pay his expenses his first year in Berea. I planned my part of the tobacco crop to pay my expenses for a year of graduate work at Vanderbilt University.

In July the heavy rains came. Our tobacco, with too much rain and not enough sun, rotted away. We knew the money crop, on which we had fastened our hopes to finance us a year in college, was no longer a reality.

In the meantime I borrowed $250 at the Landsburgh National Bank. I gave James $50 to enter Berea. I gave Mom $50, for she was in need of money, since Dad wasn't getting steady work on the railroad section. With $150 I went to Vanderbilt University to do a year of graduate work. A conservative estimate of my expenses there for one year would have been $900. I went to Vanderbilt University, because I had heard of the Fugitives. I had read poems in magazines and books written by members of this group. I wanted to take graduate courses under these men, whose poems, stories, articles, and nonfiction books I had read.

I believed that I could combine farming and writing. Since I had been six—old enough to thin corn—I had worked on the farm. There wasn't any kind of work I couldn't do. And since I could remember I had wanted to write. I thought one year of graduate work in Vanderbilt University, with classes under these well-known southern authors, was all I needed.

When my first term papers were returned to me I wondered if I could write. They were slashed to pieces with red marks. But I didn't have time enough to do research for my term papers. I worked in the Wesley Hall cafeteria for eleven meals each week. In addition to this, I worked four hours each day as janitor. Shortly after the first semester ended, Wesley Hall burned to the ground. It burned the cafeteria where I worked and where I ate my eleven meals each week.

During the second semester I lived on a meal a day. I didn't leave Vanderbilt University. I had lost all my clothes in the fire but those I had on my back. I lost all the poems I had brought to Vanderbilt and the thesis I was attempting to write for my M.A. degree. But somebody gave me a suit of clothes, and when the old suit of clothes gave out, Lonnie Maxwell, still teaching in Landsburgh High School, loaned me a suit of his so I would have a change.

During my second semester in Vanderbilt University, Dr. Mims gave us an assignment in his English class to write a brief autobiography. He asked us not to write more than eighteen pages. This was the first time I had been given a writing assignment at Vanderbilt University that wasn't about a dead man. I couldn't tell Dr. Edwin Mims what I wanted to tell him in eighteen pages, either. In the eleven days before our assignments were due, I had written 322 pages from margin to margin. Three days later he told me I had written a book. Dr. Mims took my term paper to Donald Davidson to let him read it. Then they wrote a publisher and advised me to send *Beyond Dark Hills* there. It was published six years later.

In the meantime I finished my year of graduate work at Vanderbilt. I didn't rewrite my thesis. I borrowed two dollars and left Vanderbilt, hitchhiking home, without my M.A. degree.

2

ON A Saturday afternoon in July, I was lying on the parched yard grass under the shade of a bushy-topped poplar whose broad leaves were now wilted pods drooping in the sun. Pencil-sized shafts of light from the midsummer sun filtered between these clusters of wilted leaves to make shadows on the grass. I was observing light and shadow crisscross and intermingle on the brown-parched grass.

"Is this where Stuarts live?"

"It is," I said, rising from the grass.

"Could you tell me where I could find Jesse Stuart?" said the short red-faced man with a blond mustache, standing by our yard gate. Two larger men were walking up the path behind him.

"You're talking to him," I answered.

"I thought you were an older man," said the man at the gate. "This is the man we want to see," he said, turning to the others. "This is Stuart."

"Come in," I invited him.

"My name is Mooner Bentworth," he introduced himself. "I'm Chairman of the Greenwood County Board of Education. This is William Dawson, and this is Tobias Claxton, members of the Greenwood County School Board."

"I'm glad to meet you, gentlemen," I said. "But if you've come to see me about teaching school, I'm not available. I left the teaching profession last year. I have said that I would never teach again!"

"This is something bigger than teaching," Mooner Bentworth explained. "Let me tell you what we want. We need a new Superintendent for Greenwood County Schools."

"New Superintendent for Greenwood County Schools!" I repeated, for it was hard for me to believe. "What's happened to Larry Anderson?"

"Landsburgh City Schools have pulled out of the county

system," Mooner explained. "Landsburgh is an independent
city school system like it used to be. We had a little misunder-
standing."

"The county and town had what I'd call a falling-out, Mr.
Stuart." William Dawson helped Mooner explain, as he spat
ambeer spittle on the grass. "It was never in the stars for us to
get along with them, anyway. I told the boys that, when we
went in cahoots with 'em."

"Landsburgh has taken Larry Anderson from us," Mooner
said. "He's the new Superintendent of Landsburgh City
Schools!"

"So that's the story," I said.

"Larry Anderson was a good man and we hate to lose
him," Tobias Claxton interrupted. "But Landsburgh is paying
him more money than we can pay him."

"We need somebody to lead us," Mooner Bentworth said.
"We've talked to teachers of our county school system and
we've talked to citizens from different parts of the county.
Everybody we've talked to tells us you're the right man. We
can't find anybody against you."

"I'm glad the people feel that way about me," I said.
"This is good news. But I don't think I could qualify for
County School Superintendent!"

"You have a college degree, haven't you, Mr. Stuart?"
William Dawson said, spitting again on the grass.

"Yes, I have my degree," I said. "I have college hours
to spare. But the Kentucky School Laws have changed. One has
to have four years of teaching experience before he can get a
superintendent's certificate. I have only three unless they will
accept my substitute- and practice-teaching in college."

"Are you old enough?" Tobias Claxton asked.

"I'm twenty-four," I said.

"That's the age limit," Tobias said. "You can't be any
younger."

"Can you qualify, get your certificate, and take over next
month?" Mooner Bentworth asked me.

"I don't know," I said.

"Superintendent of Greenwood County Schools," raced

through my mind. Not teaching, not a high-school principal, but Superintendent of Greenwood County Schools! This was hard for me to believe. I wondered if I were really lying under the poplar tree dreaming that three members of the Greenwood County Board of Education had approachd me. Here they stood before me. Two were leaning on the yard fence and Mooner Bentworth was standing with his hand on the gatepost. They were awaiting my answer. Would I take it if I could qualify?

"Gentlemen, will you hold the position for me until I see whether I can get a superintendent's certificate or not?" I said, because I couldn't turn this offer down. "If I'm able to qualify I'll be your Superintendent of the Greenwood County Schools."

"How long will it take you to find out whether you can qualify or not?" Mooner Bentworth asked me.

"Not more than two weeks," I said. "Maybe not that long."

"Can we wait that long, men?" Mooner asked, turning to his fellow-board members.

"Yes, we can wait," William Dawson said. "This is the man we want."

"We want you to try for your certificate in a hurry," Tobias Claxton warned. "We don't want to be without a superintendent."

"I'll start work this afternoon," I said. "I'll let you know, soon as I can, what happens."

"That's good enough," Mooner Bentworth said.

"Say, where's your other two board members?" I asked. It suddenly dawned on me only three board members had come to ask me to be Superintendent of Greenwood County Rural Schools.

"Don't even ask about them," Mooner Bentworth answered quickly. "Two new men were elected in our race last year. Benton Dangerfield was elected from the west end of the county and Manley Warburton was elected from the east end. They were elected against Larry Anderson. They're against everything we do!"

"Mr. Stuart, we don't consider them," William Dawson said.

"We run the school board," Tobias Claxton interrupted. "We have the majority. We hold together. We are your friends. We want you. Benton Dangerfield and Manley Warburton are against you because we are for you."

3

"YOU'RE not on the ground floor now, my boy," Dad beamed, as he stood before me dressed in a tight-fitting blue-serge suit, white shirt, bow tie, and derby hat. "You're on the top floor. You've amounted to somethin'. You've gone as high as you can ever go.. That's why I'm taking this day off."

"Be honest in all things, Jesse," Mom advised me. "You're going into the higgest job in this county. The County School Superintendent's Office has been the graveyard for many a man's reputation. I'll pray for you."

Then Dad and I started walking to Landsburgh over the old familiar path. He walked in front to brush the dew from the ragweeds. "Son, if you can be Superintendent of this big county school system, I can brush the dew from ragweeds to protect your clothes."

When we reached Landsburgh and started walking down Main Street, Dad was surprised at the number of people who stopped us in the street and congratulated me. They congratulated Dad, too, for having a son that would be Superintendent of Greenwood County Schools. For these people—many of them merchants—knew that my father couldn't read, couldn't write, and had such scanty knowledge of arithmetic that he had to depend on the merchants with whom he traded to do his figuring. He had to take their word for everything unless one of his children was with him. Sophia and I had to write his letters and do his figuring for him, from the time we were eight years old.

"Young man, I'm proud of you," Uncle Walt Weston said, shaking my hand. "You've amounted to something."

Uncle Walt Weston had operated a clothing store in Landsburgh for sixty years. It was in his store that I had bought my clothes when I was a pupil in Landsburgh High School. Often I would get clothes on credit and he would wait until I got returns on a batch of animal pelts. He had always given me credit in his store for anything I wanted. My father had traded with him for forty years.

Alvin Terry, Mrs. Annie Walters, Mrs. Maud Farlington, Grace Binion, Larke Spruce, and others stopped us and congratulated me and talked to my father as we walked down the street. Dad and I planned to be in the County Superintendent's Office an hour before the Greenwood County School Board met. But so many of our friends had stopped us, we arrived just in time for the meeting.

"I'm one of the school board members you don't know," said a big pink-cheeked man. "I'm Benton Dangerfield."

I did know Benton Dangerfield. He had killed two chicken thieves in his chicken roost, and his trial had been one of the most sensational trials in our county. He had come clear in his trial. But because Sherman Anderson, brother to Larry Anderson, who was prosecuting attorney, had prosecuted him (he thought, unmercifully), he ran for a member of the Greenwood County Board of Education against Albert Hix, who was Larry Anderson's board member, and defeated him. Benton Dangerfield was about six feet five and weighed approximately 260 pounds. He had bright-blue laughing eyes and a shock of blond hair. He didn't look like a killer. He was the best-looking, best-dressed member on the school board.

"I've heard of you, wondered about you. You are a very young man," he said, looking me in the eye. "I had planned not to vote for you because the other three members of this school board are for you. They are still too friendly with Larry Anderson. I'm against that man. Young man," he continued, while we stood in the courthouse corridor, "you are going into a mess. You've got something ahead of you. I know you have."

"I'm willing to tackle it," I said.

Then Mooner Bentworth called the meeting of the Greenwood County Board of Education, and we went inside. Benton Dangerfield introduced me to Manley Warburton, a small gray-eyed man wearing a gray suit, light-blue shirt, and red necktie. I greeted the three members of the majority faction of the school board that had come to my home to ask me to accept the position. I greeted Larry Anderson, Superintendent, under whom I had served for two years. This was his last day in office. Tomorrow I would be in his place, and he would be where I had once been.

The meeting was called to order. Mooner Bentworth presented to the board of education my application for the position of Greenwood County Superintendent. William Dawson made the motion that I be hired. Tobias Claxton seconded the motion. Immediately the majority faction of the board voted for me. The surprise came when Benton Dangerfield voted for me. After Manley Warburton saw how Benton Dangerfield had cast his vote, he, too, voted for me. I got the unanimous vote of the board. Members of each faction looked at each other as if there was something they couldn't understand. I was ready to take my oath of office. Outside the office door I gave my first newspaper interview. Monday I would take over, and I called an extra meeting of my Greenwood County School Board for my first day in office. There was something I wanted to know.

4

MY FIRST day in office, I was a busy man. I must have had a hundred visitors. Each one wanted something. Many were school trustees who had axes to grind with other school trustees. While I was in Vanderbilt University, I didn't know that a law had been passed to have three district school trustees instead of one. Now each little rural school district in each county in the state of Kentucky had three district school trustees. Why the schoolteachers and the educators and thinking citizens had ever allowed this bill to pass was beyond me, for this gave each teacher of the little rural school nine bosses: three trustees, five county school board members, and the county school superintendent. But the district school trustees had the power. Many of these trustees had come to see me on the first day I was in office. We now had 246 district school trustees in Greenwood County.

I wanted to know something about the financial condition of the Greenwood County Schools. The stories my school board members told me, while we were in closed session, about the financial plight of our school system were alarming. If I could rely on what they told me, we were in danger of financial collapse. They told me they hadn't been paid for months. They were waiting for the new tax revenues to be collected. I suggested to them that we should not accept opinions about this financial situation, but have a public accountant audit our books and give us the facts.

When I made this suggestion only Benton Dangerfield and Manley Warburton approved. Whatever they were for, the majority of my school board was against. And I had to keep the majority of my school board on my side. After I had talked with the board members, I knew that not one of them was a good businessman. Each man was a farmer. Not one of them owned and operated a large farm. Not one of them had handled very much money.

Finally I told them it was customary, when a new man took over a public office, for an accounting to be made so that the public would know in what condition the outgoing official had left the office to his successor. I told them the condition of the county school might be better than they thought. I hinted that there might be enough money to pay what was due them, and that my wanting the books audited wasn't anything against the character of any man that had served in the office. That this was the right thing to do, so we could build from the foundation stones of financial facts. Finally they agreed. They made a motion—and it carried by unanimous vote—to have an auditor audit our books and calculate our incoming revenue.

Two weeks later the audit had been made. The Greenwood County School System was approximately $144,000 in debt. This included the bonded indebtedness of the new Maxwell High School in the west end of the county. But of this $144,000 we owed the Landsburgh National Bank $54,000, and $26,000 of the amount we owed the Landsburgh National

Bank had been borrowed the preceding year by Tobias Claxton, Mooner Bentworth, William Dawson, and the two members of the board that Benton Dangerfield and Manley Warburton had defeated, with the promise to pay the bank from this year's local taxes when they were collected. There was even a deficit of $3,300 in our account at the bank. Our property taxes, plus state appropriations, were approximately $100,000. This was the highest figure at which the auditor could place our anticipated revenue for the year.

I asked them what arrangements had been made for the rural pupils of the east end of Greenwood County, since Landsburgh was no longer a joint county-city high school. I was informed a temporary line had been drawn across the county. All county high-school pupils west of this line would go to Maxwell High School. All the county high-school pupils east of this line would go to Landsburgh High School. I was told that we would have to pay eight dollars per month for each pupil. This tuition was exceedingly high, judging from the amount of revenue we had to spend. This temporary line was drawn with Cliff Creek, a small stream that flowed south from Big River, dividing the county in approximate one-third and two-thirds sections. According to this setup, which was made by the Greenwood County School Board before I became Superintendent, the majority of our county high-school pupils from the two-thirds section would be going to Landsburgh High School where we would have to pay tuition. Maxwell High School, our only county high school, would not have half as many pupils from the one-third section as we had space for and faculty to teach.

"I would like to suggest this arrangement be changed," I said. "Instead of paying this tuition to Landsburgh High School, I suggest we transport our pupils by bus from the east end to Maxwell High School. We can save money. We can give employment to another bus driver. We still have an extra school bus. And if we have to," I added, "we can employ additional teachers at Maxwell High School to take care of these pupils, and still save money."

"But teachers have already been hired to take care of

them at Landsburgh High School," Mooner Bentworth said, jumping to his feet. "We can't tear up their plans!"

"I would just like to ask Mr. Bentworth something," Benton Dangerfield said, as he arose from his chair. "Mooner, are you working for Landsburgh City School System, or are you working for the Greenwood County School System?"

Then I presented facts and figures to the members of the board. I showed them what the cost would be at Landsburgh High School if we paid tuition. I showed them the approximate cost at Maxwell High School.

"I make a motion we send our rural pupils from east end of Greenwood County to Maxwell High School," Manley Warburton said.

"I second that motion," Benton Dangerfield said.

"Did you gentlemen know," Mooner Bentworth said, "that there is a Kentucky School Law that says you must send pupils to the most convenient school? Did you know we cannot pass Landsburgh High School with our school busses loaded with pupils for Maxwell High School? We can't transport our pupils from this end of Greenwood County lawfully past Landsburgh High School!"

"I'd like to test that law," Benton Dangerfield said. "Laws are made for the people, not people created for laws."

"I know this will cause trouble," Mooner warned. "We will have a lawsuit if we do it. Jesse Stuart has made the wrong suggestion. I don't agree with it. I think that you," he said, pointing his trembling index finger at me, "are a dangerous man."

"Let this motion come to a vote," Benton Dangerfield said. "Let's see who is loyal to the county! We know it's a good suggestion. We know that this proposal is right. We know it's one of the best suggestions we've had made here."

William Dawson, Tobias Claxton, Benton Dangerfield, and Manley Warburton voted in favor of this motion. Then a strange thing happened. "I'm voting for it too," Mooner Bentworth said. "It's a measure I don't want to go on record as voting against."

5

SOMETHING had to be done about our financial situation. The rural schools had already begun. There were approximately a hundred rural teachers at work now. At the end of their first month, they would want their meager but much-needed pay. Not any rural salary was under $48.70 and not any was more than $79.80 per month. The two rural teachers who made $79.80 per month had college degrees and four years or more of teaching experience. Other salaries ranged somewhere between these figures. The major portion of the salaries was around $65 per month. And at the end of the first month's teaching, we were supposed to pay these salaries.

I read every book concerning finance I could find. I didn't know how to handle other people's money. I'd never handled much money. Since I was practically sure that my board members had handled less, I thought one of us would have to learn. I thought this person ought to be me. I wanted to know it, anyway. There wasn't anything about my duties I wasn't willing to learn. But I couldn't learn enough from the books I was reading. Perhaps they were not the right kind. I had to do some thinking. I had to find the way.

Then the thought came to me that there were many small but successful businessmen in Greenwood County. I reasoned if county businessmen could be successful for themselves, why couldn't they give sound advice to me and to my board of education, whose backs were now against the wall? But we could not have them unless we could get their services free.

When I asked Joe Terrill, Charles Angus, John Roberts, and James Melvin if they would meet with us in a financial advisory capacity without pay, each man felt flattered. It was the first time that local businessmen had been called in to give financial advice to the schools. There was only one thing I requested of them. That was the same thing I had requested of my board members: Not to spread the news of our impending financial crisis to the public. I thought if this news got around it would hurt the little credit we had.

When we let these businessmen see the auditor's report, know the amount of our anticipated revenue for the year, they came to one conclusion: We would have to borrow money. We would have to make new debts to pay old debts. We would have to find some place to cut expenses. I knew this wouldn't be my salary, for it had been cut before I took office. I was making as little as the state would allow a superintendent of county schools to receive, $100 per month. And I wasn't allowed any expense account.

Joe Terrill agreed to go with me to find credit for Greenwood County Schools. First, we contacted Landsburgh National Bank. Instead of extending us more credit, they asked that we pay what we owed. Then we tried three banks in Auckland. Each banker asked us what collateral we could give for security. We couldn't offer Maxwell High School Building, for it wasn't paid for. We didn't find a banker that wanted a schoolhouse, anyway. What would he do with it if we couldn't pay back the borrowed money? We couldn't offer him our school busses for security, for we had only four, and they were old. We hadn't anything to offer but our promises to pay from future revenue. We tried three banks in West Virginia and they asked us if we had tried to borrow from Kentucky banks. We tried the First National in Dartmouth, Ohio. Everywhere it was the same story. Promise-to-pay collateral was, to bankers, equivalent to the wind. We were as far from our solution as ever. We hadn't solved anything.

Since we couldn't find credit anywhere and since we owed $26,000 at the Landsburgh National Bank that would be taken from our local tax money, this is what we did to save us temporarily. In Kentucky, half of the local tax money is added to the state appropriations (the county's share of per capita money) to make up the salaries of the teachers. It was against the state laws to use this money for anything but teachers' salaries. The other half of the local revenue went to pay the county school superintendent, janitors, county school board members, bus drivers, upkeep and maintenance of school busses, maintenance of eighty-two rural-school buildings and

Maxwell High School. When we paid the $26,000 to Lands-
burgh National Bank—an obligation we were forced to meet—
there would be little, if anything, left of our local tax money
except the half that was used for teachers' salaries.

I suggested to my school board that we loan the school
busses to the drivers, let them furnish the gas and take responsibility for repairs, and let the high-school pupils pay a reasonable amount each month for transportation. The bus drivers
would not get as good salaries as they had gotten, nor would
the pupils get free transportation; but since we were in a position where we couldn't run the busses at all, it was better to
do this so the county pupils, who lived long distances away,
could still go to high school.

Only two of my board members, Benton Dangerfield and
Manley Warburton, were responsive to this idea. Mooner Bentworth was against my idea. William Dawson didn't express
his opinion. I thought he would vote with Tobias Claxton and
Mooner Bentworth. But he immediately came over to my side.
My suggestion carried by a vote of three to two. This relieved
us of the expensive transportation system. Our solution of the
bus problem was used by two of my successors.

Then I proposed we cut one month from all the schools
in Greenwood County. This would reduce all the rural schools
to six months, and Maxwell High School from nine months to
eight. I could not understand why high schools should have
nine months when the rural schools only got six and seven. For,
according to statistics, only a small percentage of the pupils
from the rural schools go to high school. Only a small per
cent of these pupils finish high school. It seemed to me that
the rural schools and the graded schools were the underpinning
of the whole public school system. So why shouldn't the public-
school tax money, paid by the people, be used for the greatest
good for the greatest number of their children? I was amazed
that members of my school board, without a dissenting vote,
agreed to slice a month from every county school. I wondered
if the Kentucky State Department would let us do this. If not,
I planned to ask them to show us a way to solve our financial
crisis.

With the approval of my county school board, I started

to remake our budget. The budget I had inherited from my predecessor had been made for an anticipated revenue we would not receive. We could not raise taxation. The state law didn't permit us to do this. In the state of Kentucky, cities and counties were governed by dual taxation laws. The maximum school taxation on property valuation of the county rural districts, was seventy-five cents per $100 valuation. The maximum school taxation in the city independent districts, where there were greater concentrations of wealth, was $1.50 per $100 valuation. We had two school systems. We had the *poor*, and the *poorer* systems. We had this great discrimination shown between the rural and city pupils of Kentucky. This discrimination made me madder than the Corn Laws of Great Britain could have made Thomas Carlyle, and, like Carlyle, I decided to do something about it as soon as I had finished with the emergency work in my office. That emergency work was to make a new school budget.

Joseph Terrill; Margaret Raridan, my secretary; Chad Hoskins, our auditor, helped make the new budget. We finally agreed—since we couldn't borrow money, couldn't raise taxes —that we make our budget with the money left us and spend within this budget. This suggestion was approved by members of the school board. In a few days we had made the new budget for six months' school instead of seven. Since this was contrary to the school laws of the state, members of my school board approved it reluctantly. They didn't think it would be approved by the state department of education.

Instead of posting the budget to Frankfort, I asked my school board for expense money to take me and the auditor to Frankfort. They voted me twenty-five dollars. Then the owner of a garage we owed a big account for operation of last year's school busses, loaned us a car. Auditor Chad Hoskins drove us to Frankfort, where we stayed at the Y.M.C.A. because the rooms were cheaper. We ate at restaurants where food was quantity and not quality. I presented my new budget to the state department of education. On a few minor items, members of this department were generous enough with their time to help make changes. We stayed in Frankfort two days. I got a personal interview with James Richmond, State Superintendent of Schools, and explained to him what we were up against. My auditor showed him facts and figures. Our budget was approved. We knew then that our per capita money— money that would go to pay everything but teachers—would soon be on the way. This was a great relief; we had weathered the first storm. I went back to Landsburgh rejoicing. . . . Margaret Raridan issued checks to one hundred rural teachers —checks that were long overdue, since these teachers had begun teaching in July.

6

WHEN I reported the success of our budget to members of the Greenwood County Board of Education, four of them applauded. But Mooner Bentworth didn't. He sat motionless, looking straight at me. There was fire dancing in his ferret-colored eyes. Then he arose to his feet.

"I make a motion to members of this board of education that we impeach Jesse Stuart for embezzlement," he shouted. Then he pointed at me, and said, "You are leading us straight to hell!"

"He's leading us out of a muddle," Manley Warburton shouted, jumping to his feet. "And you, Mooner Bentworth, helped get us in that muddle!"

"When did I embezzle county funds?" I asked, almost too stunned to speak.

"That twenty-five dollars expense money to go to Frankfort!" he shouted.

"Expenses of two men: meals and rooms for two days and nights, and expenses of a car for three hundred and sixty miles," I said. "We spent the last quarter to have the carburetor cleaned. We coasted over the last hill home."

"Gentlemen," said Benton Dangerfield, rising to his feet, and opening his mouth for the first time at the board meeting, "I make a motion that we have Mooner Bentworth removed as Chairman of the Greenwood County Board of Education. I have enough evidence here in my pocket to remove him from the board if we want to go to Law to do it. Last summer," he said, as everybody became breathlessly quiet, "he used the county school bus for a touring car. Drove it to the head of Big Sandy River to see a baseball game. He charged gasoline and repairs to Greenwood County Board of Education. I have the evidence here in my pocket. I got it this morning," he said, as he brought his big hand from his coat pocket filled with duplicate copies of unpaid bills. "I want you to look at these."

"Another thing," he continued, while the board members looked at these unpaid bills with amazement, "Mooner Bentworth is not fit to be Chairman of the Greenwood County School Board. He takes his orders before he comes to a meeting! Is that right, Mooner Bentworth?"

When Benton Dangerfield made this accusation, Dawson, Claxton, and Warburton stopped reading the bills. Mooner Bentworth sat motionless and stared at the wall. He didn't answer Benton Dangerfield's accusations.

"I watched you this morning with my own eyes," Benton accused. "I thought this was going on. I wanted to be sure. Do you want to tell your Superintendent and fellow-board members where you went early this morning? Do you want to tell them where you go to get your orders before each meeting?"

Benton waited for Mooner to answer his accusation.

"Gentlemen, I think the Greenwood County Board of Education and the Superintendent of Greenwood County Schools are plenty capable of running this county's school business," Benton said. "I move that we remove Mooner Bentworth as Chairman of the Greenwood County Board of Education."

"I second that motion," Manley Warburton said.

There were four votes cast against Mooner. Tobias Claxton was chosen for the new Chairman of the Greenwood County Board of Education. We did not bring court proceedings against Mooner Bentworth but allowed him to remain as a member of the Greenwood County Board of Education, since he had only one year to serve before his time expired. If we had brought court proceedings against him, it might have taken us a long time to oust him. It might have been better if we had. For, from this time forward, Mooner Bentworth and Benton Dangerfield never spoke again to each other. Not as long as I was Superintendent of Greenwood County Schools. They were not without guns, either. Often one could see a pistol handle showing from their pockets. We never knew, when we attended a board meeting, who would come out alive or who would be left dead.

7

ONE morning when I arrived at my office, two groups of well-dressed people were waiting to see me. The groups were standing at opposite ends of the courthouse corridor. Before I reached my office door, a man from each group rushed toward me. Each man introduced himself. One was Fred Harrison, a trustee from Samaria Rural School District. Rodney Norton, the representative of the second group, was a little disappointed when I agreed to see Fred Harrison and his crowd first. I invited both groups inside my office. I met not only the leaders of each group but everyone who had come as a representative of these fighting clans. John Harrison, brother to Fred, was with the Rodney Norton clan. He was fighting his own brother Fred now, as he had fought him in the district trustee election.

"Mr. Stuart, I want to explain the whole situation to you," Fred Harrison began. "We had a hotly contested election at Samaria and I beat Rodney Norton by three votes!"

"You mean you stole it," Rodney shouted, his temper rising.

"Now just a minute, Mr. Norton," I said. "You let Fred Harrison tell his story, then I'll listen to you. Go ahead with your story, Mr. Harrison."

"Mr. Norton and I belong to different churches," Fred Harrison continued. "He belongs to the Holiness and I belong to the Christian, and his church house is very close to the Samaria School. At night they made great disturbances, shouting and carrying on over there. And I don't say that members of their church did this, but I saw cars parked around the schoolhouse and the next morning I had to pick up the empty bottles lying on the playground. Many were broken. Last year Cief Benton's boy lost an eye when he fell on a piece of broken glass. So I put up a row of posts to keep the cars off the school-yard. Then Mr. Norton came to me, saying I was against his church, and asked me to remove the posts. I didn't remove them. But one dark night somebody else did. Then," Fred Harrison shouted, "I put posts down they couldn't dig up. I put steel rods through the ends that I set in the ground. They can't get 'em up now. But here's what Rodney Norton and my brother John did. They got up a petition against the teacher I hired. They had accused me of going to the schoolhouse and kissing the teacher in front of the pupils!"

"And look at the signers we have on this petition to oust Ollie Nuckels from that school!" Rodney Norton shouted. "Look at the witnesses we've got here, their names in black and white, who did see Fred Harrison who stole the trustee election from me, kissing the teacher he was not qualified to recommend because he stole that election!"

"That's the truth," John Harrison echoed.

"Now listen, Mr. Norton," I pleaded, for I was afraid the two groups were going after each other in my office, "you let me get through with Mr. Harrison. If you can't agree to this, I'm going to have to ask you and your group to leave my office until I am through hearing his story."

My secretary Margaret Raridan was the only other person beside myself and these two groups in the office. There would have been little we could do if a free-for-all had started. Miss Raridan sat by the telephone ready to call the sheriff if a riot broke out. She had seen these things happen many times before.

"Miss Ollie Nuckels is a fine teacher, Mr. Stuart," Fred Harrison bragged. "She's one of the best. Yet they"— he pointed toward Rodney Norton's group, whose faces were flushed and whose tempers were rising every minute while they waited and listened—"have tried to stir up a scandal. I have come to you to see what can be done about this trouble. This is my story!"

"All right, Mr. Norton, will you come forward?" I said.

"Yes, sir, gladly will I come," he said, as he took long strides across my office, with a petition in one hand and a long list of witnesses' signatures in the other. "I am bringing these to you, Mr. Stuart," he said, giving me the petition and list of witnesses. "I want you to look these over. We want action immediately. We want this Ollie Nuckels ousted from Samaria School! We can't have all this loving a-goin' on between her and her so-called trustee in front of the innocent little girls and boys!"

"This petition is very interesting reading," I said, as I turned the pages.

"But Mr. Stuart," Rodney Norton said, "I want to go back to the election. Fred Harrison voted men and women not eligible to vote. I've got the proof!"

"Didn't the election officers challenge them?" I asked.

"The election officers were Fred Harrison's friends," Rodney explained. "They belonged to his church."

"I can't do anything about your election," I said. "This is not for me to decide. You'll have to see your lawyer."

Everyday since I had been in office, district school trustees had come to see me about their problems. They took most of my time. And they kept the thriving Landsburgh lawyers busy. Another trustee spent a half-day telling me how the outdoor privy had fallen in on the teacher. And this day I had the same sort of a rumpus. I was not going to spend my entire day trying to be a peaceful mediator between these warlike clans.

"If Fred Harrison can swear I took the posts from around the schoolhouse," Rodney shouted, shaking his fist at Fred, "I'll let him do it on the witness stand. He put them posts there for spite. I know that the people of Samaria Holiness Church didn't park their cars around the schoolhouse and drink whiskey and leave empty bottles and broken glass. Brother," Rodney shouted, with dry cotton-spittle flying from his mouth, "members of our church don't do business that a-way! Bless Jesus, we've never done that sort of thing yet! But Mr. Stuart," Rodney said, his voice getting softer, "let me ask you if Fred Harrison has the right to put posts on the school property. Don't the members of the school board have to give him permission? Do the district school trustees have more power than the Greenwood County Board of Education?"

"Mr. Norton, I'm afraid they have," I said. "They have

in regard to hiring schoolteachers! About setting posts on the school ground, I don't know!"

"I'll take it to court," he shouted. "We'll see if Fred Harrison has the right!"

"I'm ready to take it to court," Fred Harrison said. "I've already got my lawyers."

"This is something that the superintendent can't settle," I said. "It's not in my power."

"The courts are too slow," said a big man of the Rodney Norton faction, who wore a big, black umbrella hat he never removed in the office. "We demand action," he said with a slow, soft drawl, as he looked at me with his slanting, black beady eyes and twirled the long horn of his black handle-bar mustache with one hand.

"I've done all I can do with this situation," I said. "You'll have to demand action from your lawyers."

"That's what we'll do," said Rodney Norton, the little sparrow-like man, who was the militant leader of his clan.

"Mr. Norton, do you have another copy of this petition?" I asked him.

"No, you have the only copy," he said.

"May I keep this petition?" I asked.

"That's why I brought it along," he said. "I want you to read it."

Miss Raridan escorted Fred Harrison and his group through the office door first. Then she very politely escorted Rodney Norton, who wanted to talk on and tell us what a terrible man Fred Harrison was, out the door. The last man from the office was the man with the big black mustache, with the slanting, black beady eyes, and the big, black umbrella hat.

This situation ended in court. How many suits were brought into court, how many lawyers were hired, I never knew. I do know that Rodney Norton and his following didn't oust Ollie Nuckels from the Samaria School.

As to the posts around the schoolyard, the courts didn't give fast enough action. Less than a month later, Alvin Barker, the big man with the black beady eyes, with the black handle-bar mustache, and the big, black umbrella hat, was found by Fred Harrison lying beside these posts at daybreak in a down-

pour of autumn rain. He had been possum-hunting and he had
a coffee sack with a little possum in it. The moonshine jug
was half empty. He had blown out two of the posts with dynamite. But the third post . . . something had happened. It was
partly blown out. Beside it lay Alvin Barker with his right
hand almost blown away, his right arm mangled, the right wing
of his handle-bar mustache nipped as clean as if it had been
done with a pair of scissors, and his right eye gone. He had
almost bled to death. He was rushed to a hospital, where he
wasn't given any chance to live. When I chose not to be rehired
for Greenwood County School Superintendent, many months
later, Fred Harrison and his clan were waiting for Alvin
Barker to return from the hospital so he could be summoned
before the Greenwood County Grand Jury to tell who furnished him whiskey on the night he had gone possum-hunting,
who furnished him dynamite to blow out the posts, who was
behind the whole thing. The fight was still carried on. It hadn't
ended nor would it end for years to come.

8

REPORTS sent beyond this state that we didn't count our
election votes until we had counted our dead, had good factual
foundation. But many people believed this statement concerned
county, state, and national elections between the two major
political parties. It did concern them, but only in a minor
degree as compared to these trustee elections, which were supposed to be nonpolitical. They were, to a certain degree, nonpolitical. But in these local trustee elections it would have been
better if they had chosen political sides. It was a certain church
group pitted against another church group. It was the "wets"
against the "drys." It was feuding clan against feuding clan.
It was a certain group for one teacher and a certain group for
another teacher, and it didn't matter which trustee was elected
and to whom he gave the school—the candidate he had defeated
and his following, who had lost their votes, made schoolteaching impossible for the teacher that had been recommended by

his trustee and hired by the county school board. They would find fault with the teacher, get signatures on a petition, and try to have him ousted.

Guns were often brought into play at these elections. Men were killed and seriously wounded. People were stabbed with knives. Men fought with clubs and rocks. Often the school-yard where one of these elections was held turned out to be the scene of a brawl. Often as many as twenty men were lying on the grass knocked senseless while forty or fifty more fought over their prone bodies, stepping on them, until the county sheriff and a posse of deputies had to be called. If the sheriff and his deputies were lucky, they could stop the fight. There have been occasions when the sheriff and his deputies knew the kind of fighters they were, and stayed away from the election grounds until the fight was over. The election of local school trustees in each of these districts was a big event in the community. Scarcely ever was there a peaceful election.

With the memories of these past experiences; with the memory of my first teaching experience at Lonesome Valley and the daily experience I had with these many school trustees since I had become Superintendent of Greenwood County Schools, I was compelled to try to do something about them. And of the 120 county school superintendents in the state of Kentucky, I may have been the first to attempt to oust the school trustees. I don't know. I seethed when I thought of the power of a district school trustee over the superintendent of county schools, over five county board members, and certainly over the schoolteacher. The local district school trustees told my school board and me what to do. Trustees who couldn't write their names, who would not know their own names if they had been printed on road signs, told college graduates with years of teaching experience how to teach school. Often these trustees visited the schools once a week and gave the teachers orders. If the teachers didn't teach according to their instructions, punish this pupil and let that one go, then these trustees came to me. They tried to make me act against the teacher in their behalf. That, I wouldn't do. Because I felt deeply for the members of my profession, I fought for them and with them, with every ounce of energy, mental and physical, that I had. If these were not injustices I was fighting against, I had never in my lifetime seen an injustice. In no other profession had I heard of one worker with nine bosses.

"Gentlemen, I have a proposition to which I have given much thought lately," I said to members of my school board. "It's the injustice of this abominable trustee system. I don't see why a schoolteacher has to have nine bosses! I propose to do away with the school trustee system."

"Well, I'll be goddamned, what else will you propose?" Mooner Bentworth shouted, jumping to his feet. With one hand, he twirled a horn of his blond mustache. With the other, he gripped the arm of his chair. "Don't you know you are going against a state law? Don't you know you will get yourself and the members of this board of education in trouble?"

"I agree with Mooner Bentworth," Tobias Claxton said. "I think he's right!"

"I never heard tell of anything like this," William Dawson said softly, shaking his head, then hit the cuspidor perfectly with amber spittle at a distance of eight feet. "Jesse," he said plainly, now that his mouth was free, "you are fooling with something *very dangerous!*"

"Any superintendent that has this trustee system to work with finds it very dangerous," I said. "It's dangerous to the whole state school system. And gentlemen," I explained, "I know this state has a law in favor of district school trustees. But we could go on record—this Greenwood County Board of Education—as being against this system and I'll send copies of our record to the state superintendent of schools and to members of the Kentucky Legislature."

"Oh, oh, no, never," Mooner shouted, louder than before. "Then we will be in hot water over our heads!"

"I'm not for this, either," Manley Warburton said. "I believe in the old way. It was good enough for me. It's good enough for the children of today. The trustee system is a wonderful thing. I was trustee for nine years!"

"Four members of this school board are against my proposal," I said. "I'd like to know what Mr. Dangerfield thinks about it!"

Benton Dangerfield had remained silent. He sat there,

looking at me with twinkling light-blue eyes. He had agreed many times on the proposals that I had suggested.

"I'm against it," was all he said.

Then I knew my proposal was doomed. It didn't get even a motion. All of my board members were against me. I wanted to leave this as a record on my minute-books. I still proposed to do something about this system. My fight about this system was just beginning.

9

ON THE morning of September 11th, our four school busses transported Greenwood County High School pupils to Maxwell High School. They transported approximately one hundred pupils to Maxwell High School whom Landsburgh High School had made arrangements to teach. Larry Anderson, now Superintendent of Landsburgh City Schools, his teachers, and members of his city school board must have been disappointed to find a few of the high-school classrooms vacant. Teachers must have been disappointed. The approximate sum of $800 per month they had expected to receive from us, went to our own Maxwell High School, where we employed three new teachers to help with the additional pupils.

On the afternoon of September 11th, John Farnsworth, elderly local politician of Landsburgh, who had congratulated me on the street, laid his arm across my shoulder.

"Jesse, you are a product of this town," he said. "You graduated from Landsburgh High School. You have been Principal of Landsburgh High School. Now you are wrecking our school system!"

"I'm not wrecking your school system," I said. "I'm working for my own."

"Now listen," he whispered in my ear, "can't we get this school business all ironed out? Can't you throw . . . ?"

"Throw what?" I broke in, before he had time to finish. . . . "Do you know that I am under oath to do my duty for my school system. If I were not under oath, do you think I'd throw anything?"

"You can be somebody or you can wreck yourself," he snapped.

"I don't appreciate your thinking so little of me as to think I can be propositioned," I told him, in cold turkey. "Who sent you here, anyway? You'd better get along!"

"You'll be sorry," he said. "We've got many good lawyers here, and they're loyal to Landsburgh!"

It took one day for the news of what had happened to Landsburgh High School to spread over the town. Pupils came home from school and told what had happened. From this time on, my Landsburgh friends would meet me on the street and wouldn't speak to me. They would turn their heads in the opposite direction when they passed me. A few of them jeered. This sort of thing cut me like a knife. I had known these people all my life and they had been my friends.

"I'm ashamed of you, Jesse Stuart," were Jason Hinton's first words when we met on the street one morning. "Don't ever come to my apartment again. You're not welcome. Mrs. Hinton and I don't want to be bothered with you!"

The majority of my high-school classmates wouldn't speak to me. I wasn't welcomed in the stores. I was sorry that my office was in the courthouse of this county-seat town. This was the first time in my life I had been shunned by all my Landsburgh friends. It cut me to the heart when people turned their heads and spat when they met me, instead of the usual "good morning" as it had been down through the years. These were the same people who had once cheered me when I played football for Landsburgh High School. I soon stayed off the street as much as possible. I spent the first part of the night in my office working and the early morning hours in my hotel-room sleeping. The light in my office was always the last to be switched off, according to Bill Hayes, night policeman; for the Mayor of Landsburgh, John Moore, and members of his city council, had voted the town in night darkness as an economy measure.

The following week when I returned, one noon hour, from the hotel to my office, Sheriff Bill Creason stopped me on the street and gave me a summons to appear in court. When I received this summons—the first one I had ever received—a warm glow came over my face and my heart pumped a little faster. I thought about what Mooner Bentworth had said at the board meeting, when I made the suggestion that we transport all our county high-school pupils to Maxwell High School. Now I knew we were up against a real fight. I had to have help and counsel.

Oscar Vinson, who was a citizen and taxpayer of Greenwood County, had brought suit against the Greenwood County School Board and the Superintendent of Greenwood County, in his own behalf and that of other taxpaying citizens of Greenwood County who were sending their sons and daughters to Landsburgh High School. They asked in their petition that we furnish free transportation and that we pay eight dollars per month per pupil for these county pupils who were going to Landsburgh High School. This petition gave the names of the parents who were behind this suit, and a list of their sons and daughters now in Landsburgh High School. I had checked the list of pupils eligible to attend high school before we sent our pupils to Maxwell High School. I had Margaret Raridan compare the two lists. Many of the pupils now attending Landsburgh High School had not passed examination to enter high school. A few of them were sixth-grade pupils. But they occupied the seats that had been vacated in Landsburgh High School. They kept the teachers whom Landsburgh City School Board had employed, busy, and would pay them as well, if they collected the tuition for them from the county.

I called the businessmen who had helped me with the school budget into my office, to meet with a special session of the Greenwood County School Board.

"I told you, young man, you were leading us straight to hell," Mooner Bentworth reminded me. "Now we are in a mess!"

"We can't talk about the mess," Joe Terrill said. "We've got to work, and work fast. We can't let them take money that is to pay our teachers. If they get it, their teachers will be paid twice the salaries our teachers are supposed to get!"

I showed the board members and businessmen the list of

unauthorized county pupils now attending Landsburgh High School, and with county school records we showed them where sixth-grade county school pupils had been accepted at Landsburgh High School.

"They haven't any right to invade our schools and take our pupils," Manley Warburton said.

Then came the problem of getting lawyers. Each board member suggested getting his favorite lawyer in Landsburgh. And I remembered John Farnsworth had told me that Landsburgh lawyers would be loyal to Landsburgh. I suggested to members of my school board that we employ out-of-town lawyers—the best lawyers in Auckland. Businessmen from the county agreed with me. Then my school board agreed to let Tobias Claxton and me employ the lawyers, with a promise-to-pay when we got the money. We hadn't made any provision in our budget for attorney fees. Tobias Claxton and I went to Auckland that afternoon and employed the firm of Tanner, Stevens, Denton, and Denton to be our attorneys.

Two of the four county businessmen who had met with us, and three of our county school board members, didn't think we had a chance of winning this lawsuit. They found in the Kentucky School laws two strong points against us. The law might have been a little on their side, but justice, all of justice, was on our side.

On the day members of the county school board, and the businessmen, and I discussed in my office how we would handle this lawsuit, Jason Spleeves, one of the largest men in size in Greenwood County and the biggest county taxpayer, heard about it and came to see me. Since this man couldn't read and write, he had my secretary Margaret Raridan read the claims against the county in the suit that Oscar Vinson had brought against us. He had her read parts of this petition over and over to him so "he could get it in his head." We were aggravated at this man, since we needed Margaret Raridan all the time; but we couldn't keep her from reading this petition to Jason Spleeves. He was a taxpayer and citizen of Greenwood County and he had a right to know facts concerning the county. She also read him the list of unauthorized county pupils attending Landsburgh School.

"B'gad, I'll do something about this," he said, when he left the office.

Before the lawyers were ready to act, he had done something about it. I was standing on the street near-by when it happened.

"Oscar, why did you bring suit against us?" Jason said, when he met him on the street. "Now you get your name off that petition and drop that lawsuit in a hurry!"

"I won't do it," Oscar said.

"Listen, Oscar," Jason reminded him, as he shook his big finger under his nose, "you have sold me the rottenest moonshine whiskey I ever drinked. You know it. If you don't get your name off that lawsuit, I'll go before the Grand Jury and indict you for bootlegging and prove it on you and send you to the penitentiary. Hate to do it, Oscar, on account of your wife and children, but, b'gad, I will if you don't drop that petition."

Oscar Vinson's face turned red as an October sourwood leaf. He got away from Jason Spleeves fast as he could run. In two weeks Oscar Vinson's name was off the petition and the suit against us was dropped.

Now that our money wasn't tied up, we paid our teachers their second month's salary.

After this suit was dropped, another week hadn't passed until Morris Thornton, another citizen and taxpayer of Greenwood County, had sued us. The old petition was retyped, and Morris Thornton's name was substituted for Oscar Vinson. The date was set for the new trial, and something happened again. On the night before the date of the trial, Greenwood County had one of the greatest electrical storms in the history of our county. Lightning split giant oak trees from butt to tip, burned barns, killed livestock. Rain fell in torrents that flooded roads and valleys and washed out bridges. Electric and telephone wires were broken. Though it was late for one of these storms, it was the greatest and most destructive the people had ever known. On this night Morris Thornton had gone to bed in good health and looked forward to the following day when he would be leader in a courthouse packed with people. But the thunder awoke him in the night when his house seemed to be falling apart. He arose from his bed, pushed aside the window blind and took one look at a world that seemed to be on fire. His heart failed him. He died.

"Even God in heaven is with us," Jason Spleeves said next day, when the second suit had ended. "It's a good token, men," he told members of the school board. "We're going to win this suit! We're not just going to fight to delay it. We're going to win it!"

Now that our money was free again, we paid our rural teachers their third month's salary. We paid them on this very day when we should have been in court.

Since the older people of Greenwood County had cause to be superstitious over the way Morris Thornton left this world, it was difficult to get another person to head this lawsuit against us. Since the person suing us had to be a citizen and taxpayer of Greenwood County, not from the Landsburgh Independent School District, we hoped that no one to head the suit could be found. But our hopes were in vain. In three weeks this man had been found. If Tom Jackson was superstitious and afraid of death, he must have thought he was prepared to die. He was a leader of his church where there were often great testimonial meetings and much shouting. He wasn't an ordained minister but he preached when they hadn't a minister. He headed the suit against us.

In the meantime Jason Spleeves must have been at work. Many of our unauthorized county pupils left Landsburgh High School and went back to their respective rural schools to finish their grade work, or, where they were eligible for high school, they went to Maxwell High School. Jason Spleeves had these names "fixed in his head" and something was happening to make many parents change their minds. Perhaps the death of Morris Thornton had something to do with it. But nothing happened to Tom Jackson. Jason Spleeves was not able to make him withdraw his name from the petition, and on the third date set for our trial, Tom Jackson was there in robust health.

Tom Jackson and a host of parents, whose names were on the suit against us, sat with the Landsburgh lawyers on one side of the courtroom. My five board members and I sat with our Auckland lawyers on the other side and we eyed each other across the courtroom. The courtroom was packed to capacity. A big trial in Landsburgh was something of a holiday, and people turned out in great numbers. It was relaxation and enjoyment. They sat in the windows. They stood in the aisles. They thought it would be something like the big murder trials. But they were sadly disappointed when, after a few court preliminaries, they heard the lawyers arguing points before Judge Whittlecomb, Circuit Judge of Greenwood and Lambert Counties. Many of them left before the day was over. The day was spent and the lawyers on both sides were not through presenting their contentions to Judge Whittlecomb.

Then came a series of long-drawn-out legal battles. It took a legally trained mind to follow the charges and counter-charges of the lawsuits that followed. After each time we were in court, people would be asking each other what had happened.

Since we believed there was so much prejudice against us in Landsburgh, we asked for these trials to be held at neighboring courts. We had hearings at Lanceville, county seat of Lambert County; Paisley, county seat of Cantrill County; and at Centerville, county seat of Benton County. On court days, we loaded our four school busses to capacity with citizens of Greenwood County who were fighting for us.

"Get up close, boys, where you can look the Judge right in the eye," Jason Spleeves warned us. "And clap your hands and stomp your feet when the Judge rules a point in our favor. We've got to win."

Jason Spleeves sat up close, looked straight at the Judge, and he kept one hand cupped over his right ear to catch every word the Judge said. If he approved of what he heard, he clapped his hands and stomped his feet. If he didn't approve, he moaned unintelligible words while he shook his head sadly. In all the courts in these different towns, Greenwood County citizens attended in great numbers—because upon these decisions depended whether or not our school system would be wrecked. These people were interested in their schools.

At first, we didn't have any way of explaining our position in these legal battles to the people of Greenwood County. I went to Lambert Reed, the editor of the *Landsburgh Leader*, a county newspaper that circulated throughout the county.

Since the city had presented its side, I asked for space to present my side—the county's side—of what had brought about this great school muddle. He would not give me space. Then I wrote the county's side of the story and took it to the *Roxford Examiner,* the only other paper published in our county. At that time it had much less circulation than the *Landsburgh Leader.* Very few copies of this paper circulated beyond the metropolitan area of Roxford. Editor Rex Milford gleefully accepted the long article I had written and gave it front page and headlines. Whatever the *Landsburgh Leader* was against, the *Roxford Examiner* was for. Then I bought personally hundreds of these papers, and they were sent from my office to all parts of Greenwood County. I let the people and teachers of Greenwood County School System read another side of the story. The newspaper fight was a fight to a finish.

Judge Whittlecomb finally decided in our favor. He decided that we didn't have to send the east-end high-school pupils to Landsburgh High School, and that we could drive our busses loaded with our pupils past the Landsburgh High School and take them on down eighteen miles beyond to Maxwell High School if we wished. That we didn't owe Landsburgh City School Board any tuition for the pupils that had gone there, and that we didn't owe anything for transportation of these pupils. His decision brought great happiness throughout Greenwood County.

"The Judge had a-better decided for us, son," Jason Spleeves said to me with a wink. "We were on the right side of justice. Besides, Judge Whittlecomb knows where the votes are." He winked again. "If he hadn't decided with us, we'd a-beat him in spite of hell next time he ran for office. There's enough votes in this county to decide his fate! Boy," he said, slapping my shoulder with his big hand, "before you start fighting, know you are in the right and fight with all the power there is in you and then fight some more!"

But Tom Jackson, his county followers, and the Landsburgh City School Board still had another chance at us, for this case went to the Court of Appeals of Kentucky for a final decision. When the final verdict was rendered, Judge Whittlecomb's decision was upheld. If my memory is correct, we had approximately thirty-two lawsuits while I was Superintendent of Greenwood County Schools, and we won thirty-one and one-half. For us, justice had prevailed over the petty, flimsy, nonessential school laws. But we had to fight for that justice.

10

THE Kentucky School Law required the superintendent of county schools to visit each rural school under his supervision at least once during the school term. At a board meeting I read this law. Then I reminded members of my school board that I didn't have an expense account. After I paid for room, board, laundry, I wouldn't have enough left from my $100 a month to pay my expenses to visit these schools. They had voted my predecessor, Larry Anderson, $160 expense account, and this was certainly not enough, considering the amount of traveling necessary. Greenwood County had a vast and sprawling network of rural schools that covered hundreds of square miles of mountainous terrain where the few roads became impassable after the autumn rains had fallen in November. My school board allowed me $50 to visit eighty-two rural schools that were from three to eight miles apart.

If they had not appropriated the money, I would have walked from school to school. This would have required more time away from my office, where the work was always stacked ahead of me. I knew I couldn't wait too long to visit the rural schools. I had to go while the roads were good. I had to beat the November rains. It was October now.

I contacted Lester Larkes, who owned an old, topless, Chevrolet roadster. Lester was a big, blond-headed, left-handed baseball pitcher, who had pitched first for the Landsburgh Owls, later for Harlan County's Coal Miners League. He lived at Plum Grove and was a near neighbor of mine. We had gone to the one-room Plum Grove Rural School together, where Lester had reached the fifth grade.

"Lester, I've had fifty dollars appropriated for me by my school board to visit eighty-two rural schools," I explained. "How much would you take—to drive me over the county?"

"Since I have the right kind of car for the roads and have nothing to do now that baseball season is over, I'll take three dollars a day and expenses," he laughed. "I know, Stuart, that in eighty-two rural schools in Greenwood County we're bound to find some beautiful young women teaching school," he said. "The only thing that I ask of you is, if I find one I can fall in love with, don't you try to cut me out!"

"It's a bargain," I said. "You be at my office at seven in the morning."

11

AT SEVEN that morning Lester and I climbed into the topless roadster. We didn't wear overcoats and we didn't wear hats. We left Landsburgh in a hurry for the school, Mountain View, which was the farthest from Landsburgh of any rural school in Greenwood County. I had heard teachers refer to this school as "Greenwood County's most distant outpost." We wanted to visit first the rural schools farthest away from the county seat. We wanted to visit them while the weather was right for us. Lester drove as fast as the road would allow up Route 1 until we reached Lost Hollow. Then we started up a road that was in the creek and out of the creek for the next five miles. Once our engine drowned out in a hole of water. We had to pull off our shoes and roll up our pant legs and wade the ice-cold water to shove the car forward. We did it easily. The two of us weighed four hundred pounds and we were strong as oxen. But from now on Lester was more careful about driving through the water holes.

It was a beautiful morning to drive. The high hills were blanketed white with frost. The brisk wind brought color to our faces. High on the hilltops, above this narrow-gauged valley, the frost was rising in white clouds, beautiful but formless, in the morning rays of autumn sun.

We were in Greenwood County's finest burley tobacco district. Every farmer in Lost Hollow raised light burley tobacco. We passed the giant tobacco barns whose tier poles were empty now of this bright-colored aromatic plant. We passed the little creek bottoms and steep hill slopes where last year's drought-dwarfed tobacco plants stood unharvested. The harvest had been too worthless to reap. Through the shallow holes of blue water our car wheels rolled on the slick slate-rock bottom. Then we came to the end of our creek-bed road. A water-gap fence spanned the creek. Here we stopped. Lester finally turned the car in this narrow-gauged valley until it was facing the direction we had come. Then at a near-by farmhouse we asked directions to Mountain View School.

"Go through the drawbars yander," said a housewife at a little log shack, "then go up the pint until you come to the old road. My husband says it's six pipes of tobacco or two miles from here to the schoolhouse and that you follow your nose instead of your right or left hand. Straight ahead!" she laughed. "Straight ahead!"

"I'll bet this is some school," Lester said, as we hand-sprung across the drawbars. "Not even a wagon road leading to it! Wonder how they get coal up there to burn?"

"I don't know," I said, as I followed Lester up the well-worn path that was getting steeper all the time. "This is some climb up to the school!"

I knew that this was the one rural school district in Greenwood County where a rural merchant, approximately eight miles away, drove in each year in late September with a truckload of shoes. And since he couldn't get to the people, they came to him, for he announced the day of his coming. At the same place where we had parked our car, the parents in this district brought their children to the shoe truck, where their summer-brown feet were fitted into brogan shoes. In normal times each child received one pair of shoes for the year. This was the only district in Greenwood County I knew that still did this. Buying shoes for the winter was a great day for everybody. They could all get together and have their feet fitted into shoes and make a holiday of the affair.

When Lester and I climbed halfway up the hill, though

it was getting near noon the October sun was just lifting the frost from the deep valley. We stopped to catch our second wind and looked down over Lost Hollow. Clouds rising from this narrow valley streamed skyward, thin white sheets of vapor, like fresh-laundered sheets buoyed by blue crisp wind. While up around us on the hill, the leaves on the autumn trees were clouds of a different color. The leaves were dried by the sun and they rustled in the morning wind. There were red clouds of leaves, brown leaves, golden and light-golden. There were leaf-clouds of many colors, depending on the direction one looked. And there was still a patch of world above, just a little island of high hilltop and not another house on it but a schoolhouse.

"This is something to see," Lester said. "But if I had to climb this mountain every morning to school, I wouldn't have my fifth-grade education."

Before we had reached the top of this little island in the highlands, we had whetted up an appetite.

"Boy, am I hungry," Lester said.

"There's not anyplace here to buy sardines and crackers," I said.

Less than a hundred yards from the hilltop, we followed the ridge path around a curve. Here was the schoolhouse. Just as we reached the schoolyard, school dismissed for noon. We crossed the yard filled with barefooted, ruddy-cheeked, husky pupils. Many of them were larger than high-school pupils. They eyed us suspiciously as we greeted them and walked over to the schoolhouse. We found Mrs. Ethel Henthorne inside.

"I'm Jesse Stuart, Mrs. Henthorne," I said.

"Oh, our new Superintendent," she smiled. "I've heard a lot about you."

She was a large, elderly lady, with a shock of gray hair piled on her head.

"This is Lester Larkes, who is driving me around to visit the schools," I said.

"You young men haven't had any dinner, have you?"

We didn't have time to answer her.

"We'll share with you," she said. "You know you're far-

away from a house or a country store up here. Wait a minute.
I don't have enough for all three of us."

She moved slowly across the schoolhouse, for walking
seemed to be difficult for her.

"Our County School Superintendent, Jesse Stuart, and
his friend Lester Larkes are here without their dinner," I
heard her telling the pupils. "We must share with them."

While Ethel Henthorne was outside, I looked over the
inside of this one-room school. The blackboards had been
washed before school was dismissed for noon. Above the blackboards and between the windows were decorations of autumn
leaves, clusters of red shoe-make berries, bittersweet, pale-blue
and white farewell-to-summer. They were artistically arranged
in contrasting colors, flowers and leaves, shoe-make berries,
bittersweet, and mountain laurel. I had never seen a room in
any high school as well decorated. It was the prettiest schoolroom I had ever seen.

"Ain't this room sumptuous?" Lester said. "Never expected to find anything like this up here! Who is this Mrs.
Henthorne, anyway?"

I didn't have time to answer him, for she came through
the door with many pupils following her. Each pupil offered
to share his lunch with us. Dry corn bread never tasted better
to me. Very few of these pupils had anything besides dry corn
bread. There were no cakes or candy. No food delicacies. Only
the rough, solid food for the body's subsistence. Yet here was
the strongest-looking, most handsome group of pupils I had
ever seen in a rural school. Lester ate dry corn bread too.
Later, he said he wished he'd had a half-gallon of cold butter-
milk with his corn bread.

After we had shared lunch with the Mountain View pupils
and Mrs. Henthorne, Lester went out on the school ground to
play baseball with the boys. An eighth-grade pupil who had
heard of Lester Larkes got his catcher's mitt and asked Lester
to pitch for him. And while Lester pitched and he caught and
the boys tried to hit the left-handed drops, I talked to Mrs.
Henthorne.

"How long have you been teaching here?"

"Four years, Mr. Stuart," she said.

"Isn't it a very inconvenient place for you to teach?"

"Yes, very inconvenient," she admitted. "But for every inconvenience, there is a compensation. And I've taught many rural schools in this county. I have met many fine people, but here"—she spoke with enthusiasm—"are the finest people I have ever known. I don't have a discipline problem. My pupils know I am trying to help them. They love me for it."

"How do you get coal up here?" I asked.

"We don't burn coal," she said. "We burn wood. My boys here in school, and their fathers, cut it. There's plenty of wood here."

"Mrs. Henthorne, do you live in Mountain View School District?" I asked.

"Oh, me, I don't," she said. "I board in this school district. I room and board at Praters' down at the foot of the mountain. My home is over at Oldham."

"I don't see how you are able to climb up here every morning and go back down in the afternoon," I said.

"It would have been much better if the trustees of one of the rural districts had given me a school somewhere on a highway . . . but when one gets old"—she sighed . . . "when one gets old, one cannot choose. One has to take what is given him. I was glad to be hired to teach Mountain View. One year, you know, none of the trustees in this county would hire me. Superintendent Larry Anderson and the members of the Greenwood County School Board wanted me, but the trustees didn't. I didn't get a school. When they hired me for Mountain View, I didn't grumble. I knew I had a mountain to climb. But I figured out a way to do that," she continued. "Willis Prater has two large boys in school. And each morning one of them takes me by the hand and helps me up the mountain. Sometimes," she explained, "John Phillips, one of my large eighth-grade boys, who lives near Praters', gets behind me and shoves. Myrtle Phillips often carries my books. My pupils are good to me!"

"But when the snow falls?" I questioned.

"Get up the same way I do when the weather is good," she answered quickly. "The boys help me. Getting down the mountain is another problem. Mr. Stuart," she whispered, bending over closer to me, "when we have sleet and the ground is slick, my pupils have to let me down the mountain with ropes. I keep the ropes here in the schoolhouse, for winter emergencies."

I didn't ask Mrs. Ethel Henthorne how heavy she was. I guessed her to weigh between 240 and 260 pounds. Her shock of high-piled hair was the color of frosted crab grass. Her eyes sparkled like water in the sunlight when she talked to me.

"I have to teach school, Mr. Stuart," she said. "I've taught all my life, and I've never been able to put anything away for a rainy day. See, summer after summer, I've gone to Morehead College and have worked off a few college hours, until I now have my degree. Oh," she laughed, "I didn't get it until I was nearly seventy. But I got it. I'm a college graduate now. I wanted all my life to be one. My ambition was finally realized. I started teaching after I finished the fifth grade. Later, I finished high school and finally college. It has taken me more than fifty years to do it," she laughed. "But it's better late than never. Now when you leave the mountain, you stop at the hickory grove on your right and look down and you can see the shack at the foot. That's where Praters live. The path that bends back and forth up the hill is the one I climb every morning and go down every afternoon."

Mrs. Henthorne talked on. She told me that this would be a hard year on her pupils, since the drought had destroyed the money crops—tobacco and cane—and the food crops. She apologized that her pupils were barefooted this late in autumn. She said the truck hadn't brought them shoes yet. She told me that she had often seen red spots on the frost where her pupils had come to school ahead of her. And she said she guessed many would have to stop coming to school as soon as the snows fell on this mountain.

Before the noon hour was over, I went outside to watch the boys and girls play ball. They had chosen sides and Lester was umpiring the game for them. They were having the time of their lives. Pupils too small to play had divided into groups, and each group was rooting for one of the teams. I watched the ball game for a few minutes and then I went around the schoolhouse and looked it over. This schoolhouse had once been painted, but now it was weathered gray with many strips of weatherboarding gone, until one could look inside and see the studding. This building was not as good, not half as good, as some of the barns owned by little one-horse farmers in rural Greenwood County. I wondered how it held together during the great windstorms that swept this mountaintop. I wondered if the time wouldn't come when it would blow apart and instantly kill these pupils and their teacher.

While I was looking the schoolhouse over and, down below me in every direction, at the multicolored clouds of autumn leaves, the bell rang for books and the ball game ended. The pupils lined up outside and marched in. There were smiles on their sweaty red faces. They were happy in Mountain View School. They hadn't any thought of a storm that might blow their ramshackle schoolhouse to pieces and kill all of them! This was the place they loved to come. It was not a task for them to climb the mountain to school. It was a recreation. Corn bread was all right for them to eat, too, and it was all right to come barefooted in the frost! While Lester and I joined the line of boys and marched inside with them—boys that had shared their lunches with us—I wished many of the Landsburgh High School pupils could have been there. I wished they could have compared their educational opportunities with those of the Mountain View people.

Soon as the pupils were seated, Mrs. Henthorne asked me to say something to them.

I faced this group of sturdy, stalwart, and eager youth, and spoke to them for about twenty-five minutes. I told them they could further their education without any more of a struggle than they were having now, if they were ambitious and willing to try; that education was not a commodity to be bought and sold but something that gave one more realization and enjoyment of the many things that life held in store. That with more education, the mysteries and the beauties of life would unfold before them like the buds of leaf and flower in the spring. I told them they would even see more beauty in their natural surroundings than they now saw. Then I sat down.

For the next thirty minutes or longer, Mrs. Henthorne's

pupils entertained us. One of the sweaty-faced ballplayers stood up and recited Keat's "To Autumn." Another recited Whittier's "The Barefoot Boy." A girl recited "Annabel Lee." One recited Longfellow's "A Psalm of Life." At least a dozen good poems were recited by these pupils. Then they sang "Beautiful Dreamer" by Stephen Foster, and followed it with a number of familiar folk songs. When they had finished Mrs. Henthorne gave a reading: James Whitcomb Riley's "Little Orphant Annie." Lester Larkes sat spellbound at this entertainment by his ballplayers. I never enjoyed school entertainment more than this spontaneous program by Mountain View rural pupils and their teacher.

Lester and I said good-bye to her and her pupils. We had to hurry. We had to stop at five more schools. We had to visit Upper Lost Hollow, Lower Lost Hollow, Hopewell, Cane Creek, and Oldham Rural Schools before this day was over. I had to make the time count while I was spending the fifty dollars appropriated by my Greenwood County Board of Education for this purpose.

12

LESTER LARKES had driven us over the Rock Creek boulders, up a shallow stream that shone brilliantly in the autumn sunlight. We had looked at this ribbon of water until there were spots before our eyes. Lester had driven us where few other cars had been, for the rock-ribbed hills came down to the stream. There wasn't anyplace for a road except in the middle of the stream, and the cars before us had traveled it only when the stream was dry in summer. The few autumn rains had not caused the stream to rise enough to drown our engine. We had reached Upper Rock Creek Rural School. This was our sixth and last school for the second day.

"Don't see how in the world Sophia can stand to live in this forsaken place," said Lester, who knew my sister well. "She must have been in love to marry a man and live here,"

Lester laughed jovially. "It'd certainly take a good-looking gal to hold me in this forsaken hole!"

We left the car in the creek bed with the swift blue water flowing around us, and stepped on big boulders until we reached dry land. Then we went up a little bank to the schoolhouse. When we walked in the teacher arose from her seat and faced us. And she was beautiful. She had soft brown hair and large blue eyes. She didn't wear any make-up, but her lips were as red as October sourwood leaves. Her desk was loaded with apples, wild grapes, and pawpaws—gifts her pupils had brought her.

"Miss Binion, I'm Jesse Stuart," I said. "I've come to visit your school."

"You're our new Superintendent," she said. "I've heard about you. And I know your sister, Mrs. Kenneally, very well. See, I followed her to this school!"

"Have you been here that long?" I asked.

"Five years," she laughed.

"Your trustees must like you," I joked.

"They wouldn't let me leave if I wanted to," she said. "My pupils wouldn't, either!"

Then I looked over a schoolroom filled with fifty or more handsome pupils. Girls were on one side. Boys were on the other.

"Miss Binion, I'm Lester Larkes," Lester said, as he came forward and introduced himself. "I drive Mr. Stuart over the county to visit schools."

"I've heard of you. Baseball-pitcher, aren't you?" she said.

"Right," Lester beamed.

The boys had heard of Lester too; for they started whispering to each other.

"And Mr. Stuart, I've never seen you but you don't need any introduction here," Olive Binion said, turning to me. "We first heard talk of you when Winston High School defeated Landsburgh High School in a scholastic contest. Pupils, this is Jesse Stuart, Superintendent of Greenwood County Schools. We'd like to have him speak to us."

I didn't have long to speak for it was only a few minutes until the school day ended.

When I had finished talking, Olive Binion dismissed school. The pupils swarmed around us. They wanted to meet Lester and they wanted to meet me. Finally they departed, going up steep paths in many directions. A few wore brogan shoes. The majority of them were still barefoot. While Lester and Olive talked I looked over the schoolhouse. It was in worse condition than the Mountain View Schoolhouse. There were holes in the walls. It looked ready to fall apart. But Miss Binion kept the schoolroom very clean. The walls were decorated with autumn leaves and flowers. The tiny yard, where fifty pupils played, was clean too. This schoolhouse was typical of so many of the rural schoolhouses I had visited in Greenwood County.

Inside the schoolroom Lester and Miss Binion were still talking and laughing.

"This house needs painting badly," Miss Binion said.

"I wish we had the money to paint it," I said. "I'd love to have every rural school in this county repaired and painted. They're all going to seed!"

Before we left, Olive Binion invited us to come to the Rock Creek Singing-School that evening. Lester had told her that we were spending the night at my sister's home. She went down the path above the shallow, blue Rock Creek waters that lashed white spray of foam against the boulders. After she had turned the last bend and was out of sight, Lester followed me to the car.

"I've seen many beautiful women," he confessed. "Olive Binion is the prettiest girl I ever saw. I could fall in love with her. I believe I am in love with her! She's prettier than any woman I ever saw on the screen!"

"But you thought Lucinda Sprouse, the teacher at Mount Carmel, was beautiful too," I reminded him. "You've raved about her since we visited her school!"

"Oh, boy, but this Olive Binion!" he said. "Just to have Olive Binion in my arms," he sighed, as he kept his eyes fastened on the stream of water before us, "would be a greater thrill than winning the championship of Harlan County's Coal Miners League."

"Think you could live the rest of your days here with her in this forsaken hollow?" I asked.

"Could if I couldn't persuade her to leave with me," he said.

"Hank wouldn't leave with Sophia," I said. "These people love this narrow valley, their rock-ribbed hills, and the song of water over rocks that lulls them to sleep at night. My sister wants to move where there are better schools for her children when they grow up. But Hank won't leave."

My sister couldn't believe her eyes when we drove up in front of her little cottage with a car. She and Hank and their two little girls greeted us. Sophia asked me about Dad and Mom and the family. She didn't get home very often, though she lived not more than thirty miles from us. During the winter when Rock Creek was landlocked, she never came home at all. We heard from her only by letter. A telephone was unheard-of in this country. When Lester and I sat down at the table, we stopped worrying about how people on Rock Creek lived.

After supper while we sat and talked, Blake Pennington, one of the trustees of the Upper Rock Creek Rural District, came to the house and called Hank outside. Blake said something to Hank. Then Hank called Lester and me outside.

"Schoolteachers wantin' dates with you fellows," Hank laughed. "Blake Pennington here was afraid to ask you. I told him I would. Ain't it right, Blake, two teachers are dying to have dates with 'em?"

"It shore is," Blake said seriously. "That's why I'm here. When Miss Olive wants anything I always do it. She's a perfect mother to the little ones, and all she has to do to the big boys is smile at 'em once. Best teacher in Greenwood County and I don't bar none. She's as decent and honorable as she is pretty."

"She's the one for me," Lester shouted. "I agree with you, Mr. Pennington. I agree with every word you've said."

"I'm sorry to disappoint you, young man," Blake said, "but she wants to date her Superintendent. She wants him to take her to the singing-school."

Lester looked at me. He looked at Hank. Disappointment clouded his ruddy-complexioned face.

"Lucinda Sprouse of the Mount Carmel School fell for you today," Blake told Lester. "She thinks you're the best-looking young man she has ever seen."

"What do you say about it, Stuart?" Lester said.

"Let the teachers choose," I said. "I'm satisfied."

Then Lester reluctantly consented to take Lucinda.

"At seven-thirty you will meet the girls in the Upper Rock Creek schoolyard and go inside with them," Blake directed us. "It's too late for you to go to their homes and get them. Besides, you don't know where they live!"

"That's all right with us," I said. "We'll be there, won't we, Lester?"

"Sure," he answered in a subdued tone.

"We'll see you this evening," Blake Pennington said, as he hurried away.

At seven-thirty Lester and I were back at the school-house. Lucinda Sprouse and Olive Binion arrived just as we did. Lester took Lucinda by the arm, and they walked in front of Olive and me into the schoolhouse. When we walked inside all eyes were turned upon us. The house was packed to capacity and Blake Pennington was up front with his tuning fork in his hand. He turned his back to the audience and faced his choir, a mixed group of men, women, boys, and girls. He registered the tune on his tuning fork. For two hours we heard this choir sing hymns and folk songs. They sang beautifully, even if the choir members didn't know a note of music; and often the people in the audience sang with the choir. When everybody sang I thought the singing was as beautiful as a high wind among the winter oak tops. So many people often turned toward Lester and me, strangers in their midst, that it seemed they were singing for us.

It was half-past nine when the singing-school was over and we left the schoolhouse. Lester and Lucinda went up a path along one of Rock Creek's narrow-gauged tributaries. It was not in the direction of Mount Carmel. I didn't have far enough to go to take Olive home. We walked along the path beside the ruffled waters of Rock Creek until we came to a very large loghouse. This was the house where Olive Binion was born and where she had lived all her life, except for four nine-month periods when she had been in the Morehead Training School.

She invited me inside. There I met her father and mother, and her brothers and sisters, all younger than Olive. After we had talked for an hour or more, Mrs. Binion served hot biscuits, wild honey, and coffee. She also served homemade pickles at intervals, to take the taste of wild honey from our mouths. Then Olive and I went into the parlor, a big room with an open fireplace and a blazing wood fire. Here we had the late evening all alone. The room was spacious and beautiful, and Olive was beautiful, too, in the soft glow of firelight. I wondered if Greenwood County's Superintendent of Schools should be dating one of his teachers. Then I decided the position that I held shouldn't interfere with personal affairs. It was about midnight when I said good night to Olive and left Binions'.

While I was walking up the path, with pleasant thoughts of an evening well spent, a pistol barked six times from somewhere near the schoolhouse. I had to pass the schoolhouse to get to my sister's. At least, I thought I did. Another pistol was emptied in my direction. The bullets went high. I heard two hit among the black oak branches above my head and sing off into space. I didn't have time to think what to do. Pistols barked again. Dirt flew up in the starlit path ahead of me. I started running for my life. Not in the direction of the schoolhouse, either. I went back the way I had come. Now I heard the screams of my pursuers. There must have been a half-dozen men after me.

I ran part of the way back to Binions'; I made for the steep hill. I ran like a fox over the autumn leaves that carpeted the earth. After my pursuers got away from the noise of the singing waters, they could hear me in the leaves. I think they must have shot in the direction of the sound, for bullets whizzed by too close for safety. I got behind a big oak high on the mountainside, and I let them shoot. More than once, oak bark flew all around me. I let them shoot until I thought they had wasted their bullets. Then I walked as softly as a cat around the steep hill slope until I reached Hank's cow pasture, and I went down the backway to the house. When I got home it was two-thirty. My clothes were ruined. There was a hole torn in the back of my coat. I thought my pant leg just below my knee was ripped in two places, until I discovered a bullet had gone in and had come out again! I was so scared I didn't know when it had happened.

When Lester got back at three-thirty I was in bed. He woke me.

"Look at me," he said, after he lit the lamp. "You're a lucky dog!"

There was a pump knot on his forehead big as a guinea's egg. His face was red with blood.

"What's happened to you, fellow?" I asked.

"I was rocked," he said. "First I stood my ground. I threw rocks at them fast as bullets, must have upended a half-dozen the way they screamed. But there was too many of them! They hit me with three rocks. One nearly busted a panel of ribs and one caught me squarely behind, then I realized it was time for me to take off."

"Did you have a good time?" I asked.

"Oh, I had a wonderful time taking Lucinda home," Lester said. "Had to walk four or five miles. She lives in a place you ought to see. Rock Creek is a paradise compared to the place where she lives."

"You didn't get rocked all the way home, did you?" I asked.

"Just the last two miles," he said. "Was lucky it wasn't all the way. I know you had a good time."

"That's right," I said.

After breakfast I wore Hank's clothes while Sophia darned mine.

"What happened to your clothes?" Lester inquired, as he watched my sister darn the holes.

"You got off easy last night," I said. "Rocks are easier to dodge than bullets."

Lester laughed as I had never heard him laugh before.

He must have thought he had been richly rewarded by not dating the teacher of his choice, since he had only been hit with three rocks and I had come so close to the call.

"Lester, I don't think it's anything to laugh about," Sophia said. "Just an inch closer that bullet might have made Jesse a cripple for life. He might have lost his leg."

"I think it's funny when the Superintendent of Greenwood County Schools gets a bullet in his pant leg when he has a date with one of his teachers." Lester screamed with laughter.

"I told Hank, after you boys left last night," Sophia said, "that something might happen. The young men around here are awfully funny about strangers coming in here and dating their girls. Four or five young men in this district are in love with Olive Binion."

13

SPRAY of water splashing from the car wheels was bright as polished silver in the bright October sunlight as we dashed up the Little Cavern Creek Road. A sweep of October wind that had slept during the night arose early from the narrow valley and rustled slowly the frosted clusters of leaves still hanging to the tough-butted white oaks. The wind was cool and soothing against our faces. A cool breath of this wind into the warm lungs made one feel wide-awake and happy to be alive on such a morning.

"Step on it, Lester," I said. "Little Cavern is one school I am anxious to visit."

"What's the attraction?" he asked jokingly. "Beautiful teacher?"

"Don Conway is teacher," I said. "I used to teach him at Lonesome Valley. Since then he's finished the grades, high school, and has two years in college."

"Must be a smart boy," Lester said, as we left the creek road and started climbing the hill.

"Not too smart," I said. "He's ambitious and eager."

As Lester drove up this difficult road, where only wagons and mule teams traveled, I thought about Don Conway. I had persuaded him to attend school so as to get some practical education before he got married. I thought he would be a good man to have on my side, since there was Guy Hawkins, a pupil I was sure I'd have to fight before my school term was over; and his friend Ova Salyers would help him do his fighting. After Don returned, he got so interested in his schoolwork, he forgot to marry. He kept going to school. Now he was teaching school.

"Gee, this is a nice schoolhouse," Lester said, as we reached Little Cavern and parked in the schoolyard. "House painted and the yard is clean! Best-looking schoolhouse we've visited."

I stepped inside and was facing Don Conway. He didn't look like the Don Conway I used to know. He was a big, broad-shouldered, handsome man. He was wearing a new suit of clothes. I don't believe I would have known him if I had met him somewhere on a city street.

"Mr. Stuart," he said, when he looked up and saw me standing in his schoolroom, where his pupils were making a working noise like honeybees in a hive.

"Don Conway," I said, "there's not anything that pleases me more than this. Remember our days in Lonesome Valley, when we surveyed farms, figured amounts wagon beds would hold!"

"Practical education," he laughed. "That's what I'm giving the pupils and their parents in this community! Pupils, here's your Superintendent and my old teacher I've been telling you about."

"Another one of Mr. Stuart's pupils?" Don asked, when I introduced him to Lester.

"No, I used to go to school with him at Plum Grove," Lester said. "I'm his neighbor and drive him around to the schools. I'm as old as he is."

"Don, how did you get this house painted?" I asked.

"Had a pie social and made enough money to buy the

paint," he answered. "And don't you know I can paint? Remember?"

"I certainly do remember," I said, as I looked over at the new water fountain in the corner.

"Mr. Stuart, we've been looking for you to visit this school," Don said. "You don't need any introduction here. I introduced you the first day I came here. But we do want you to make us a talk. On any subject. Just talk to us."

"How about the subject of Don Conway?" I said.

I told Don Conway's fifty-five pupils about their teacher.

After talking briefly to Don about schoolteaching and the needs of Greenwood County Schools, and about the people we knew in Lonesome Valley, Lester and I moved hurriedly to Love Branch Rural School, where Juanita Cowley taught. I had taught her English in Landsburgh High School. She was a tall girl with curly auburn hair and with a handicap that didn't keep her from being one of the progressive young teachers of Greenwood County. She had a withered arm from infantile paralysis. I had never thought of her as being a schoolteacher. But her schoolhouse was clean and well decorated, and her school records were up to date. There was a sign on the wall: *Order is Heaven's First Law.* She could teach school. She had something more in her school than discipline.

I then visited Center Valley School where Ann Bush, another one of my Landsburgh High School pupils, was teaching. When Lester drove the car onto the school ground, we heard considerable noise and confusion in the schoolhouse. When we went inside Ann was sitting at her desk crying, while a group of small children stood around her. Another group of pupils was huddled over in a corner of the schoolhouse, and, judging from the looks of their eyes, most of them had been crying.

"What's the matter, Miss Bush?" I asked, when I walked up the broad aisle to her desk.

"Mr. Stuart, I'm goin' to resign this school," she said, weeping.

"Why, what's wrong?"

"That old Tom Anderson come back to school again today and whipped Miss Ann," said a little girl who was standing beside Ann's desk. "This makes four times he's come to school and whipped Miss Ann!"

"Who is this Tom Anderson?" I asked.

"Son of Cief Anderson, district school trustee, who was against hiring me to teach this school," she said.

Then I asked Ann Bush to go out into the yard with me where we could talk. We went out into the bright autumn sunshine and left Lester Larkes with the pupils. Ann had been a brilliant pupil in high school. I thought she would make an excellent teacher. I wanted to know the story behind this boy's fighting Ann.

"Ann, straighten up your face and smile," I said. "Don't you ever cry in front of your pupils! Have more spunk than that!"

"But Mr. Stuart, I can't discipline Tom Anderson," she said.

"How old and how large is he?" I asked. "What grade is he in?"

"Fourteen years old, and not large for his age," she said. "He's in the first grade."

"Why doesn't his father do something with him?" I asked.

"His father doesn't like me," she said, "I think he puts Tom up to do what he's been doing."

"Why don't you expel Tom Anderson?" I said. "You don't have to put up with him. You don't have to have your life made miserable by one pupil."

"I did expel him," she said. "But he comes back. He won't stay away from the school. He sits inside the schoolroom about an hour or two, makes remarks and disrupts my classes. Then when I say something to him, he starts a fight. He has fought me four times in the last two weeks."

"Where do Andersons live?" I asked.

"Right over there," she said, pointing to a shack not more than three hundred yards across Center Valley.

"Ann, go back to your pupils," I said. "I'm going to Andersons'."

"Mr. Stuart, they are fighting people," she said. "If I were you, I wouldn't go."

Ann went back to her pupils. I walked across Center

Creek and up the low rolling slope to the little log shack at the foothills. I knocked on the door. A middle-aged woman came to the door.

"This where Andersons live?" I asked.

"Yes, I'm Mrs. Anderson," she said.

"I'm Jesse Stuart," I said. "I'm Superintendent of Greenwood County Schools. I'd like to see Mr. Anderson!"

"He's working across the hill," she said.

"Mrs. Anderson, I've come to see why your son Tom isn't in school," I said.

"Tommie didn't feel very well this morning and he came home about eleven o'clock," she said.

"He felt well enough to whip his teacher," I said. "I'd like to take Tom back to school with me."

"We're not having any school over there," Mrs. Anderson said.

"It's not because we don't have a good teacher," I said. "I used to teach Ann Bush. She's a good student and she's a fine young woman. The parents need to cooperate with her. One of the district school trustees needs to help her. I'd like to see Tom."

Mrs. Anderson brought Tom to the door. I was surprised. Here stood a fourteen-year-old boy that wouldn't weigh over 110 pounds. I wondered if I had bragged too much and too soon on Ann Bush. I didn't see why she couldn't discipline this boy.

"Tom, I want you to go back to school with me," I said. "Come along. I'll take care of him, Mrs. Anderson. If your husband comes in, you send him over to the school too."

Then I took Tom by the hand so he couldn't run and we walked across the valley and talked pleasantly together. However, Tom did tell me he didn't like Ann Bush and that his parents didn't like her. He told me he didn't like schoolteachers and that he wasn't going to let old Ann Bush finish teaching the school. When we walked into the schoolroom, approximately fifty pupils became breathlessly quiet.

"Now where did you fight your teacher, Tom?" I said.

"Right here's the spot," he said, marking the spot with

his big toe. "Here's where I lambasted the daylights out of the old thing!"

"Miss Bush, have you a paddle?" I said.

"You ain't a-spankin' me," Tom warned, trying to jerk his hand loose from mine. He tried to bite my hand.

"I don't have a paddle, Mr. Stuart," Ann said.

Right on the spot where he had fought her that morning, I sat down in a chair and put him across my lap and started to spank him. Even Guy Hawkins, bully of Lonesome Valley School, did have the decency to come back after school to whip me. He didn't try it in front of the pupils. I never believed in punishing a pupil in front of others. But I wanted this lesson sent home in this district. This 110-pounder squirmed on my lap like a worm. He was the strongest pupil, for his size, I had ever tried to punish. He reached up and grabbed the end of my necktie and yanked on it with all his might. The necktie was tied in a loose knot, and when he pulled on it my tongue came out of my mouth an inch or more, and I gasped for breath. Then his brother Little Cief Anderson leaped over a school desk to get me. And he had a sister in school that started screaming and grabbed a geography book.

"Would like to help you, Stuart," Lester Larkes laughed, "but I'm not allowed to touch a pupil!"

Ann Bush grabbed his brother Little Cief and held him. I got up from my chair and held Tom with one hand while I pulled at the necktie with one hand and Tom pulled at it with two. We broke the necktie and I was free. But before we broke it, I almost fell to the floor. That was the nearest ever a pupil came to getting me. I caught a few long breaths while Tom kicked my shins with his feet and pounded my stomach with his fists. When I was through with Tom, he was willing to sit down. He was willing to behave. Then I put Little Cief across my lap. I used my left hand on him.

Mrs. Anderson must have gotten word to her husband. He arrived at the schoolhouse just when I had finished spanking his sons.

"What's goin' on here?" he asked.

"Now let me tell you all something," I said. "This goes

for you, Mr. Anderson, too. If ever another pupil fights this teacher, that pupil is going to be sent to a school where he won't be able to fight the teacher. Miss Bush is not going to resign. Miss Bush is going to teach this school to the end, and we—the Greenwood County Board of Education, and I—will see that she does. The first boy that attacks Miss Bush will go to the Kentucky Reformatory!"

Big Cief Anderson's face turned crimson.

"Miss Bush, I want you to promote Tom Anderson to the second grade," I said. "If he does well enough in the second grade, promote him to the third. You got anything more to say, Mr. Anderson?"

"You had no right to come to my house and get my son," he said.

"He has no right to come back to this school and fight this teacher after she expelled him," I said. "He's not going to be expelled any more. Next time he tries to fight Miss Bush, we'll have you and your son in court!"

Cief Anderson went out and picked up the double-barreled shotgun he had left leaning against the wall outside the door. He laid it across his shoulder and walked silently away.

The last school we visited on this day was Winston Rural School, where Betsy Sutton was teaching. Betsy had been one of my fourteen pupils in Winston High School, and I had taught her again in Landsburgh High School. She was a plump redheaded girl with plenty of temper when properly aroused. Once she had reported my brother James to me in Landsburgh High School for pulling her hair. "I'll slap his face until it's red," she told me, "if you don't make him behave." She was now probably the best teacher in Greenwood County. Her Winston Rural School was a model school. When I spoke to her pupils, I told them of my experience in this community teaching my first high school and how their teacher and the other thirteen pupils had made me study to keep ahead of them. Betsy's pupils laughed. Then I told them to pay her back, that I wanted them to make her work. I told them to make her study ahead as she had once made me.

When Lester and I started back to Landsburgh over a

familiar road, I asked Lester to stop at a little low house, beneath some elm trees, near the Tiber River.

"Stuart, why on earth do you want to stop here?" Lester laughed. "Nothing in that old ramshackle house but hay! Look" —he pointed at the hay bulging through the windows on each side the house—"it's even got a pair of ears! It's even got dark, sightless eyes!" he laughed again, as he pointed to the windows with broken panes.

I was sentimental enough to stop and stand before this old house and look over the little schoolyard and think about the fourteen pupils I had taught here. I thought, in a few years all the houses I had visited in Greenwood County would be gone. Large consolidated schoolhouses, with spacious playgrounds, big athletic fields, large libraries, and big gymnasiums would, I hoped, replace these barnlike structures. This tumbling-down lodge hall, with hay bulging through the side windows for ears that listened to the wind, and the sightless, dark window-eyes that looked at exactly nothing, would be a sundown symbol of the schools of yesterday. Don Conway, Betsy Sutton, Juanita Cowley, and Ann Bush were the sunrise symbols for tomorrow's teaching in consolidated schools. This was my thought. This was my dream.

14

THERE was never a doubt in my mind about my chosen profession now. I rode beside Lester Larkes in our topless roadster, bareheaded, without an overcoat, through the blue chilly wind of morning that whipped color into our faces while blankets of innocent frost covered the earth and made the trees look like tall white ghosts. We rode through the golden rays of October and November sun, through the wind-driven swishes of icy rain, through the bullet-pelting grains of sleet that stung our faces, and through the millions of flakes of soothing snow. We often lost our way in the storm clouds on the ridges. But we visited the schools.

As we went from school to school, I could not help wishing that members of the Kentucky State Department of Education were in automobiles following us; and as we walked the little paths to these one-room schools, where it was impossible to take a car, I wished members of this department would have walked with us. I had visited the state department of education in Frankfort. I had been in their well-heated, well-lighted, and comfortable offices. I thought they were too far-removed from the front-line schools. In all they had written and sent to me—a Superintendent in their vast school system—not one sentence had any red blood in it. Their pamphlets were too dry. They were without guts! One of them might have written a red-blooded book with plenty of guts in it, instead of bloodless, dry-as-dust pamphlets, if he had been along to see the ground roots of American democracy. Ground roots that penetrated deeply into this rugged American earth.

Where was their vision? What was to be the future progress of our schools? What would we teach to improve our people? How would we teach it? How would we lift the qualifications of our teachers? How would we build for a greater, happier, and more prosperous tomorrow? How would we conserve our natural resources? There were a thousand and one things that needed to be done.

There were ten thousand things I wanted to say about schools and schoolteaching. I couldn't begin to say all the things I wanted to say; I couldn't begin to do all the things I wanted to do. The need was too great. One couldn't be away from these things and figure the needs. One had to be with them, see them, be a living part of the whole. For when one was a part of the rock-bottom reality, then he could have vision for vast improvement. The thought must precede the action. Vision: first, good roads until we could have consolidation of schools, then, consolidated schools, well-qualified teachers, who would teach pupils how to get along with one another. Teach them elementary principles of health. Help them find a vocation in life and work toward that vocation. Not let the talent of any pupil born upon this earth with a fair amount of intelligence, be lost to the whole of humanity. Teach them to protect, and where possible rebuild natural resources that had been selfishly destroyed by lust for the dirty dollar. Teach them to think about good, honest government *of the people, by the people, and for the people.* Teach them, thousands and thousands of them with good minds and character, to be teachers. Pay them a living wage and not the death-colored wages they now received. Teach those who went into other professions to give support to the school system in their communities. And, above all, teach them this: Whatever talent you have as a schoolteacher, governor, or shoe repairman, do your job well and honestly and with fairness to all people. And, teach him who didn't have any talent at all that he could at least be a good citizen. He could be an asset to human society instead of a liability.

"You know, Stuart," Lester Larkes said, as he drove us up the last mountain (steering clear of the stumps in the road) to visit the last school, "what I would like to do? I'd love to go back to school, finish the grades, go to high school, and become a teacher and a coach. To see all of this makes me want to do something besides pitch ball. You know," he continued with enthusiasm—for he had caught the spirit of the schools—"I'd organize a baseball team at every rural school in this county for July, August, and September. Then I'd teach these boys and girls basketball if I had to put baskets on the schoolyard trees for the sunny days and in the schoolhouse for winter days. I'd buy each school a basketball. Look at the baseball players and the basketball players that would feed the high schools! These boys can really play baseball," he bragged. "And how they would love the game of basketball! They put their hearts into the game and they love to play and they play hard!"

But Lester Larkes didn't live to realize his ambition. This physically powerful young man contracted tuberculosis in the coal mines the following summer and went too soon to a Plum Grove grave. If he were alive today, he could tell you he was the first man ever to drive a car into two of the rural districts of Greenwood County. When he drove me to the Lookout Ridge Rural School, teacher and pupils came outside the schoolhouse, for they couldn't believe it possible for anybody to drive an automobile to their school. When we got ready to leave the road we had come over was so difficult and treacherous, we didn't go back the way we had come. In the valley far below us, we could see a little county road winding down between the high hills of Blackoak Valley, and we wondered if we could get down the mountain to this road. If we could, we knew it would save miles and miles.

Two men took axes and cut the saplings we couldn't get around or go over. They rolled the big stones away. They opened up fences around pasture fields and took down panels of paling from gardens. People were cooperative enough to let us drive through yards, and pigpens, and barn lots. They helped us choke wheels and use handspikes. They helped us take this car where never a car had gone before or since, down to the valley road. This was the last school in Greenwood County that we visited.

After we reached the valley road, Lester had difficulty driving his car, for it shimmied from one side of the road to the other. Finally we reached Landsburgh, where a garageman discovered that the brake rods were bent, one spring broken, the steering gear out of order, and that the radiator leaked. Lester sold his car for twenty-five dollars; the engine was all that was any good. He had received from me seventy dollars for himself and expenses. My school board was generous enough to allow me twenty dollars more, after I had spent the fifty dollars they had appropriated, to complete my enjoyable visit to eighty-two Greenwood County Rural Schools.

15

ON DECEMBER 3rd, the regular meeting of the Greenwood County Board of Education was held. Four of my board members seemed to be in a jovial mood. They laughed and joked with each other—all but Benton Dangerfield and Mooner Bentworth. Margaret Raridan had carried from her home potted geraniums and placed them on my desk. With the attitude of my school board changed, and with flowers to brighten the atmosphere of the room where members of my school board and I had battled with many school problems, I thought something was about to happen.

Soon as Tobias Claxton had called the meeting to order, three members started to rise at the same time. Benton Dangerfield was the first to his feet.

"Members of the Greenwood County School Board," he said, his blue eyes twinkling brightly, "I have an important motion to make. I make the motion that we raise our Superintendent's salary to $125 a month!"

"That's too much money to pay him," Mooner Bentworth interrupted angrily. "He's not worth it!"

"This man doesn't have regular office hours," Benton Dangerfield said, disregarding Mooner Bentworth's interruption. "He works all day and half of the night. He has pulled us through a financial crisis. He has made a budget that will stand. We are operating from within that budget. We're not overspending now! And gentlemen," Benton Dangerfield continued, with enthusiasm, "if there was ever a man worth his salt, by his works, deeds, and actions, it is this man. I say we give him a raise!"

"I second that motion," Manley Warburton said.

"I'm against it," Mooner said. "We can't afford it."

Tobias Claxton, William Dawson, Manley Warburton, and Benton Dangerfield voted for upping my salary.

"I'll go along with the school board," Mooner agreed. "I don't want it recorded on the minute-books I voted against this raise. But I still don't think he's half the man that one of my fellow-board members thinks he is. He's caused us more trouble than any man we could have put in this office! I think of all the lawsuits he's caused us. I can't go to sleep at night for thinkin' about these ticklish lawsuits."

Then, on this day, I received my third check since I had been Greenwood County School Superintendent. I had received two $100 checks already. This, my third check, was for $125, which made me a total of $325 since I had taken office. This was the last check that I was to receive. Little did I know, on this day when I got my check cashed, that it would be five years later before I got the remainder of my pay for the services I had rendered the Greenwood County School of System. Little did I know that the rural teachers of Greenwood County had gotten their last pay when they received the checks for the third month of their six months' school term. Maxwell High School teachers got half their pay and that was all.

One morning I looked from my office window at a great crowd of angry people milling around the Landsburgh National Bank. Many were weeping. A few were shouting oaths at the banker behind the locked doors. One woman fainted and fell on the hard concrete. Many people were almost in hysterics. The Landsburgh National Bank had closed on all debts, deposits, cash, and collateral. But one thing, our $26,000 debt had been paid. We had thought this bank was as strong as the rock cliffs on the palisades south of Landsburgh. Now we faced the greatest problem we had ever had to face. We were entirely without funds. There was $40 in our office which we had drawn out for office expenditures. I told Margaret Raridan to take this, since she was a widow with a son in the University of Kentucky and a daughter in Landsburgh High School.

Despite all that could be done, I thought our entire county school system would collapse. I thought the Maxwell High School teachers and the rural teachers of the one-room schools would not work without pay. We didn't know when the insolvent bank would be solvent again. Many of the parents whose pupils attended Maxwell High School could no longer pay the bus drivers to transport their pupils.

Now, without any expense account, I started revisiting the rural schools. I got there any way I could. I caught rides, walked, rode horseback, any way I could get there. What I saw amazed me. I learned what the members of my profession were made of. They were working with their backs to the wall. I hadn't known members of any profession, up to that time, who had worked without pay, and without knowing that they would ever get their pay. I thought of the time when I helped build the Landsburgh city streets, and Bill Patton, contractor, went broke and couldn't pay his men. I remembered how suddenly the men stopped working and how his paving machinery, concrete mixers, his trucks, picks and shovels, plows, scrapers, all his tools, were tied up. We didn't work without our pay then.

But the members of the most underpaid profession in the United States did not whimper nor ask too many questions about their salaries. They kept on working, harder now, it seemed to me, than ever before. They didn't try to tie up anything to get their money from the county. I thought I had to visit these rural schools for morale purposes. But I discovered that the morale was higher than ever. General George Washington's soldiers, according to our history books, went barefoot during the hard winter at Valley Forge and lived on baked potatoes. We, members of the teaching profession in Greenwood County, didn't exactly do this. But we lived on scant rations, wore the best clothes we could afford, worked on and on without a promise of a dime for our labors, and kept our big school system from collapsing. Pupils who attended these rural schools often did have only baked potatoes and corn bread to eat and braved the elements, to get to these little barnlike schoolhouses, scantily clad and often with makeshift shoes. I was thinking that George Washington and his men fought to make this a country and we were fighting to maintain what he had fought for. If he and his men could have seen us, 150 years later, fighting to carry on what he and his men had given us, I think the General would have been proud. I think he would have said with a smile, "The spirit of America is not dead!"

If we didn't have coal at a rural school, the pupils and their teachers and parents from the district cut wood to burn. If the hole in the schoolhouse wall became too large to hold in the heat from the potbellied stove, somebody fixed it. Somebody volunteered to clean out the wells. There were volunteers everywhere to help us. And another great thing happened to us. The county businessmen I had called into my office, these men who had helped us to fight for our survival, who knew the financial condition of our county school system, gave extended credit to our teachers, janitors, bus drivers . . . to all of the people employed in our school system.

"If you go down, we'll go down with you," one said.

These men gave credit until their supplies were exhausted. If ever a group of people worked in unison, we did. We battled the great problem before us. We, the teachers, superintendent, and schoolworkers, didn't let down the youth, who depended upon us, and the county, state, and nation, who depended upon these youth. I visited schools and made talks to the teachers and pupils saying that we would survive, that we could not fail, that as long as teachers would work without pay and do as good work if not better than when they got paid, when pupils would come to school thinly clad and live on corn bread and baked potatoes, hell couldn't stop us. Washington's men at Valley Forge hadn't anything on us.

I had one criticism to make of my teachers. I had heard a few of them say, "Oh, I'm just another schoolteacher!" This burned me up. I told my teachers never to say this. I told them to walk proudly, with their heads high, and to thank God they had chosen the teaching profession—the mother of all professions; that they were members working in the front line of American democracy, that they were the ground roots and not the brace roots of American democracy. I believed this deep in my heart and brain. That the teaching profession was the greatest profession of them all. Of course, they and I and everybody had heard the remarks about the "old-maid" schoolteachers. In stories, books, and in the movies, the old-maid teachers were caricatured.

If only our producers, I thought then and have thought since, could make a powerful movie to show what the teachers in America are doing, it would be one that couldn't miss. If some writer could spring from the teaching profession and do a great book to honor his profession, he would be immortal. For no other profession in America has directly or indirectly influenced the destiny of so many people as has the teaching profession.

16

ONLY once while Margaret Raridan was my secretary, did I see her afraid. She was so accustomed to hearing people's quarrels in our office that she regarded it as a part of her daily work to try to settle them. Often two men would come into the office to settle a problem. They would be mad enough to fight. When they left the office, they would often be laughing and talking to each other. Margaret had brought them together. She had the wit, the humor, and the diplomacy of her Irish race. But one morning there was a loud knock at the office door. It sounded like somebody was beating the door with a big wooden mallet. This was unusual, for most everybody opened the door and walked in. It didn't take appointments to see us. We were always ready to see the public. That's why Margaret rushed to the door.

"Good morning, Mr. Bledsoe," Margaret said, with a trembling voice. "Won't you come in?" And she added before he had time to answer, "Anything we can do for you, Mr. Bledsoe?"

"Naw, you can't help me none," he answered. "I'm here to see your Super!"

I looked up from where I was seated behind my desk. There stood "Bad John" Bledsoe in the door. He was almost as broad as the door was wide, and tall as the door was high. Once, at the Lawson Hardware in Landsburgh, when he was bragging about his strength, he rolled up his sleeves and showed some young admirers his bulging muscles. Then he stepped onto the scales and tipped them at 296 pounds. As he stood looking at me, his black eyes shone like glowing embers in the dark.

"Can I help you, Mr. Bledsoe?" I asked.

"Yeah, why ain't I been paid for hauling that coal last year?" he shouted angrily. Then I heard behind him, in the dim-lighted courthouse corridor, men talking in low tones. I heard oaths and laughter. Perhaps Margaret Raridan had seen these men when she had opened the door.

"We don't have the money, Mr. Bledsoe," I said. "If we had the money we would have paid all these old bills. I know we owe them. We'll pay them soon as we can."

"Don't give me that old song," he snarled, showing two rows of imperfect teeth. "I've heard that before."

"Well, have you heard that the Landsburgh National Bank has closed its doors on all the funds we had?" I asked him.

"That ain't none of my business," he said. "I've come for the seventeen dollars you owe me. A lot of the other boys are here with me too. They want their money. I want mine. And by God," he swore, "I'd better be getting my money too!"

"We can't pay you," I said. "Every teacher in this county is working without pay. Miss Raridan and I, and all the rest, are working without pay."

"I don't believe it," he shouted. "If you's a-workin' without pay you wouldn't be wearin' that nice suit and that pretty collar and tie."

There was a roar of wild laughter in the corridor behind him.

"I've come after my money and I'm goin' to have it," he said. "I'll give you five minutes to pay me!"

"I've told you we don't have the money," I said.

"If you don't pay me," he threatened, "I'll take it out of your goddamned hide."

When he said these words it suddenly became very warm. I walked across the floor toward him. He had not moved from the door.

"Listen, Bad John," I said, getting close enough for him to strike me and looking him straight in the eye, "I'll tell you what I'll do. Miss Raridan, listen to this bargain. If you whip me, I'll go borrow the money and pay you myself. If I whip you, then this county has paid you the debt it owes you for hauling coal!"

Bad John Bledsoe was stunned. Few men had talked to this man, who had once been sentenced to the Kentucky State Penitentiary, as I was talking to him now. I meant what I said. I was not afraid of him now. I knew how I would fight him.

I'd never try to slug it out with him. I intended to throw my 222 pounds at his long legs, knock them clean from under him with a surprise tackle that would flatten his face on the oily floor. I didn't care for my white shirt and good suit. I wouldn't be bluffed by Bad John. When I talked up to his threat, the laughter behind him stopped. There was a sudden hush and then there were whispers among the men behind him.

"Do you mean that?" he said, looking me over.

"I mean every word of it," I said, looking him over. "But before we fight, we must make an agreement. We'll make the contract that if you win, I borrow the money and pay you seventeen dollars. If I win, Greenwood County has paid you. You and I will sign this agreement, in the presence of witnesses. Miss Raridan and one of your men can be witnesses to our agreement."

Bad John looked me over again. He looked at me from my feet to my head. He turned and walked away.

"What's the matter, Bad John?" one of his men asked. "You ain't afraid of 'im, are ye?"

"Come on," he told them. "Follow me."

"If any man wants to take the debt Greenwood County owes him out of my hide, I'll pay it that way," I said, as I stood watching these men go down the steps. "That goes for the banker at the Landsburgh National Bank too!"

That was the last time any man ever came to my office to bully me about a debt Greenwood County couldn't pay.

17

ON THIS winter night, when darkness came early, I called Naomi Deane from my office and asked her if I could stop to see her on my way home. I told her I wanted to bring along a surprise that I hadn't shown to anybody. She told me over the telephone that she would be delighted to see me. Then she warned me to ring the bell on the door that opened from the front porch into the parlor. There was another door on this porch that opened into the living-room, where members of her family spent winter evenings before an open fire. I knew what she meant when she told me to be sure and knock on the first door and she would be waiting there for me. This meant I would go into the house and not come in contact with any member of her family. For the time had come when there wasn't anyplace in Landsburgh where we could go together. The only place that I could see her was in the parlor of her home. Landsburgh was her home town and it was my home town, if I could claim a home town upon this earth.

Soon as Naomi Deane told me I could come to see her, I was overcome with joy. It was certainly important that I see her on this night. Then I picked up the manuscript I had put together. These were the poems I had written at the plow when I had farmed at home last summer. These were the poems I had written on leaves, red-horse tobacco sacks, and scraps of old paper that I had picked up here and there. When I became Superintendent of Greenwood County Schools, I used the typewriter in my office during the night, since Margaret Raridan used it during the day. Our office had a good supply of high-grade and beautiful paper that we used to record minutes of the school board meetings. But I found another use for this paper. My poems looked beautiful and neat typed upon this paper. At least I thought they did.

With this manuscript under my arm, I switched off the lights and closed the door. I walked up the dark street for approximately a half-mile. Then at this familiar house, where I had been so many times before, I walked upon the porch and rang the bell on the first door. Naomi Deane opened the door.

"Come in, Jesse," she greeted me.

But I stood a few seconds and looked at her. I had never seen her more beautiful than she was on this night. She was wearing a dress of bright colors that reminded me of a sunny autumn day when all the leaves were ripe. There were orange, yellow-green, maroon, deep-purple, brown, and dark-brown against a tan background in this dress. The designs were so small that the colors ran together like the trees, rocks, houses, and hills run together in a winter sunset. All of the colors, except the maroon and deep-purple, were the colors of autumn leaves. The maroon and deep-purple were the colors of morning-glories that I had seen blooming from the fields of corn in Lonesome Valley. I had never seen Naomi Deane as beautiful as she was now, wearing this bright-colored dress.

"This is the surprise I have to show you," I said, after I'd stood there looking at her for some time.

"What's this, Jesse?" she asked, as she took the manuscript. "More articles about education?"

Before I had time to answer her, she had turned the first page.

"Oh, poems!" she exclaimed. "Are these yours? All of them?"

"Yes," I admitted. "And I want you to see them. I want to know what you think of them!"

Then we sat down on the divan and she turned the pages and read. I sat and watched the expressions on her pretty face while she read poem after poem.

Often she laughed as she continued reading. Sometimes she smiled. More than once she wiped tears from her blue eyes.

"Jesse, I've always thought you had something to you," she said, turning away from the poems toward me. "But I didn't know you had this. I think these poems are excellent! This reads like a novel! Maybe I'm wrong. Maybe I'm not a good judge, but I've read poems in the big magazines not any better than these!"

"Then you really like them?"

"I certainly do," she said. "These poems stir me. It wouldn't surprise me that you don't have a book here. I like this title too—*Man With a Bull-Tongue Plow.*"

"I'm glad you like the poems and the title," I said. "Not anything could please me any more!"

"Would green apple pie and hot coffee?" she said laughingly.

"You know what pleases me most," I said.

For I did like her pies and cakes. Other people in Landsburgh did too. When Naomi Deane's church had a "bake sale," her pies and cakes brought the most money. They were often sold to customers who were not members of her church. I had been one of those customers.

"You'll have to help me make the coffee," she said. "Come along."

We went into the kitchen, where we laughed and talked while we made the coffee. We had made coffee and had eaten pie and cake in this kitchen many times before. Tonight the wall of darkness fenced us in. We were in a cozy little kitchen. And we didn't talk about schools. We didn't mention Greenwood County's fight against the city of Landsburgh. We didn't mention any of my enemies who were her friends. We forgot all of these things as we sat down at the kitchen table to eat pie and drink coffee.

"This pie's the best I've ever tasted," I said, soon as I'd taken the first bite. "It's the best pie you've ever made."

"I'm glad you like it," she said, smiling at me across the table.

"This coffee is wonderful too," I said, after I'd downed my first swallow.

Then we sat in silence and looked at each other. On this night Naomi Deane was lovelier than any one of the best lyrics in the English language. I had been striving since I could remember to write one or more of these lyrics. The years had flown by like young winds over the empty fields of spring since I had met Naomi Deane. I had dated many girls but I always returned to her.

"Wouldn't it be wonderful if you and I had a little house with a kitchen like this one where we could sit in the evenings and eat green apple pie and drink hot coffee?" I said. "There's peace and beauty within these walls with you."

"That's a nice dream," she answered, smiling sweetly. "But how could it be a reality?"

"Why couldn't it be a reality?" I asked.

"Well, maybe some day it will," she answered.

Maybe some day, I thought, but when?

Thoughts flashed through my mind. Naomi Deane knew that I was making $125 a month but I wasn't getting my salary. She knew I didn't have any promise of ever getting it. I was working for exactly nothing. I couldn't pay a barber to shave me. I shaved myself. My cousin Glenn Hilton cut my hair for exactly nothing. I shined my own shoes and pressed my own clothes. Naomi Deane knew this too. She knew that on more than one occasion she had put her money into my hand to buy tickets to see a movie. She had paid for the coffee and sandwiches after the show.

Naomi Deane knew the value of a dollar too. She, too, knew what it was to have ambitions and to want to do something constructive and worth while in the world. She had borrowed money to pay expenses of her first year in college. Not many, if any, of the young girls that had grown up in Landsburgh had done this.

After she attended college for one year at Morehead State Teachers College, where she made excellent grades, she was granted a teaching certificate and taught her first year, Lower Lambert Rural School, which was not far from Mountain View. Often when she returned to her home in Landsburgh, she rode horseback eighteen miles through the rough winter weather. She paid back the money she had borrowed. Then she borrowed again and went back to Morehead State Teachers College to finish her second year. She returned to teach for a second time in Greenwood County's Rural Schools. She taught school to pay her college expenses until she graduated.

Then, there was a vacancy in the Greenwood Graded Schools. She applied for this position and got it with a raise in salary now that she had teaching experience and her college degree. She received eighty dollars a month. On this salary, she bought her clothes, helped put a bathroom in her home, and had helped her family financially. By the practical experience of educating herself and working for her money, she had learned the value of a dollar. She knew that it was next to impossible for two people to live on one teacher's salary. She knew that, regardless of our love for each other, each of us would have to work and each of us would have to get paid, before we could be self-sufficient. This was the reason we hoped and prayed, same as the other young members of our profession, that we would get a raise in salary someday.

"You know, Jesse, we have educated ourselves for the teaching profession," Naomi Deane said, to break the silence

that now engulfed us. "We are supposed to be intelligent people. We have to look at this situation intelligently. We have to
face the facts."

I didn't answer her, because I didn't like the facts. She
knew that I didn't.

"Come and let's clear the table," she said, smiling at me.

Then she carried the few dishes from the table to the
sink. While she washed them I dried the dishes and put them
in their places. I knew where to place each one, for we had
washed, dried, and put away the dishes many times before.

"You play records while I read the poems," she said,
after we had finished with the dishes. "Would you like to?"

"I would love to," I said.

We went back into the parlor where I played recordings
of Schubert's music slowly and softly while she read aloud
from the poems I had brought her. I played over and over
Schubert's "Serenade," Strauss's "Voices of Spring," and Men-
delssohn's delightful *Overture to Midsummer Night's Dream*.
Often tears came to Naomi Deane's eyes when she read some
of the poems. She found the mood of winter in them. She
found the sadness of Schubert's "Serenade" in them for I had
played this record over and over while I composed them.
When she read the poems about spring, her mood changed to
be as delightful and as gay as that in "Voices of Spring." I
had written poems while I played this record over and over too.

Her voice was soft and beautiful and the poems took a
new and different meaning they did not have for me when I
wrote them. I listened to her read them while I kept on winding
the phonograph and changing records until midnight. This was
the time for me to leave. Then I left a dream of love and the
peace and beauty behind these sheltered walls. I faced the
winter wind for five miles through the cold and windy darkness
over the high and rugged range of hills that lay between Landsburgh and my father's home.

18

I COULDN'T stay any longer at the Landsburgh Hotel. Not after I had failed to pay for my last month's room rent and board. I had left laundry and dry-cleaning bills unpaid too. The Landsburgh Hotel was owned and operated by Landsburgh people who were not in sympathy with one who had fought their school system. And this made it very inconvenient for me, since Landsburgh—the county seat of Greenwood County—was in the north-central part of the county, and all the main county roads led there.

I knew that when I went home to live again, my walking five miles to and from my work in winter weather would often be very difficult. My not getting credit at the Landsburgh Hotel would not squeeze me from my nonpaying position as Superintendent of the Greenwood County Schools. I would stay with my work. There wasn't anything but sickness or death that could stop me. I was fighting to the bitter end.

I walked proudly, with my head high, to and from my work. I walked proudly, but a little afraid, through Landsburgh, where I was at that time the most despised person that ever stepped on their streets. I walked happily through the mud, sleet, rain, and snow, over the path that wound around and over the high hills to my home. I walked to the log shack that my grandfather Nathan Hilton and I had built. He was seventy-five years old and I was a boy of fourteen when we built this house. We put every log, plank, and stone into it while my father worked on the railroad section to pay for the land. In this shack, which was not the best and certainly not the worst in the community, I knew that I would always have a bed. I knew that I would always have food, because we had saved the surplus from the fat years to tide us through the lean. There couldn't be any squeeze put on me, forcing me to leave my job, because of food and shelter. My legs and my wind were good. Ten miles a day wasn't any walking for me.

Often I walked to my office with ice frozen in my hair,

for I went bareheaded regardless of rain, snow and sleet. When I reached my office in the morning, I would have a sheaf of almost indecipherable poems I had written in the winter rain so I could catch the exact sounds of the water hitting oak leaves. When I saw something along the way that excited my brain to poetic moods, I sat down on a stump, log, or rock, and jotted down the ideas that came to me, just as I had done when I worked on the farm the summer I was elected Superintendent of Greenwood County Schools. This was the only time I had now. I could not write these moods in my office. I was too busy. But after my day in the office—after the city was blanketed in darkness—I would remain in the office, and use the county typewriter and the county's minute-book stationery, and type these poems.

Lacking one day of eleven months from the time I had written the first of these poems, I wrote the last one. It was number 703. Writing these poems had been my recreation. They had been great enjoyment. While I was working on the farm and writing them, it was something different from farm work. While working as County School Superintendent, writing them was a change from my school problems. Writing them gave me mental rest.

After the rural schools had successfully ended, and grades from the thousands of rural pupils had been recorded and were filed in my office, I launched a four-point school-reform program. I gave everything I had to this writing. I threw every ounce of creative energy I had into this fight for reform in the public school system. This was practically the last thing I did while I was Superintendent of Greenwood County Schools. I first tackled the dual school system in Kentucky. I couldn't understand why we should have a city school system and a rural school system, with two different kinds of taxation, with different school laws, yet both school systems subject to the same state department of education.

I couldn't understand why a child born in the city or town should have a better education than a child born among the valleys or on the hills. Why shouldn't a boy at Sassafras, Kentucky, be as well educated as a boy in Louisville, Kentucky? Why shouldn't a boy in Chugwater, Wyoming, be as well educated as a boy in Boston or Manhattan? It seemed to me, the democratic public school system needed some democratic reforms.

If ever any man was to see the need of this reform, I was in the right place to see it. The four independent city school districts in Greenwood County paid their teachers a decent wage, which was exceedingly high in comparison with the salaries of our rural teachers. The superintendents of these independent districts had office and personal expense accounts, and salaries approximately three times the amount I received. Yet I had the largest school system. My school system covered hundreds of square miles while their school systems were small and compact. They didn't have to drive their cars in the mud to visit a school. They didn't have to worry about ragweeds coloring their pant legs. They didn't have to worry about too much of anything. One of these independent districts in Greenwood County, located where railroad wealth was concentrated, hardly knew what to do with the public tax money it received. This independent school system could spend as much on football and basketball teams as we paid to operate fourteen rural schools, where at least five hundred rural pupils got their education. It could, and did, invest its surplus money while county rural teachers were unpaid. Teachers in this independent system received more than twice the salary of our teachers; furthermore, when their salaries were due they got their money. This all came about by unfair distribution of taxes. For we helped to support the railroad company who paid them this big local tax. This railway company hauled freight from Greenwood County farms, timber from Greenwood County slopes, coal from Greenwood County mines. This railway company hauled Greenwood County passengers. Perhaps the Greenwood County people supported this railway company more than the people living in these cities. This railway-company's lawyers tried to get as much of their possessions into the county because of the law that allowed us to tax them only half as much!

If we hadn't had the dual school system, Landsburgh would not have been fighting us. We would not have been fighting Landsburgh. We would have been sending our east-end high-school pupils to Landsburgh High School. I knew that this system—as long as it lasted—would be a source of trouble. Because Kentucky is predominantly rural, and, in this case, the tail was wagging the dog.

I offered instead of this dual school system, a county-unit plan. In this county-unit plan, the school system was simplified. This was to put independent school districts and rural school districts under the county system. Let the county school superintendent be over the whole system. Let the school tax be equalized in all the districts. Pay all teachers upon the basis of qualification and experience. By this system, we would have 120 units in Kentucky, subject to the state superintendent of schools and the state department of education. This would have simplified the whole system. Pay our local school taxes to the state and let the state return this money, similar to the per capita money, on a fair and equal distribution, to all the counties of the state. Let them receive so much for each pupil enrolled in the school census. In this way, the wealthy counties, such as Greenwood County, would be helping one of the many pauper counties in our state which couldn't support its schools. I worked days and nights on this article. After I had finished it, I could not find anyone who would print it.

Then I wrote an article about seniority rights for teachers. I was not familiar with the teacher's tenure systems then in effect in many states. I borrowed "seniority rights" from my father. It was a common expression among the railroad laborers where he worked. But I had seen teachers—excellent rural teachers—in Greenwood County, pushed from rural school to rural school, pushed completely out of the system, for no good reason, by ignorant school trustees. I had observed, in my county school system, that the teachers who were doing the greatest work were those who had been allowed to stay a few years in one school. There could be good reasons for ousting a teacher from a school; but to have them pushed around, without a justifiable reason, by persons who hadn't the faintest idea what schoolteaching was all about, by school trustees who never had what it takes to make teachers themselves, didn't make sense to me. This article was rejected everywhere I sent it.

If only members of the state department of education and members of our state legislature and of our state senate could have gone with me when I visited the Greenwood County Rural Schools, if they could only have been on the front line for a while and not so far-removed from the actual scenes, I think we would have gotten old-age pensions for teachers much sooner; and I think it would be for more than it actually is today. I was not one of the first to start fighting for the old-age pensions for teachers. Others had fought before me. But not any one of these fighters had been more dynamic in his fighting than I had been.

One teacher in my system, who had taught fifty-five rural schools, told me that he prayed each day to keep his health so he could continue teaching. He said he prayed that when he did die he'd go suddenly, with a stroke or a heart attack. He confessed he had never been able to save a penny and teaching was his only means of support. He had a fear of being sent to the county poorhouse. I wrote a separate article about this man as an argument for old-age pensions for our teachers. None of these articles were accepted.

The bitterest denunciation I ever made in print was in regard to the school trustee system. I wrote many articles about school trustees. In these articles I said the state should pass a law to do away with this system, for as long as members of the teaching profession in the rural school districts of Kentucky had to be subject to, and controlled by, these little self-important dictatorial drones, we could never have a school system. I sent articles to newspapers and to a local educational magazine. They were returned as fast as I sent them.

If I had sent these articles to magazines of national circulation instead of to little local magazines, my fight against these evils might have been different.

I didn't succeed in getting a single one published; and here is what happened. Two weeks before I left the County School Superintendent's Office, I gathered all these articles together. Also, a 450-page MS, *The Cradle of the Copperheads*, a nonfiction satirical denunciation of certain educators who fought against school reforms for their own personal gains,

was included among them. I carried the coffee sack filled to
the top with all these manuscripts, and burned them by the big
rock in our pasture where we salted the sheep. This labor went
up in flame and smoke.

19

ON THE morning of our regular board meeting, which
might be the last one for me, I called Benton Dangerfield into
a vacant room in the Greenwood County Courthouse and had
an hour's talk with him. I knew that if any man had ever
known danger, this man had. I knew that he could feel danger
better than any man I had ever known. If anybody could give
me advice, Benton Dangerfield could.

"Do you think, Mr. Dangerfield," I asked him point-
blank, "that I will be in danger if I attempt another term as
Superintendent of Greenwood County Schools? Do you honestly think I shall be killed?"

"Jesse, you have asked me to tell you what I believe,"
he answered. "I'm going to be frank with you. I think you are
in great danger all over this county, except in the west end
around Maxwell High School. There you are well liked and
respected. In the east end of this county," he explained, "I
think many a man that doesn't understand what you have done
for this county thinks you are an enemy and will consider it
an honor to kill you. Not just one but many would do it."

"But why do they feel that way toward me?" I asked.
"The east end is my part of Greenwood County. These are the
people I have known—most of them—all my life!"

"You've done too much good in too little time," Benton
answered my question. "You're honest. The politicians can't
handle you."

"Will members of the school board re-employ me if I
ask to continue my work?" I asked.

"Four members will vote for you," he said. "Of course
Mooner Bentworth will be against you!"

"Could you be re-elected if you support me for a second term?" I asked.

"To tell you the truth," he said, "we will all be defeated when we run again, if we support you. We've talked that over. But that doesn't matter," he explained. "We've agreed among ourselves to stand by you to the last ditch. You've stood by this county; there are a few honest men in the world, and you are one."

"Thank you," I said.

I had made up my mind what I was going to do. I wasn't going to leave the teaching profession. Not me.

20

TOBIAS CLAXTON called the regular meeting to order. While they were seating themselves I thought about what Benton Dangerfield had just told me! I knew the gift of life was the greatest thing on earth. I didn't want to lose it now. There was too much for me to do. There was too much living ahead of me.

"Members of the Greenwood County School Board," said Manley Warburton as he arose from his chair. "I make the motion that we re-employ Jesse Stuart, County School Superintendent of Greenwood County Schools, for another term."

"I'm against it!" Mooner Bentworth shouted. "Heavens, no"—he stomped his feet as he stood beside his chair—"not another term with him. Another term with him will run me crazy!"

I arose from my chair before Tobias Claxton could rise to his feet and second Manley Warburton's motion.

"Members of my school board, with whom I have worked so long," I said, "this time I am inclined to agree with Mooner Bentworth. I think it is the first time."

Everybody laughed except Mooner. He couldn't understand that we were agreeing for once.

"I do not want to be re-employed as Superintendent of Greenwood County Schools," I said.

My school board members stopped laughing and looked at each other in amazement.

"But while I am Superintendent of Greenwood County Schools," I said, "and since Maxwell High School is without a principal for next year, I should like to recommend myself for that position."

"Did you ever hear tell of a thing like this?" Mooner screamed. "You can't do that! You can't recommend yourself!"

"Why not?" I asked him. "I *am* doing it, am I not?"

"I make the motion we hire Jesse Stuart for Principal of Maxwell High School for next year," Manley Warburton said.

"I second the motion," Benton Dangerfield said.

Then Mooner Bentworth laughed as I had never heard him laugh before.

"What's so funny, Mooner?" William Dawson said.

"I'm going to vote for him," Mooner said. "Get him that faraway from this office this time and next time maybe we can vote him out of Greenwood County!"

"You don't have to vote for me, Mooner," I said. "Because I'm leaving this office doesn't mean you will ever again work with a little handful of corrupt politicians to betray the county school system."

"I say he won't," Benton Dangerfield said. "I'll stay on this school board long as he stays, if I can be re-elected to see that he doesn't!"

The motion was put to a vote. I received all five votes. I was made Principal of Maxwell High School for the following year.

PART V

MANY A SCHOOL HAVE I LET GO

I

TO BE Principal of Maxwell High School was something like a dream. I was getting better pay than I had ever received since I had been in the teaching profession. I was making $1,200 my first year, with a promise of an additional $100 per year for the next three years. After my past experiences, I couldn't believe I was principal of a high school where there was a telephone in every room. There was a large gymnasium which we used for athletics and also as our auditorium. There were shower-rooms for the girls on one side of the gym and for boys on the other side. And this was something for those who came from the rural sections of the west end of Greenwood County; for not more than 2 per cent of the homes had bathrooms!

The walls of this Maxwell High School Building were so thick not a sound could be heard unless a classroom door was open. If one walked through the corridors during a class period, one wouldn't know school was going on; that there were 350 pupils and twelve teachers in this building. One wouldn't know school was in session except when the bells rang at the end of class periods and the pupils moved from classroom to classroom and to library and study hall. Though a double-tracked railway was not more than four hundred yards away, down in Big River Valley, where more coal trains passed perhaps than on any railroad in America, we never heard the moaning whistles of the big engines speeding down the valley with their 160 loaded cars or bringing back their long trains of empties.

This citadel of architectural beauty was built upon a little hill, where the ground sloped gently in all directions. Maxwell High School was built to face the north. In the front yard was beautiful landscaping, with many kinds of evergreens. Between this yard and the national highway were acres of pleasant meadows, donated to the county by Dr. Maxwell, for whom the school was named. Farmers in Big River Valley mowed and raked these acres without cost. Beyond the highway was the railroad, and beyond the railroad were river-bottom farms. Beyond these farms was Big River, and beyond the river were the steel mills in Ohio.

To the east of Maxwell High School were the low-lying Kentucky hills. To our west, Tiber River wound like a white ribbon down from the hills to join Big River. Between our football field and the Tiber was a forest of young willows, wild plums, water birch, silver maples, and elms, while beyond the Tiber was a palisade that lifted toward the Kentucky sky. I had never seen a finer high-school building in all east Kentucky or in southern Ohio than the Maxwell High School Building, and I had never seen a school anyplace in more beautiful surroundings, with as many acres of playground. Dr. Maxwell, a citizen of Ohio, who had given all these valuable acres, also gave Maxwell High School a fine library. After he had seen our football players playing without headgear, he bought equipment for our athletic teams.

Now for the first time, I had the opportunity to recommend my own teachers. Charles Manson, who had succeeded me as Superintendent of Greenwood County Schools, asked me to do this before I asked him if I might have that privilege. Charles Manson was a clean-cut, middle-aged man with twenty years of teaching experience behind him. He had taught rural schools, village schools, and in independent city school systems. He had once been Principal of Maxwell High School. After he had been elected Superintendent of Greenwood County

Schools, I made an appointment with him to discuss the plans for Maxwell High School. The one-hour's appointment was expanded into a full day. We discussed public schools—the needs and the future—and never before had I met a more kindred spirit whose ideas so coincided with my own. He felt the way I did about the school trustee system, about the old-age pensions for teachers, teacher's seniority rights, and the unfairness of the dual school system in our state.

My real problem came when I tried to find myself a faculty. Only 25 per cent of the teachers who had taught in Maxwell High School when I was Superintendent of Greenwood County Schools reapplied for their positions. Their salaries had averaged less than $100 per month; they had received only half of this amount and one month had been eliminated from the school year. One of these teachers—a brilliant young man—was employed by the New York City School System. Another found teaching employment, with better pay, in Massachusetts, while a third teacher found employment in an Ohio Public School System. The remaining half of the faculty—six teachers who had spent their early years preparing themselves for the teaching profession—gave it up entirely and sought other kinds of employment. They were excellent teachers and I tried to persuade them to return to teach for me, but they wouldn't return to a salary which was less than $800 for eight months. High school had begun and I was still short of a science and an English teacher. And one of these teachers had to be able to coach football and basketball.

One day in our first week at Maxwell High School, a car pulled up at the noon hour and a nicely dressed young couple got out. They walked into the corridor and asked a pupil where they could find the principal.

"I'm the Principal," I said, wondering what they wanted.

"My name is Charles Meyers," the young man introduced himself. "This is Mrs. Meyers, my wife. We heard you had two vacancies here. We've been to see Mr. Manson, Superintendent of Greenwood County Schools, and he sent us to see you. He said a recommendation had to come from you."

"What's your major?" I asked him.

"I have a couple of majors," he said. "Science and math, but I prefer to teach science."

"Can you coach?" I asked him.

"Five years of experience," he said. "Football and basketball."

"And what about you?" I asked Mrs. Meyers.

"I have majors in English, music, and languages," she said.

"Well, come into the office with me," I said, for I wondered if this could be true.

We went into the office and talked the rest of the noon hour, and I learned the reason this couple had applied. Due to the age and illness of Mrs. Meyers' father, she had returned to her home in an adjoining county from an excellent teaching position in Illinois. Thalia Meyers was a graduate of the Cincinnati Conservatory of Music. She held B.A. and M.A. degrees from the University of Kentucky. She spoke two languages fluently. Charles Meyers had done enough graduate work for his master's degree. The thing I hated most to ask them was whether they would accept the salaries we paid. Thalia would be the only one on my faculty to make more than $100 per month. She would make $103. Charles would get $96 a month for teaching science and coaching football and basketball.

"Yes, we'll take it," Charles agreed. "With both salaries we can get along all right."

"You know, Mr. Stuart," Thalia interrupted, "after you once start teaching school, it's hard to leave the profession. When I see a high school building along the highway, I am homesick to start teaching again."

That afternoon, Charles and Thalia Meyers became members of my faculty. They were officially hired, shortly afterwards, at a special meeting of the Greenwood County Board of Education. My faculty was complete. I was proud to have a faculty of college graduates. Now we could remain an accredited high school. If we were compelled to use a teacher who did not have a college degree, we were dropped from the accredited list of state high schools.

2

MY SUPERINTENDENT granted me permission to carry out any idea that I thought would have future consequences for the education of the people in my county. I extended an invitation to the rural teachers of Greenwood County Rural Schools who had not finished high school, or who had never gone to high school. I opened the doors of Maxwell High School to any person, regardless of age, who was qualified to enter. Mr. Manson invited older people to the rural schools if they wanted to get a preliminary education. This made it possible for an older person who had been deprived of an education in his youth to return to school and to receive an eighth-grade and a high-school education.

Two of my teachers were skeptical about bringing back older people and putting them with pupils of high-school age. This idea drew criticism from many parents who had sons and daughters in Maxwell High School. But I believed it to be sound and that it would do good to a great number of people. I knew that it wouldn't hurt us to try it. Kentucky stood second from the bottom (where it still stands today) educationally, of all the states in the Union. There was one state below us. There was a popular expression among Kentucky teachers at that time, as there is still: "Thank God for Arkansas."

If our plans worked, I secretly believed many Kentucky counties might follow what we were doing, and reduce illiteracy in Kentucky to a minimum. I wanted to make Maxwell High School not a model school, but one that would do a great service to the community. I wanted to make this high school a beacon of light to eradicate the illiteracy of the older people and to educate the young.

3

THE ages of our pupils in Maxwell High School ranged from eleven to sixty-nine. Rural teachers came to Maxwell High School. Many of these rural teachers had taught the pupils in Maxwell High School that we were now teaching. It was interesting to observe the competition between pupil and former teacher.

One morning before schooltime, Cooge Baines came into my office with his *First Year Algebra* in his hand. I pitied this tall, lanky, rural schoolteacher, who had taught the same little one-room school for forty-one years because his blood kin lived in this district and had elected the school trustees that had elected him to teach members of their clan. The majority of his pupils had been relatives. I knew when Cooge walked into my office he wanted to drop first-year algebra.

"Now, Mr. Stuart, I hate to take your time," he apologized in his slow drawl, "but I have to see you about this algebra. . . ."

"That's all right, Mr. Baines," I said. "That's what I'm here for. I, too, had trouble with algebra . . . don't feel too badly about it. . . . You've sent me some of the best high-school pupils I ever taught."

"But Mr. Stuart . . ." Cooge Baines tried to interrupt.

"Now we are glad you are here," I broke in, "and we'll be as easy with you on this algebra as we can!"

"But Mr. Stuart, this problem is not what you think it is," Cooge Baines said. "Mrs. Laird says that she can't teach me."

"Then stay in the class this year, absorb as much as you can, and take it over again next year," I advised him.

"But I can work every problem in this book," he said. "I could work every problem in this book before you were born."

"You can work every problem in that book?" I repeated.

"And the *Second Year Algebra* book too," he said. "And everything in plane geometry!"

"Where and when did you take algebra and geometry?" I asked.

"I've never had them in school," he said.

I sat and looked at this man. How I had been fooled! I had seen him many times in Landsburgh when I was a high-school pupil. I had taken my first teacher's examination with him; for I remembered his razor-hacked, half-shaven bony face and his flaming red hair, and I wondered then how he would ever pass a teacher's examination.

"You know, Mr. Stuart," he said, breaking the silence, "I have always thirsted for knowledge like a man thirsts for water. I grew up in the mountains where they didn't have schools in my day. The closest school was eight miles. I got very little education from schools. But I have sat many a day on the beam of my plow and let the weeds take the corn while I read books and solved problems. I wasn't sure that my methods in algebra were right until I went over both first- and second-year algebra with Mrs. Laird. And"—he spoke softly and modestly—"she told me that I knew as much algebra as she did. That's why she sent me to you."

I talked to Mrs. Laird about Cooge Baines.

"He's the best algebra student I've ever seen," she said. "This man can work college algebra. There's no use to have him in my class. It's a waste of time for him and for me. He could teach my classes."

"I'd better call my Superintendent and ask him what to do with a pupil like Cooge," I said.

I called Mr. Manson, and he referred me to the Kentucky School Law which required a pupil to have so many lessons in the prescribed course before he could earn the unit in high school. I wrote to the state department of education about Cooge Baines, and I got a letter referring me to a certain section, on a certain page, of Kentucky School Laws. This was the same law my Superintendent had referred me to.

All we could do with Cooge Baines was let him read every book in the library. We gave him the highest number of credits he was allowed to make in a year, and when we needed a substitute teacher in plane geometry, algebra, arithmetic, we used Cooge Baines. We didn't use him as a substitute teacher in

English or in any of the social sciences. We had other rural teachers we could use in these subjects.

Martha Binion, who had returned to high school as a Sophomore, at the age of sixty-nine, had been for many years a rural teacher in Greenwood County. Five of her grand-children (three of them A pupils) were in Maxwell High School, and they referred to her as "Grandma" Binion. Soon many of the other high-school pupils affectionately called her "Grandma." Every grade that she made in Maxwell High School was an A. She perhaps knew more grammar than any high-school teacher in Maxwell High School, including the Principal and the County School Superintendent. She carried five subjects, but we used her very, very often as a substitute English teacher, and we didn't have a teacher who could handle a study hall as well as "Grandma" Binion. She graduated with honors at Maxwell High School, then went back to teaching in the rural schools.

Then there was Vernon Madden, twenty-eight years of age, who returned to finish three years at Maxwell High School. This man had finished only one year of high school. Then he had done considerable boxing. He had played professional baseball and football. He had ended up as a leather-cutter for a shoe factory in Dartmouth, Ohio, and somehow he lost his job. I never asked him why he lost his job, when he came to enter high school. I had heard about his reputation for drink-ing, and I had a long talk with him. He was quite frank with me when he told me about the episodes of his life, which was like reading an adventure story. Now he wanted to put the past behind, like one would throw a bucket of ashes onto the heap, and to become a new man; and that was his reason for returning to school. I believed his story and allowed him to return to school despite criticisms from many people who knew his past life.

He was an excellent athlete and he helped Coach Meyers with football, basketball, and baseball practice. He took care of all the athletic equipment as well, and he took as much interest in the athletic teams as if he were the coach. This man, also, carried five subjects in high school. He didn't graduate with scholastic honors, but he was perhaps one of the most valuable citizens to his county, state, and nation that we ever graduated from Maxwell High School. Our high school didn't help him any more than he helped the school. This man knew right from wrong, for he had lived on both sides of the fence; and when he advised one of our athletes about breaking a training rule, the athlete listened. The Tarlington citizens were later glad that I had taken Vernon Madden back to high school. He served the school and the community with honor.

Another pupil, Charles Watson, twenty-five years of age, entered high school after he lost his job as a railroad engineer. He was bald-headed, and the pupils called him "Pop" Watson. He, too, helped Coach Meyers with the athletic teams. He, like many of our other pupils, was regarded as a faculty member by strangers. When we followed the football team or basketball team away from home, many comments were made about our having such a large faculty. Many of the high-school teachers were taken for older pupils, and Martha Binion, with her head of white high-piled hair, and all her dignity; Cooge Baines; Vernon Madden; and Charles Watson were always regarded as faculty members along with dozens of others.

Taking older pupils into Maxwell High School helped younger pupils. They saw these older people coming back to pick up the opportunity they had missed in their youth. They watched them working hard to learn all they could while time was with them. Never once did one of the older pupils that had come to Maxwell High School by invitation give us a discipline problem. Instead of their giving us trouble, they were of great value to us, and it was a pleasure to have them in our classes.

4

IN MY Freshman algebra class, I gave my pupils daily assignments. I thought they would cover the assignments if I required them to work all of the problems on paper. I graded these papers. I recorded the grades but I did not return the papers. Then I read the grades to the pupils. But on this day, after the bell had rung and my pupils were dismissed to go to other classes, one little girl, Eustacia Pratt, remained in the room.

"Mr. Stuart, I didn't make ninety on my paper!" Eustacia said.

"Yes, you did, Eustacia," I said, looking at my gradebook again to be sure.

"Not disputing your word," she said politely, "but I made a hundred."

"But I graded those papers," I told her.

"You graded mine wrong," she said. "Where is my paper?"

"Over there in the wastepaper basket," I told her.

"May I get it?" she asked.

"No, I put it in there and I'll get it to convince you," I said.

When I got the paper from the wastepaper basket, Eustacia Pratt was right. She had made a hundred. Every problem on her paper was solved correctly.

"I don't make mistakes, Mr. Stuart," she said, looking straight at me with soft blue eyes.

"That's wonderful," I said. "You come to my office during your study-hall period. I can use you. I need student secretaries who don't make mistakes!"

"I'll be there," she said.

I stood watching this girl, straight as an arrow, with all the determination and self-confidence in the world, but who looked a little undernourished, rush from my classroom to her second-period class. And for the next four years Eustacia was one of my student secretaries. She was one of the most efficient student secretaries I ever had in my office. She made all the transcripts of credits for Maxwell High School graduates going away to college. She made the transcripts when pupils transferred from Maxwell High School. If she ever made a mistake, I never knew it.

I wondered about Eustacia Pratt's background after she challenged my grading her algebra papers. Once, I asked her where she lived.

"In that little house on the west bank of the Tiber," she told me. "You can see it from the schoolyard."

"Is either one of your parents a teacher?" I asked her.

"My father is dead," she said. "My mother isn't a teacher."

Eustacia didn't like to talk about her people, and this made me curious. I wanted to know more about her and her two sisters, who were also in Maxwell High School. All three were A pupils. They were approximately the same size. All of the little things that I had observed made me want to visit them. Though I had never been invited to visit this home, one sunny Saturday afternoon when I was walking along the Tiber, I made it a point to pass by.

I walked slowly up the dusty road that wound between the Tiber River and the rocky palisade. Below me, down on the cool, crystal blue autumn water, I saw the leaves of the sycamore, birch, poplar, willow, oak, and wild plum, like an armada of multi-colored ships moving restlessly to some far-away place. I had seen similar scenes when I had taught Winston High School, which was approximately twenty miles up the river, and it was at Winston when I walked beside this river, that I thought the future of my country's thinking, action, and progress rested squarely upon the shoulders of the nation's schoolteachers. I still believed I was right. Now as I walked along toward the little shack at the foot of the palisade, I was wondering what was the background of three sisters who were among the best pupils in the school. The winding leaf-strewn path led to the little house, where I saw one of the biggest wash of clothes hanging on clotheslines I had ever seen. And many of the dresses on these clotheslines, I knew Eustacia, May, and Lucinda didn't wear.

Eustacia introduced me to her mother, Samanthia Pratt, who was washing clothes. She was a tiny, blue-eyed woman, smaller and thinner than any of her daughters. I met Samanthia Pratt's son Danny, of high-school age, who didn't like school and refused to go. . . . And I met a daughter, older than Eustacia, a Maxwell High School graduate, who clerked in Dartmouth, Ohio, at the five-and-ten cent store.

I later learned that Eustacia's father, Theopolis Pratt, had been dead for several years. Samanthia Pratt had supported herself by doing housework, cooking for families, scrubbing and mopping floors for two dollars per week. This little woman had worked during the day in people's homes, brought back a wash to do in the late afternoon, evening, or night. And her young daughters helped her. There were times when all the Pratts had to eat was bread. . . . Yet Samanthia Pratt had given to Maxwell High School three of its highest-ranking pupils in character and in brains. So this was where the girl came from who had stood up and faced me in the algebra classroom, and told me she didn't make anything but hundreds!

This is not all concerning Pratts. One evening late, I was walking over the valley farm land along Big River. I saw a clump of trees growing in the center of a big bottom. I wondered why this clump of trees had been left. When I walked over to this matted thicket of brush, briars, and trees, I saw some ancient, leaned-over, and fallen tombstones. I looked at the names on these headstones that dated back to the Revolutionary War. On one slab, I read the name Theopolis Pratt. The inscription beneath his name and dates of his birth and death said that he fought valiantly in the American Revolution. I learned later it was he who had come to the west end of Greenwood County when it was a wilderness. He had helped to pave the way for a Western civilization spreading across the continent. Now I had three of his descendants in Maxwell High School, who wore each other's dresses, who often ate bread alone because they didn't have anything else to eat with it.

Eustacia's father, Theopolis Pratt, was named for his Revolutionary forebear sleeping over in Big River bottom. This Theopolis had done another type of fighting. He had fought the building of the new Maxwell High School. It was he who had dared the contractors to lift a spade of dirt for the new high school that was to be erected across the Tiber River in front of his house. He had threatened with a rifle bullet the first one to lift a spade of dirt. And it was he who, at this time, was selling moonshine whiskey. When local and federal officers went to arrest him, they took twelve men and surrounded the house. They were afraid of Theopolis Pratt, who slept with two revolvers under his pillow. He kept other firearms near-by, for longer range shooting. They arrested Theopolis Pratt. He was waiting trial when he walked, one day, down to the Farlington Railway Station. There, three young men tried to bully Theopolis. Theopolis fought back against odds, killing one of these young men and chasing the other two away.

He had two indictments against him. One was possessing and selling illegal whiskey. The other was for murder. Death released him from these indictments. He died one night in his sleep.

Eustacia Pratt put all the fight she had inherited from her father—and she had inherited plenty—into her school-work. She directed all of her energy and ability into learning and good citizenship. She finished second in her class. She was nosed out of first honor by a small fraction of 1 per cent. About the time of Eustacia's graduation, her uncle, T. J. Pratt, found a job for her in a Dartmouth shoe factory. I had a different idea for Eustacia's future. T. J. Pratt threatened me after we had quarreled over what Eustacia should do. He said for her to work in the shoe factory and pay the accumulated rent of the house they were living in, which belonged to him; and I said the rent of this house wasn't her responsibility, and she was the type to go to college. "But she won't have the money to go to college," were his last words.

Then I wrote a short story, titled "Eustacia," and sent it to *Household Magazine*, where it was accepted.

This story is now read by thousands of high-school pupils, for it is in many *Literature and Life Books*. I endorsed the check and gave it to Eustacia for her first year's expenses at Berea College.

"Mr. Stuart, when will I pay this money back?" she asked.

"Pay it to May when she enters Berea College," I said. "Then let May pay it to Linda when she enters Berea College. All you girls will be college graduates."

All three graduated with excellent records. Today, two are teaching in Ohio and one is teaching in Virginia.

5

BEFORE I went to Maxwell High School as Principal, Charles Manson had told me that probably the only difficult problem I would have there would be: Maxwell High School *versus* Community. He said if the school won the fight, there would be a fine community of citizens in the west end of Greenwood County someday, but if the school lost the fight, it might take the community a long time to shake off ignorance and superstition.

At first, it looked as though the community might win. At our football games, men from the steel mills and shoe factories in Dartmouth, who made twice as much money as the teachers, refused to pay our small admission fees. They forced their way in. When boys saw older men doing this, they did likewise. There were too many of them for us to handle, without the help of the county sheriff and his deputies.

When the basketball season began, even though we were inside, we were unable to keep these people from coming in through doors and windows. A crowd would overpower the pupils who tried to stand guard. I notified Deputy Sheriff Bill Windsor, and for three nights he came to help us. Then he said he missed his sleep and could not guard the schoolhouse every time we had a basketball game.

Coach Meyers thought of an idea to stop the intrusions. He stapled large chains to the walls inside, put a staple in the door, and fastened the chains to the staple with a padlock. Before a game, or a school program, we checked every window to see if it was locked. But our windows were broken, and our doors were pounded and kicked until the panels were broken. I saw my students fight to keep their school building from being destroyed. They took pride in the building; before this had been built they had had to attend school in a building a little better than an ordinary Kentucky barn.

We continued to be harassed by outsiders, however, until

April of my first year there. On this April evening, we were presenting an operetta under the supervision of Mrs. Thalia Meyers. About a hundred pupils were taking part in it, and we had advertised it widely in the local papers.

People came from Dartmouth and Landsburgh and other sections, and all the seats in the auditorium were filled. Every available chair was brought from the classrooms. I had asked Sheriff Windsor to come, but he told me he couldn't.

Some minutes before curtaintime, I saw two men sitting behind me wearing broad-brimmed cowboy hats. I went back and asked them if they would remove them so that people sitting behind them could see. They mumbled something and removed their hats, but before I got back to my seat the women sitting in front of them got up and moved to back seats. The men had been putting the toes of their shoes in the open space between the chair seats and backs. I knew they were here to make trouble, and I asked them to do us the favor of leaving before the operetta started.

They said they would leave if they could have their money back, and Mrs. Laird, who had been taking tickets, came over and told me they had forced their way in without paying. I told her to pay them, and they arose, cursing the school, the teachers, and pupils, and everyone in the audience. At the door one turned and shouted obscene words that I had often washed from Lonesome Valley's outdoor privy walls.

A silence fell over the audience. I left my coat in my chair and went outside. I had decided that if there was no law to protect us, it was time we began to protect ourselves. A young fellow who didn't look to weigh more than 135 pounds followed me out. The two men were standing there in the moonlight.

"Why are you coming out here, you educated son-of-a-bitch?" the larger man asked, as he started to put his hand in his pocket. "I'll show you——"

But his hand did not quite reach his pocket, and he didn't finish his sentence. I caught him on the chin with a haymaker that really connected. I put all of my 222 pounds behind it. If we had been in the ring, he would have gone over the ropes—not under or through them. I lifted him over the row of spirea that grew behind the schoolhouse, and he slumped against the wall. Pains shot from my hand to my shoulder.

Now the other man started for me, and the little man who had followed me out tied into him. When I turned, I saw Coach Meyers coming out, and with him was Robert Wigglesworth, the county's agricultural agent. They immediately decided to phone the sheriff.

By the time he arrived, the man I had hit was just coming to his senses, and the second man had been whipped by my small friend. During all this time the operetta was going on smoothly. The audience didn't know what went on outside the schoolhouse until they read it in the papers the next day.

Superintendent Manson sent for me to come to Landsburgh.

"Mr. Stuart," he said, laying three newspaper clippings before me, "this is bad publicity for Maxwell High School, for the Greenwood County School system, for me, and for you. Schoolmen shouldn't fight."

"Only if they're forced to fight," I said. "I was forced to fight. We can't get protection from the Law. I've reported this more than once to you."

I told him what this man had said when he left the auditorium, and that every man, woman, and child had heard it.

"This Bascom Reffitt you hit is from a fighting family," he said. "They are on the dangerous side. You may have a lot more trouble with him."

"I know we will if he comes back to Maxwell High School and tries to repeat what he did and said last night," I replied.

"Now I want you to know I am back of you," Mr. Manson said. "But I don't believe in members of the teaching profession fighting. You fractured his jaw, broke two molars off even with the gums and loosened two more. I've already heard his side of the story. I'm glad he can't be considered a boy. He lacks only a year being as old as you, and is only twenty pounds under your size. This will be in your favor when it gets to court." Then he continued more softly: "I am going to do all I can to see that your trial is postponed from one term of court to another. Just don't have any more fights like this one."

I was never tried for assault and battery. It took Bascom Reffitt more than a year to cool off and to be my friend. Mr. Manson and I did not know that this April night was the turning point in our fight against the ruffians of the community. From that time on, we were not bothered. This was big news in Farlington, and it circulated to the people living in the valleys and hollows and on the hills and ridges.

Our candle burned brighter in the community because we had fought for our own self-respect and for our belief in the cause for which we stood—the cause of right.

6

IN MY second year at Maxwell High School something happened about an injustice I had fought against with every ounce of mental and physical strength I had when I was Superintendent of Greenwood County Schools. All I had written then against it was now cold ashes, supplementing nourishment to the roots of our pasture grass. Perhaps a few of the letters and the spoken words had lived and had some effect, but the main reason for it was the mounting death toll every time there was an election. "Legislation permitting the abolishment of subdistricts, thereby doing away with the trustee system." I read these unbelievable words carefully. This was the catch: "Legislation permitting." In other words, this piece of legislation threw the responsibility for doing away with the subdistricts and the school trustee system directly upon the county school superintendents and the members of their boards of education. The state's lawmakers didn't assume the responsibility. And here is what happened.

After this legislation was passed, Charles Manson, Superintendent of Greenwood County Schools, called a special session of his board, and they did away with the trustee system. Of the 120 counties in Kentucky, Greenwood County was the first to do this. If Charles Manson had had the school board I had when I was Superintendent of Greenwood County

Schools, it would not have been done. They would have voted "against" it.

But Mr. Manson was fortunate enough to have on his board three young men who were high-school graduates. I had taught these young men in Landsburgh High School, and even in those days we discussed the school problems, especially the trustee system, of our state. One of these young board members was Walter Harrison, son of Fred Harrison of the Samaria School District, and Fred Harrison and Rodney Norton were still locked in legal combat over a school trustee election when Fred Harrison beat Rodney Norton. Years were passing but the fight was still going on. Charles Manson and his school board members were threatened with reprisals, but Charles Manson was diplomatic enough to call the trustees "local advisors" and leave them in each district. However, they were left without power. Thus ended, for us, a school system worthy of the Dark Ages.

In many sections of the state, when county school superintendents and members of their school boards tried to do away with the system, they were faced with problems. Darter County, which joins Greenwood County, voted the trustee system out. But this started a young war. The fight was so intense they had to return to the system. Other counties gradually eliminated it. Not all. Even today seventeen of our 120 counties still hold to it.

Later came more important pieces of legislation. Teachers Tenure Law was passed. Then came the Teachers Retirement Law, with the highest monthly allotment of $100 and the lowest of $8.33 per month going to teachers too old to teach any longer. This law came to benefit the schoolteachers in my state long after railway-section men were drawing their old-age pensions. My father was one of them. He was retired on physical disability. Even he, though he could not read or write, could not understand why teachers too old to teach had not been given pensions long ago.

For many years I had blamed the members of the state department of education for our standing second from the bottom in education of all the forty-eight states in this Republic. After much reading and investigating the facts, I learned that members of our state department of education had to obey the laws created by the state's lawmakers. The shocking thing I learned was that the superintendent of public instruction—the highest educational office in our state—drew only $4,000 a year, while the superintendent of one of the small independent city school systems in Greenwood County drew $4,200. This injustice made me feel desperately for the men of my state department of education, grooved in the tightening clutch of Law and fighting an uphill battle! Even in Kentucky, we have a law that will not permit any state official to make more than $5,000 a year. This includes the president of the University of Kentucky.[1]

7

COACH MEYERS, Vernon Madden, and Charles Watson came to my office to discuss what we were going to do with Toodle Powell. Toodle was the best fullback in Maxwell High School's football history. He weighed only 156 pounds. This small, bowlegged, broad-shouldered boy, with a head of shaggy, coarse black hair, could punt, pass, carry a ball, block, and tackle. But Toodle Powell had a serious fault. Every time he tackled a man, he would bite like a dog.

"Look what he gave me down on the field awhile ago," Coach said, pulling up his pant leg. "Bit me through all that padding!"

There was a big red spot on Coach Meyer's leg just above his knee, and there was in this red spot the print of a full set of teeth.

"See, we divided the team to have a little skirmish,"

[1] On November 21, 1947, the Court of Appeals, in the case of *Pardue, et al.* versus *Miller*, Commission of Finance, handed down a decision declaring that presidents and professors of the University of Kentucky and other state colleges were state employees and not officials, and, therefore, the constitutional limit of $5,000 did not apply to state employees—only to officials. This will be found in the report of the Court of Appeals Ruling, Citation 306, Kentucky 110 and 206 SW (2d ed.), p. 75.

Coach explained. "When I started through with the ball, Toodle upended me with a shoestring tackle. Then he socked his teeth in my leg! I screamed and he let loose! Then he apologized. But you know, Mr. Stuart," Coach admitted, "apologies are not worth a hoot in a football game. When a player lets out a scream—like a lot of 'em have—that Toodle has tackled, the referee gets us for roughing the game."

"I've been bitten by three dogs in my lifetime," Vernon Madden admitted, "but not one of them bit me as hard as Toodle Powell did the other afternoon when I skirmished on the side against the Coach."

"Look here," grinned Charles Watson, pulling up his pant leg. "He bit me last week. See the print of his teeth still there!"

"See, Mr. Stuart," Coach Meyers said, "we have more yardage in penalties than any team in the O.K. Football Conference. Toodle bites so hard sometimes he makes the man drop the ball. It's happened a lot of times. Of course it looks bad for the school and it looks bad for me—the Coach. That's why we've not won a game. Yet if I lose this man, there's not a chance of our winning a game this year. He's a fine boy and a wonderful football player! If he just didn't have that awful habit."

"Have you talked to him about it?" I said.

"I've lectured him every day at practice," Coach answered. "He says he can't help it. I don't believe he can. I don't believe Toodle Powell wants to bite anybody."

"I suggested to Coach Meyers that we get rubber pads and put them over his teeth," Vernon Madden said. "But Coach doesn't think it'll work."

"Looks like we could do something," Charlie Watson said.

"I've lain awake at night," Coach Meyers said, "and tried to think what to do with him. See, we've got to play Landsburgh High School this Friday. Since we've not won a game this season, I'd like for us to win or tie this game, if we could. Landsburgh's not lost a game, and we've not won a game! I need Toodle in this game."

"Do you reckon I'd have any influence if I'd talk to 'im?" I asked.

"Not one bit," Coach Meyers said. "Talking doesn't do any good."

"Then we'll have to cover his mouth with something," I suggested.

"I have it," Vernon Madden shouted. "What about using a baseball-catcher's mask?"

"But how about keepin' it on 'im?" Coach Meyers asked.

"Use adhesive tape," Charlie Watson said. "Strap it to his headgear."

"But how could we explain a football fullback in a lineup with a catcher's mask taped to his headgear?" Coach asked.

"Couldn't we put a patch or two on his nose, as if he had hurt it?" I suggested.

"We could," Charlie Watson said.

"Well, looks like that might work," Coach Meyers smiled.

"Coach, I can fix the gear for Toodle," Vernon Madden said. "I know just what you want. I'll go fix it right away!"

"If it'll only work," Coach Meyers said, for he was still skeptical.

While Vernon worked in the athletic room, combining the headgear and the baseball-catcher's mask, I went down to the athletic field to watch the team practice. Toodle had been pulled out and was sitting alone on the bench.

"Get back in there, Toodle," Coach Meyers shouted. "We're going to use you! We're not putting you off the team."

When the two lines clashed, I watched Sid Callihan start around the end with the ball. And I saw Toodle miss two would-be blockers and make for Sid. Sid thought he had an open field, but Toodle picked him up from the rear with a long plunge through the air and a perfect tackle below the knees. When he tackled, I saw him grab Sid's leg and hold on like a bulldog. Sid screamed.

"See, what I've been telling you about," Coach said. "And when he bites, believe me, you are bitten!"

"I'm sorry, Sid," Toodle said, helping Sid up from the ground and putting his arm around his shoulder. "Honest, I couldn't help it!"

Sid didn't say anything. He limped back across the field where his men were forming a huddle.

Toodle Powell didn't go back into the skirmish. He sat on the bench until Vernon Madden and Coach Meyers put this mask-headgear combination on Toodle and strapped it behind. Then Coach put Toodle back into the skirmish. And it worked. When Toodle tackled and the boys piled up, we didn't see one flop from the pile like a fish on dry land and hear him let out a wild scream. Toodle nuzzled them with his mask, like a horse with a muzzle trying to get green corn.

"Boy, am I proud!" Coach Meyers said.

"And fellows, am I glad!" Sid Callihan said.

Then his teammates sang: "Coach has found a way! Toodle will get to play!"

8

ON FRIDAY afternoon, just before we started to Landsburgh to play the most important football game of the season with Maxwell High School's old rival, Toodle Powell came into my office.

"You want something, Toodle?"

"Yes, Mr. Stuart," he said, his black eyes burning like wind-fanned embers in the dark. "I want to tell you before I dress for the football game, that I've not got anything against you. But your first cousin Fenton Hoskins is playing fullback for the Landsburgh Wildcats. He's the one that's made most of the touchdowns for Landsburgh this year. But he's not carrying the ball over my goal line this afternoon! I just want you to know, before I get hold of 'im, that I've not got anything against you."

"It's all right with me if you stop 'im," I said. "I'll be glad. Just don't get your mask off and do any biting!"

Our cavalcade of school busses and automobiles, nearly a mile long, followed the bus carrying our Maxwell High School Bulldogs. With the football team were Coach Meyers, Charlie Watson, and Vernon Madden. Vernon Madden had the clippings from three newspapers. One sports writer gave Landsburgh High School thirty points average over us. Another sports writer predicted Landsburgh would win by twenty points, while the third favored us by saying Landsburgh was only two touchdowns better. Among the thirty-odd players of our football squad sat Toodle Powell, our hope against Landsburgh, with his "muzzle" already on. The bridge of his nose was plastered with tape as if it were broken.

There was no stadium at Landsburgh High's athletic field. Nor were there any seats. People had to stand to watch the game. Both sides of the athletic field were packed to capacity. There was hardly standing room left. The Landsburgh fans had turned out in great numbers. Stores had closed. They had come to see Landsburgh trounce their old rival, Maxwell High School. We had brought with us about one-fourth of this capacity crowd.

When the two teams came onto the field, it looked—judging from the size of the players—like the sports writers might have made the right predictions. Landsburgh Wildcats outweighed Maxwell High School Bulldogs, on an average, fifteen pounds to the man. Fans waited impatiently for the sound of the whistle to see these rival teams clash. The air was cool and crisp, and the day was sunny. It was beautiful football weather. Excitement ran high among the fans on both sides. They screamed until many of the older people put their fingers in their ears.

The ball was put in place. The whistle sounded. Toodle booted the ball, end over end, the length of the field while the players streaked toward each other. The ball was brought to the twenty-yard line. Landsburgh tried their first play with Fenton Hoskins carrying the ball. He was stopped for no gain. Again Fenton carried the ball and broke through the line for four yards. Toodle Powell made the tackle. He nuzzled Fenton's leg, through the muzzle. The third try, a Landsburgh back carried the ball. Sid Callihan made the tackle. They gained another yard. Then Fenton Hoskins dropped back to punt. He barely got the kick off. It was taken by Toodle Powell who ran it back from the ten- to the thirty-five-yard line.

In the first and second quarters, this football game was a punting duel between Fenton Hoskins and Toodle Powell. Fenton was six feet one and weighed 197 pounds. He was one

of the best football players Landsburgh High School ever had.
But in the first half he was punting against the wind, and
Toodle was punting with the wind. That might have been the
reason Toodle's punts were outdistancing Fenton's. . . . In the
first half Maxwell High School didn't get any deeper into
Landsburgh High School territory.

In the second half Maxwell High came roaring back.
Lanky six-feet-five Sid Callihan took Fenton Hoskins' punt on
the ten-yard line and it looked like he was going all the way.
He passed all Landsburgh's men but one. That man was Fenton
Hoskins. Hoskins came from behind and spilled him on the
two-yard line. There, Landsburgh's Wildcats dug in. When our
Toodle started around right end, Landsburgh's Hoskins spilled
him so hard with a high tackle that Toodle fumbled and
Landsburgh recovered. Fenton dropped back to punt. He punted,
with the help of the wind, to Maxwell's forty-yard line. Big
Tub Mosher took the ball from the air but he didn't take more
than a step until Landsburgh's fast left end upended him with
a shoestring tackle. During the third quarter it was a punting
duel. Maxwell High never got beyond Landsburgh's thirty-yard
line. Once in the third quarter Landsburgh got to Maxwell's
twenty-two-yard line and fumbled. Maxwell High recovered,
and Toodle punted out of danger.

"If Toodle will only keep that mask on," Coach Meyers
whispered to me, "we've got a chance to win this game."

The Landsburgh High School pupils and the local fans
had yelled themselves hoarse in the first half: "We want a
touchdown!" In the third quarter they had changed to, "Wildcats, hold that line!" And every time Toodle Powell made a
tackle—and that was very often—Coach Meyers bit his finger-
nails. "That muzzle," he'd say, and shake his head.

In the first part of the fourth quarter we watched the same
kind of football we had seen throughout the first three quarters. It was the same punting duel between Toodle and Fenton,
and the lines clashed and struggled on the field anywhere between the thirty-yard lines. This was the way the game was
played until the last two minutes of the game. Maxwell's quarterback Dave Hatfield thought it better to punt from Maxwell's
thirty-yard line than to try to make twelve yards in the fourth

down. Toodle dropped back to punt for the last time in this game. He angled the punt for out-of-bounds. But he punted against the wind. Fenton Hoskins hooked the ball from the air on the forty-yard line and he found a hole. Men were strewn on the field. We had only one man left. That man was Toodle Powell. And he had to come from approximately four yards behind to tackle Fenton, who was heading for pay dirt. This race brought every person to their toes.

Fenton Hoskins was a fast man. Toodle Powell was a little faster. At about the twenty-five-yard line, Toodle leaped wildly through the air. The strap broke that held his mask, and the mask-headgear went high into the air. Coach Meyers jumped to his feet! For Toodle Powell was riding Fenton Hoskins piggyback and Fenton was still going. But only for a step or two! Toodle's mouth was against Fenton's back. Suddenly Toodle wrapped his legs around Fenton like a wrestler. He brought Fenton to the ground. Fenton came down on top of Toodle, and they rolled like two logs. Then the referee's whistle.

When the referees ran to untangle these two men, Fenton still held the ball in a death grip. He was knocked out cold. Toodle was knocked out, too, and two of his teeth were knocked out as well, for they were sticking in Fenton's shoulder pad. Another front upper was broken off even with the gum line, and two more uppers were knocked loose. The referee carried the ball fifteen steps closer until it rested on our five-yard line. The evidence against us was left in Fenton Hoskins' shoulder pad.

"We'll lose the game now," Coach Meyers sighed. "I had a feelin' all the time Toodle would get the muzzle off."

"But what a game he's played, Coach!" Vernon Madden said.

Maxwell's line dug in. Each man was crying while Landsburgh rushed to take advantage of their time. First they tried a line plunge. They made one yard. Then they tried a quarterback sneak. They made two yards. The ball was on our two-yard line. Time was running out. Seconds to go. One of their halfbacks dropped back for a pass. When the ball was in the air, the referee put his whistle to his lips. Sid Callihan leaped high into the air and batted down the pass. The whistle sounded. The game ended. It was a victory for us. Landsburgh's players wept on the field. Their fans left the field weeping. Toodle had made good his words. Fenton Hoskins—Landsburgh's greatest fullback—did not cross the goal line he defended.

9

WE HAD a terrific snowstorm in the high hills of northern Kentucky in December. There were deep drifts in the narrow valleys that made it impossible for our school busses to bring the country pupils to Maxwell High School. We dismissed school for two days until the snowplows could clear the roads.

While I was waiting for the snowplows, I attempted to write a short story. Now that my first book of poems, *Man With a Bull-Tongue Plow*, had been accepted, I was no longer content to believe that I could not write one. In two days I wrote three short stories.

To my surprise, Martha Foley and Whit Burnett, coeditors of *Story Magazine*, accepted "Battle Keaton Dies." Helen McAfee, editor of the *Yale Review*, accepted "Head O'W-Hollow." Paul Palmer, editor of the *American Mercury*, accepted "Three Hundred Acres of Elbow Room."

I waited until each magazine had paid me for these stories, so I could cash the checks at the same time. The evening after I had cashed my short-story checks, I was sitting in the living-room with Mr. and Mrs. Kingston. Suddenly I got down on the floor, on the hand-woven carpets of this colonial house, and started stacking my money in three piles. Forrest Kingston stopped smoking his cigar as he watched the strange actions of this high-school principal. Once I saw Lydia Kingston, who was holding back her laughter, look at her husband and wink.

"This is 'Battle Keaton Dies,' my Grandpa," I said, pointing to the two tens and the five. "This is 'Head O'W-Hollow,'" I continued, pointing to five tens. "And this is 'Three Hundred Acres of Elbow Room,'" I said, pointing to the largest stack— six twenties and a five.

"What's the matter with you?" Lydia Kingston asked. Then she began laughing. Forrest Kingston let the fire die in his cigar. He sat looking at the piles of money on the floor. There was a puzzled look on his face.

"What are you doing, Stuart?" he finally asked me. "What's this all about?"

"Each pile of money is for a short story that I wrote the two days we were snowbound," I told him.

"What are you going to do with that money?" he asked me.

"Carry it in my pocket," I said.

Lydia and Forrest Kingston had loaned me money many times before, for when I first went to Maxwell High School I was badly in debt. And this money for the short stories was the first surplus money I had ever had in my hands, that I could call my own, since the days I had worked at the steel mills.

"Don't you carry that money around in your pockets," Forrest warned me. "You put it in the bank."

"I don't know how to put money in the bank," I said. "I never put a dollar of my own in the bank in my life."

"I'll show you how," he said, looking strangely at me.

Then Lydia and Forrest Kingston stopped laughing. What I had said and done was no longer funny to them. They explained to me the difference between a savings account and a checking account. The following Saturday morning I deposited my first money in the bank. I had the strangest feeling that I ever had in my life. The bank had always been the place where I had borrowed money. That's the way I looked upon banks—as a place to borrow money. Now I was out of the red, was in the black for the first time; and to have something ahead, something that meant a little security, gave me a feeling I could not explain.

Nearly every teacher I knew gave his best to teaching. But he had a sideline, such as farming, tobacco-growing, carpentering, raising chickens, selling insurance, clerking in stores on Saturdays, or selling books or products from door to door, in order to supplement his meager salary. Finally I had found my sideline to earn myself some extra money. It was writing. And it was paying off. Two hundred dollars to me was a pile of money. I thought if I could sell the first stories I had ever written, I could sell more. And I wondered about some of the things I had already written. I thought they were about as good as the stories I had just sold.

"Nest Egg," a theme I had written in high school and had taken with me to Lincoln Memorial University, Peabody College, and Vanderbilt University, and used it in the various English classes, I later sold to the *Atlantic Monthly*. Sixteen of my old high-school and college themes, I later sold to *Harper's, Collier's, Esquire, Commonwealth, Household, Progressive Farmer, Scribner's, American Mercury*, and *Southwest Review*.

I thought I had found the solution to my financial problems. I had found a sideline that gave me great enjoyment. I knew now that I could remain in the profession that I had been trained for. I could remain in the profession that I loved. Besides the sale of stories, I would have some royalties coming from *Man With a Bull-Tongue Plow*.

10

IN THE spring following the publication of *Man With a Bull-Tongue Plow*, I received a letter from H. L. Donovan, President of Eastern State Teachers College, who asked me to come and speak at college chapel. He said he was sorry that twenty-five dollars was all the honorarium he could offer me. When I received this letter I called my Superintendent, and read the letter to him over the telephone.

"By all means take it," he advised me. "Don't miss an opportunity like that. I'm proud to have a teacher in my school system who is asked to speak before a college assembly."

I hired Rank Meadows to take me in his car. It was approximately 120 miles to Eastern State College. I gave him all that I was to get for my talk to take me there and bring me back. We left long before daylight and arrived at Eastern early in the morning. I met President H. L. Donovan, who was a very friendly college president. I told him I had never before spoken to a college group and that I wasn't sure that I could do it.

"You take it easy," he advised me. "I'll go up on the platform with you myself. You rest in your room until about ten o'clock. Be at the chapel by ten-fifteen. We'll start promptly at ten-thirty. You know," he then said to me, "you've written a fine book, and I want you to get up there and tell them about it and how you did it. Tell them how you got it published and a little bit about your background."

It would have been much easier for me if I hadn't stopped at the bulletin board before I went into the college chapel. Here I stood before a little notice on the bulletin board which read: "Jesse Stuart, farm boy and schoolteacher from Greenwood County, will read some of his farm rhymes." Some husky football player stood beside me and read the bulletin same time I did. "Hell," he said, turning to me, "if Eastern can't furnish us with a better chapel program than this, I'm not going, are you?"

"Hell, yes, I'm going," I said. "I have to go. I want to see what this is all about."

This Eastern student, who thought I was a student also, and I walked into the chapel together.

"We'd better grab a seat," he said, as the chapel started filling up.

Just then President Donovan walked over to me.

"Are you ready?" he asked.

"Much as I'll ever be," I answered, while the fellow I'd met at the bulletin board looked strangely at me.

I followed President Donovan onto the stage, where I faced a sea of approximately 1,700 faces.

"Take it easy," President Donovan whispered during chapel preliminaries. "I'm going to make my introductory remarks short so we can give you the full thirty minutes."

President Donovan didn't take more than three minutes to introduce me. He told the Eastern pupils this was my first time to appear before a college group, that I was a native of the state, a farmer and schoolteacher, and that he had asked me to tell them something about my background and how I wrote *Man With a Bull-Tongue Plow*, a book, he suspected, judging from the size, was a lifetime's work. After I had talked to President Donovan, I had outlined my talk on the back of an envelope. I was ready to start talking soon as he was through with his introduction.

The first thing I told was my reception at the bulletin board. There was a roar of applause. From this time on, everything I said, though it was serious to me, was funny to them. In that sea of faces before me, I never saw a serious face. I told of my schooling, grades, high school, and college, and of my teaching. I told them of the education my parents had. I told them how we had lived, renting farm after farm until we finally managed to buy fifty acres. I told them the truth; yet they laughed. Perhaps not any other speaker had talked to them as frankly as I had. I told them I had written *Man With a Bull-Tongue Plow* mostly on leaves, while I farmed on my father's farm and while I was Superintendent of Greenwood County Schools. When I told them it had taken me lacking one day of eleven months to write it, that I wrote it for pleasure and recreation while I farmed and was County School Superintendent, they laughed as I had never heard people laugh before. They bent over in their seats and laughed and wiped their eyes with handkerchiefs at the serious, truthful talk I was trying to give them. Often I had to stand on the platform and wait many seconds for the laughter to subside before I could go on. When the bell rang for the chapel to end, the shouts went up: "More! More!"

"Go on," Dr. Donovan signalled me when I looked toward him. He was laughing.

Classes were postponed and bells rang until I had spoken eighty-seven minutes! And the laughter was stronger at the end than it was at the beginning. The applause seemed endless. There was not a serious face among the faculty members. Dr. Donovan laughed as heartily as his students. At the end of this program, pupils and teachers came forward. I was hot, and wet with perspiration. I met pupil and teacher until Dr. Donovan made it possible for me to leave the stage. Scarcely a person left the chapel until Dr. Donovan took me through a side door. Somebody had ripped the farm rhymes announcement from the bulletin board for a souvenir.

11

WE PUT the responsibility of schoolwork upon our Maxwell High School pupils. We gave them the responsibility of providing entertainment at the chapel periods. We let the pupils do most of the work. Our work was to guide and to teach them. We let them do the rest.

For instance, we let our pupils direct one-act plays. They chose their own cast. They selected their own pupil or pupils to direct the plays. If they didn't have a one-act play, we let them dramatize a short story. They arranged their own musical programs, Seniors competing against Juniors, Sophomores against Freshmen.

We let pupils who needed to earn their noon meal help run the high-school cafeteria. One or more pupils did the buying of supplies. One of the commercial pupils kept the financial books. One operated the cash register. Home-economic pupils helped the home-economic teacher prepare the food.

We let the young men in our agricultural classes dig wild trees from the woods and bring them to our school ground and plant them. They, with the aid of their teacher, arranged the trees that are standing there today. They looked after mowing the grass on our spacious acres. They raised a garden and truck patches. Our home-economic pupils canned vegetables that we later used in our cafeteria. These were lessons of practical experience for our pupils. We gave them plenty to do. In every subject we taught, we gave our pupils all the responsibility we could for practical application. Instead of our constantly reminding our pupils to do more work, they were constantly seeking direction from us.

Track was an unheard-of sport when I went to Maxwell High School. Coach Meyers and I organized the first track team. I coached the runners, and he coached discus, javelin, shot-put, pole vault, broad jump, and high jump. In the first year I ran with my pupils. I ran the half-mile, mile, and cross-country. When one could beat me, I rejoiced. My first year at

Maxwell High School, I gave them plenty of competition. But as time moved on, I was going out of the track competition and they were coming into their prime. The last half-mile I ran with four of my men, two beat me, and if there had been twenty feet more to go, the other two would have passed me. They were slender and fleet of foot.

We competed with each other, and the result was we never lost a quarter, half-mile, or cross-country race to a track team in southern Ohio or northern Kentucky. We never missed taking first, second, and third places in the mile and half-mile in the four years I was at Maxwell High School. Our third-place miler, transferred later to Columbus, Ohio, where his parents moved, captured first-places in every meet in which he participated. Our best half-miler tied the state record: two minutes and three seconds. Our timing on the mile was usually under the college time. The reason we had a good track team was our athletes enjoyed the sport. They enjoyed the spirit of friendly competition and believed in fair play. This, above winning O. K. Conference Football Championship. We never won it. This, above winning the district basketball championship. We never won it.

We believed in play and we believed in plenty of it, and we fought hard to win. But we put sportsmanship above our winning a game. Coach Charles Meyers, who played with his men all the time he was Coach at Maxwell High School, stressed sportsmanship above winning a game. This Coach built character and sense of fair play into his men.

12

COACH MEYERS came into my office. His face was radish-red.

"Mr. Stuart, it's Lyttle Brier again," he said.

"What's he done this time?" I asked.

"I want you to go up to the science room to see for yourself."

I followed Coach Meyers upstairs.

"You know, Mr. Stuart, I am held responsible for these science notebooks," Coach Meyers said.

When we walked into the science room, all the pupils were exceedingly still. Lyttle Brier, smallest boy in the class, sat on a highstool. His thin bird-legs dangled from the stool. He didn't look up when we entered the room. He continued to move his feet restlessly and look at the floor.

"Look at this, Mr. Stuart," Coach said, handing me five pages Lyttle Brier had torn from his notebook. "Destruction of school property!"

There was a poem written on each page. In some places Lyttle Brier had selected eight to ten words before he chose the right one. Coach Meyers had caught him before he revised the last poem.

"Coach, this is not verse," I said, after I finished reading the first one. "This is poetry." After I had read the second one, I said: "When a poetic mood like this strikes a pupil he should be given a chance to get paper. If he doesn't have it, let him write on his notebook." When I had finished reading the five poems, I told Coach Meyers: "If any pupil can do this, let him tear up his notebook and I will pay for it!"

And here is what happened. I told Lyttle Brier where to send his poems. The poems were accepted by a nationally known magazine. This does not end the story. When we entered the district scholastic contest at Auckland, Coach Meyers entered Lyttle Brier in general science. He not only won the district scholastic contest in general science, but he won over the entire state. Coach Meyers' face was red. But his face was not as red as mine at a later date.

When we were running on the track one April evening, I thought this tiny bird-legged boy was in the way. I suggested he stay off the track when we were running. We overtook him going around the track on his second lap when we were on our third. Little did I know that this small boy, who weighed ninety-eight pounds, was running eight miles to and from school, night and morning, and timing himself by a watch on his wrist.

Lyttle Brier had never been in a race until his Senior year. We had to have first, second, and third places in the mile to win the meet against a crack Ohio track team. One of our milers had Charley horse and was unable to run. We hoped Lyttle Brier could take a third place. He won first place, running the fastest mile that was ever run on our track. He ran the mile in four minutes and twenty-nine seconds. We took first, second, and third places in the mile. We won the meet in a close finish.

13

IN MY fourth year in Maxwell High School, scarcely a week passed I didn't get a letter asking me to come to speak to college and high-school students in chapel assemblies, to grade, high-school, and college groups of teachers, and before various school organizations. I couldn't begin to fill all these engagements. If I had done this, I would have had to resign as Principal of Maxwell High School. The publication of *Man With a Bull-Tongue Plow* had given me my first chance to speak before a college audience; and after this chapel program at Eastern State Teachers College, Richmond, Kentucky, somebody had told somebody about the talk and the news had spread.

Here is the way I managed the speaking engagements. First, I had to get permission from my Superintendent before I could leave Maxwell High School. I had, in the meantime, spoken to the high-school assemblies of approximately all of our neighboring high schools, in exchange for my fellow principals and superintendents speaking to the pupils of Maxwell High School. This had worked beautifully. It had brought about better relationships between our schools. So, if and when some inter-high-school difficulty did arise, we could get together and iron out our troubles. Mr. Manson had been sold on this idea. But now I was getting invitations to go far beyond the local high school and various organizations in Big River Valley.

Mr. Manson suggested that I take one talk per week. He

wanted me to search for new school ideas and to bring them
back to Kentucky. I had another idea that I didn't tell Mr.
Manson about. I was afraid that it might not work. The majority of my requests for talks came from colleges and universities. I even got so many requests for talks that I arranged my
first tour East during the week that teachers would attend
Kentucky Education Association in Louisville. I booked a talk
a day, beginning with a college in Ohio, going on to three
teachers' colleges in Pennsylvania, and ending with a talk at
Princeton University.

During each school week I went somewhere to give a talk.
I went East as far as New York, South as far as Georgia, West
as far as Illinois, and North as far as Michigan. When I spoke
at a college or university, often the presidents of these insti-
tutions of higher learning asked me about pupils I had taught
in schools. They would ask me if I could recommend one of
my pupils to them. If they didn't ask me, I brought the subject around about my pupils. I found that everywhere they
were interested in the education of the hill boys and girls.
But they were not as much interested as I was. They had not
seen what I had seen. I knew the value of an education, for in
the part of America I was from, education had never been
overstressed.

Of course, this was the catch. My pupils were from poor
families. I didn't know a single wealthy family among the
people in Greenwood County. When the president and I ended
our talk, I often had made an agreement with him to send one
or more of my pupils to work their way at his college or university. I asked only for a chance for a young ambitious Kentucky hill man or woman.

By doing this, I helped place thirty-seven young men and
women in colleges and universities. These young men and
women had little money. Their parents had practically nothing.
I thought when a young man or young woman was ambitious
enough to attempt to work his entire way through college or
university, he should be given that chance. And I found Americans sympathetic, generous, and kind. Often, upon my recommendation, one of my pupils would be given a scholarship.

I never begged for anything. I never asked alms for any pupils. I gave the history of the pupil's life. I stated the facts. This brought results.

Illiteracy in my state was high. My portion of my state— the high hill country of eastern Kentucky, settled by the pioneers who had helped to make this country, who had won the Northwest territory, and who had fought for the very life of this country in every war—had remained static intellectually while the progress of a nation had swept around them like a great cyclone. If there was ever a man who wanted to obliterate illiteracy from the hill country, I was that man. I thought that if any pupil I might get into college would graduate and return to the hills to work, his influence would be like the dropping of an acorn into a deep pool of mountain water. The little waves would spread from the acorn the entire breadth and length of the pool.

When the term paper, *Beyond Dark Hills*, which I had written while a student at Vanderbilt University, was published as my third book, I got a long letter from faraway Boston, Massachusetts. The letter read like this: "On the strength of a *New York Times* book review, I bought your book, *Beyond Dark Hills*. Since I could not help the boy who wrote this book while he was in college, I would like for him to recommend some pupil for me to send to college and pay all of his expenses." The letter was signed "Henry Lee Shattuck."

I was so elated over this letter that I read it many times to be sure it wasn't a dream. I couldn't decide on the pupil to send him. I had taught three boys, two at Landsburgh and one at Maxwell High, whom I was positive should go to college. These boys had only one parent living. They had home responsibilities. There wasn't a chance for them unless somebody made one possible. I wrote a long case history of each boy and sent them to Henry Lee Shattuck. I told him that I couldn't decide which one to recommend. He would have to make the choice.

He answered that he would send all three to college and pay their expenses. Who is this man? I wondered. I studied the proposition. I didn't think that these boys should have all their ways paid. I had another idea. I wrote to Mr. Shattuck and suggested he pay three-fourths of each boy's college expenses. Taking one-fourth from each would make another three-fourths and that would educate another youth. Mr. Shattuck was pleased with the idea. He wrote me that he had a friend, whose name he would not disclose, who wanted to send a pupil to college and to pay all expenses. This made five pupils.

Robert and William Hampton were the Landsburgh youths I recommended. They were the sons of John Hampton, rural teacher for more than a half-century, who passed away leaving many debts his sons managed to pay. It was John Hampton who had helped me get Lonesome Valley Rural School to teach. It was he who had driven his T-model Ford backwards up the high hills to Lonesome Valley in the night. It was he who had told me that when he had started teaching he had tried to turn the hills over to see what was under them. The third boy I recommended was Lyttle Brier, a brilliant youth, who was well remembered for writing poetry in his science notebook and for running the fastest mile at Maxwell High School. May Pratt and Helen Artner were the girls. These boys later distinguished themselves in the armed forces in service for their country. May Pratt and Helen Artner graduated from college and became teachers. They were acorns dropped into a pool. They owed their little waves of influence to Henry Lee Shattuck and his unnamed friend for doing this kind deed for American youth.

14

IT WOULD take a book to give my observations of the schools I visited in other states. I borrowed many ideas from northern schools. I saw with my own eyes what the members of my profession were doing in other states. I saw the vastness, purpose, and greatness of America's public school systems as I had never seen them before. The dream I had had walking beside the Tiber River, when I taught fourteen pupils at Winston High School, I saw in reality in America's Midwest, where industry and agriculture are well balanced. I saw the posterity of every race under the sun, every color and mixed color of humanity, of practically every religious creed known to Americans, playing, studying, rejoicing with strong life, under the same roof together. I saw democracy in the making—a strong and vital democracy—in a powerful and husky Republic.

I visited high schools, from the janitor's room to the superintendent's office. I looked for virtues. I hunted for faults. I wanted to know the answers. I wanted to know everything about America's schools in every state in the United States. I wanted to heap the information up before me like cords of wood and throw out the bad sticks and accept the sound and the durable. Here are a few of my observations.

Even in these northern and eastern states, where teachers were so well paid in comparison with those in their sister states of the South, these unbelievably high salaries were not high at all in comparison to the wages received by the skilled men of northern industries. They were often not as high as the wages paid unskilled labor. In one northern high school I visited, the janitor received a higher compensation for his sweeping and dusting than the teachers who had spent years of their lives preparing themselves for their profession, and upon whose skill in teaching American youth, depended the future of this Republic. This revelation was a rotten stick of wood that I immediately threw from the heap of sound and durable sticks I had gathered.

In one state—one of the most progressive states in the Union, where agriculture and industry are well balanced—I found rural pupils getting seven-months' school, while in cities within these counties pupils were getting nine-months' school. It was the same as in Kentucky. There was the dual school system. One drew on the big taxes from the accumulations of concentrated wealth, paying its teachers better than the teachers in the rural districts, and giving the city pupil far more advantages than the rural pupil. This was happening in Ohio, one of my favorite states of this Union. I love the state of Ohio because the people move. They do things. They don't wait. They believe in progress. And at this time, it was debatable whether Ohio or California rated tops in the nation's schools. I visited the border state of West Virginia, where the unit system was in its infancy. This system paid a minimum state wage to all teachers. It gave the rural pupils approximately equal opportunities with the city pupils.

In all of the northern states that I visited, and the border state of West Virginia, I found teachers from the southern states. I could not visit a school system anywhere in the North I didn't find one or more southern teachers. Often I found southerners heading northern school systems. Why, I asked myself, had the southern teachers made such headway in the northern states? The answer was very simple. The northern teachers were leaving their profession for better-paying positions, skilled and unskilled, in industry. They were going into businesses of their own. At least the majority of native northerners were practical people. If they couldn't make a living teaching school, they would try something that would pay them better. When these northern teachers left their profession by the thousands, teachers from the South, who had received death-colored wages all of their lives, migrated North to replace them. And as soon as they had taught a few years— soon as they saw so many better-paying positions than were offered to them in the northern school systems—they, too, left the teaching profession for better pay.

Of all the southern or border states, the one that had the greatest number of teachers working outside its borders, was my own native state of Kentucky. In one county in West Virginia, Kentucky furnished 70 per cent of the teachers. Throughout the length and breadth of Ohio, in almost every school system of any size, I found native-born and educated Kentucky teachers. In Illinois, Indiana, Michigan, Pennsylvania, I found an amazing number of Kentucky teachers. I found them in Tennessee, New Jersey, and New York. They could always double and often treble their salaries. One teacher that worked in my system for $96 a month went to West Virginia where he received $387 per month.

If one is a native-born Kentuckian, and his profession is schoolwork, he knows why there are so many Kentucky teachers. In this state, where teachers receive approximately the lowest salaries paid by any of the states, we have four excellent large state-supported teachers' colleges. We encourage youth to become members of the teaching profession. We run them through our four great mills, stamp them, and send them to our bordering states, since we do not pay them a decent living wage. We do not pay them enough to hope to hold them. It has often been said, Kentucky's greatest export is not her fine whiskies, not her racehorses, but her schoolteachers!

In the deep South, I visited colleges, universities, high schools, graded schools, and rural schools. Before one sits in far-off places and makes rash statements about the deep southern states, offering suggestions of how to solve their problems, one should go there to see with his own eyes. He should go there to feel the tempo. The situation is tragic. If it were not for the race problem, I believe that southerners would be the most liberal people in America. While it is true what we hear about the education of the Negro being held to a minimum, we do not hear as much about the hundreds of thousands of white people held to just a little higher minimum. The southern states are poor financially. They do not have the concentrated wealth of northern, eastern, and of many western states. Their school buildings are inadequate. Their teachers are poorly paid. If the South could have financial help, if both white and black could have opportunities of better education, this could be a step toward solving their problems. I believe this is the only way the problems can be solved. The southern problems will have to be solved by southerners or by people sympathetic to the South. The South must be led. The South cannot be driven.

I traveled, in my fourth year at Maxwell High School, more than I ever traveled in my life. I paid my way by the small honorariums I received for speaking. I rode the trains across the flatlands of the Midwest when the corn was green and when it was buff colored in autumn. I rode trains along the rivers and through the deep valleys of Pennsylvania when the leaves had turned multicolored on the mountains. I saw the apples ripen in the great orchards of upstate New York.

I rode into south Georgia in May when it was more comfortable to close the car windows to keep out the hot wind from the fields of cotton. I felt the sting of winter in Michigan's upper peninsula when snow was twenty-two inches deep and the thermometer was thirty degrees below!

15

IN APRIL I received a letter from Henry Allen Moe of the Guggenheim Memorial Foundation. When I had attended Peabody College for my last and third summer, Dr. Alfred Crabb suggested that I apply for a Guggenheim Fellowship.

After my application was sent to the Guggenheim Memorial Foundation, I received a letter from Allen Moe, asking me to send him any books I had-written. I sent him the only two books I had written. That had been months ago. Now I wondered what was the committee's final decision. I had applied for a Guggenheim grant so I could go to Europe. All I had to do was tear open the thin little letter to learn I had been accepted.

When I reported this to my Superintendent, I was, upon his recommendation to the Greenwood County Board of Education, given a year's leave of absence to travel and study abroad.

PART VI

BECAUSE I WANTED YOU

1

WHEN I went home after fourteen months in Europe, many startling changes had taken place. Charles Manson, Superintendent of Greenwood County Schools, had been ousted. He hadn't been ousted by the popular vote of the people. Three of the five members of his school board had run for re-election. Thomas Dixon, who had aspirations for the position Charles Manson held, also ran three men to oppose Mr. Manson's school board members who were seeking re-election. When the votes were counted, Mr. Manson's school board was elected by a substantial majority. In the petitions filed by Mr. Manson's school board members when they were seeking re-election, each had made the simple mistake of failing to state his place of birth. Two of these were native-born sons of Greenwood County. One was born in Pike County, Kentucky.

Upon these minor technicalities, a petition was filed in the Greenwood County Court to keep Mr. Manson's school board members from serving on the Greenwood County Board of Education. It sought to oust those men who had been re-elected by the popular vote of the people and to replace them with the men they had defeated. The defeated candidates were favorable to Thomas Dixon.

This legal battle started in the Greenwood County Courts shortly after the November election. After a decision had been handed down by Judge Whittlecomb, Judge of the Circuit

Court, in favor of Mr. Manson's school board members, the case was sent to the Kentucky Court of Appeals, where there was a reversed decision the following spring. Thus, the candidates who favored Thomas Dixon, and who had received the minority of popular votes in the election, were given the legal right to serve as members of the Greenwood County Board of Education. Since three board members were a majority, Charles Manson was ousted as Superintendent of Greenwood County Schools. He was replaced by Thomas Dixon.

My leave of absence from Maxwell High School was disregarded. Sturdie Roundtree had been employed to replace me as Principal of Maxwell High School. His father, a minister of one of the old and well-established churches, was one of the new school board members who had won his right to serve on a technicality of the law. Only one of my faculty members, Thalia Meyers, was re-employed at Maxwell High School. She was a talented teacher that any principal would find difficulty in replacing. Charles Meyers was employed to coach at Landsburgh High School, a school whose athletic teams he had so many times in the past five years tied and defeated. One of my teachers found a college position in Georgia. Another teacher found employment in an Indiana School System. Two were employed in an Ohio School System. Two were sent to Greenwood County Rural Schools. The remainder left the teaching profession. Thus ended one of the finest high-school faculties I had ever known. They had been scattered to the four winds. Mr. Manson, who succeeded me as Superintendent of Greenwood County Schools, and with whom I had worked peacefully and progressively for four years, was retired to his farm. Larry Anderson, whom I had succeeded as Superintendent of Greenwood County Schools, was no longer connected with schools. He had left the teaching profession to become an undertaker.

When Thomas Dixon took office as Superintendent of Greenwood County Schools, there were many surprising shakeups. Teachers were afraid to express their opinions. Because many of these rural teachers didn't qualify to teach in the Ohio School Systems. And if they could have qualified, it would have been too late for them to find positions in Ohio.

The Ohio School Systems had already engaged their teachers for the coming school year. It was hard for many of them to leave the hills where they were born, to seek employment in another state. They were sentimentally attached to their neighbors, hills, little narrow-gauged valleys, rivers, shacks, and fields. They loved their own country. They were willing to keep their mouths shut—to hold their little positions and their little salaries. But the Maxwell High School teachers were well qualified to teach anywhere in the United States.

I knew how these rural teachers felt toward Thomas Dixon. They didn't like the methods he used to get himself elected Superintendent of Greenwood County Schools. Of the one hundred rural teachers now teaching in Greenwood County, I had taught seventy-one. Many of my pupils were teaching in Ohio, Indiana, Tennessee, West Virginia, and Michigan. Eight of the fourteen pupils I had taught at Winston High School were now teaching school. Pupils I had taught at Lonesome Valley, at Landsburgh High School, and at Maxwell High School, were now teaching. My brother, James Stuart, was teaching Mountain View Rural School. The W.P.A. had built a road to this mountaintop. A car could be driven there now. Budge Waters was teaching a rural school. These young teachers had the highest average in scholastic qualifications of any group of teachers in Greenwood County's history, before or since. They averaged two years in college. Many were college graduates. Many of the pupils I had taught had equaled, or bettered, the scholastic qualifications of their Superintendent, Thomas Dixon. They had as much college training and as many years of teaching experience as he.

2

WHAT I had seen in Europe disturbed me greatly. Little men had risen to high places. They had risen to positions of power and influence. They were controlling countries. They were torturing people they didn't like. A man was not safe in his own home. Constitutional law didn't mean anything.

Could this happen in America? Could men usurp their fellow-men to obtain high places of power? Could this happen in Kentucky? Could it happen in Greenwood County? Could it happen here? After I had seen Europe, I believed anything could happen anywhere to strangle the freedom of man, the right and dignity of man, unless enough freedom-loving people went to bat for the causes of right, fair play, and justice. Why was I not back as Principal of Maxwell High School? Why was Charles Manson, able educator that he was, retired to his farm? This had not happened because the people didn't have faith in Charles Manson. They had voted an overwhelming majority for men who ran in his favor. Why should many excellent teachers not be returned to their positions? Why should they be scattered East, West, North, South?

To me, this was a fight for justice. To me, this meant to fight back. It meant to hit fast and to hit hard. And what was the best way to reach the people? I remembered how I had reached them when I was Superintendent of Greenwood County Schools. The best way was to print the truth in a newspaper. But the newspaper? Lambert Reed, editor of the *Landsburgh Leader*, remembered the old newspaper battle when he fought for Landsburgh and I fought for Greenwood County. He was still smarting, though the years had passed. Naturally, he would not print anything that I would write. Whatever I was for, he was against. Nor was there space in Rex Milford's *Roxford Examiner*. However, Rex Milford was sympathetic. He had already attacked, in his editorials in his *Roxford Examiner*, the situation in the Greenwood County Schools. I had to have more space than he could offer me.

Then the idea occurred to me to start a paper of my own, the *Greenwood County Citizen*. I made arrangements with Rex Milford to print my paper in his shop. *It couldn't happen here! It couldn't happen in Greenwood County!* I made ready for an attack. Naomi Deane said: "Jesse, don't do it. The forces are too powerful that are against you. Besides," she added solemnly, *"you might be killed."* My mother advised against editing this paper. "Is it worth it, Jesse?" she asked me. "If you had seen what I have seen," I told her, "you'd know it's worth every effort I make. You don't know what freedom is until you lose it." "Jesse, I have heard talk," James said. "You will be in great danger. The situation here is more dangerous than you think."

Despite the repeated warnings of my relatives and friends, I started my paper. I was absolutely fearless in my attack. I wanted them to retaliate. And they did, with "The Pouting Poet from W-Hollow." We were off. The fight was on. And it was a fight. It split Greenwood County—even the town of Landsburgh—into fighting camps. Housemaids working in Landsburgh homes shook their fists at each other across yard fences. The fight ranged from Washington, D. C., to Frankfort, Kentucky, to Mountain View, the farthest outpost rural school in Greenwood County.

There was never an indecent thing said in my paper. There was never anything said in it that could have kept it from getting a post-office permit. Yet I could not get a permit. Why? I shall never know. This was one good way to block the truth. I had just returned from other countries, which were giving jitters to the world now, where this sort of thing had happened! But in my own country, in my own state, in my own county, right in my own door, how could it happen? My papers were distributed by hand. They were sold on the street. Many people who believed as I did, who thought I was right, were afraid to be seen buying my paper. They were afraid of losing their jobs!

In one instance, a store that gave me ads was boycotted in a polite way. Business wasn't business as it had usually been. Business politely dropped. The store was nicely shunned. After this happened, I never solicited ads from this good merchant again. My paper was taking me deeper and deeper into debt. But I continued the fight for what I thought was right and for what I believed. The teachers of rural schools, who were very silent in the beginning, came out of their hiding. They brought me editorials and I printed them without using their names, so there would not be any reprisals. The *Landsburgh Leader* mustered up all its strength to offset the power of the *Greenwood County Citizen*, a paper without a permit to go through the mail. My circulation jumped from 200 to 800. But my paper was short-lived. It ran approximately from July until November.

In the meantime, I crossed the Mason-Dixon line. My ideas of helping to educate my own people were shineless stars in a background of memory. I was following the road sixty thousand Kentuckians followed annually. Among these thousands leaving Kentucky were hundreds of schoolteachers. I had found a position at Dartmouth High School, Dartmouth, Ohio. Lydia Leonard, my first high-school teacher, had told her brother-in-law, Grant Hale, about me. Grant Hale was Principal of Dartmouth High School. Though his faculty for the coming school year had long been engaged, Grant Hale had special work he wanted done in his high school. He thought I would be qualified to do the job.

3

MY SPECIAL work in Dartmouth High School was to teach remedial English. I was not allowed to use any published textbook. Not a grammar nor a *Literature and Life Book*. I had to make my own textbook and to teach five classes per day. I wondered why there were so many failures in English. Pupils kept coming to my classes until there was not room to seat more. Dartmouth High was a large school. There were 1,937 pupils enrolled. Yet even with this enrollment, I should not have so many remedial English pupils.

The very first thing we did in remedial English was to have a testimonial meeting. I asked each pupil to tell me why he was in my class. Believe me, this worked. We did it behind closed doors. When it came his time to speak, each pupil snapped to his feet. He didn't waste any words. He had something pent up in his heart he'd been wanting for a long time to express. I let him say it in my class. I thought it would do him good. It did. And it did their teacher good to know these things. Why were they in remedial English?

William Shakespeare, though he had been sleeping peace-

fully in the church at Stratford on Avon a few hundred years,
had driven the majority of my pupils from their regular English classes in Dartmouth High School. In these testimonial
meetings, very few pupils held grievances against their English
teachers. A few admitted they couldn't get English. There were
all sorts of testimonies, and there was much good laughter.
But why should the mental strength of the average high-school
pupil be pitted against the genius of the English language?
Why should a pupil be forced to make low marks because he
couldn't *get* Shakespeare? Why should the ghost of this great
genius haunt the youth in the high school of a steel-mill city,
who were trying to get a speaking and writing knowledge of
the mother tongue?

These were not the first youth to have trouble with Shakespeare's plays. They would not be the last. Members of my
class in Landsburgh High School had had the same trouble
many years ago. High school almost wrecked Shakespeare for
me. I wasn't ready for him. Not until I was in college could
I appreciate this writer. I was honest with these pupils when I
told them my difficulties with Shakespeare's plays. They felt
better too. I proceeded to teach them on the basis of: *They
must control the language regardless of written and spoken
errors they made. The language must not control them. They
must not have fears. They must enjoy English.*

Here is how I arranged my class work.

On Mondays I asked my pupils to give current events.
I asked them to do this so they would be able to stand on their
feet and speak the language without fear. In the beginning
there was fear. There was plenty of it. I could hardly get one
of them to rise. Some pupil gave a current event about the
labor situation, and, since Dartmouth was having its troubles,
each pupil had an opinion. I asked each pupil who wanted to
express his opinion to stand on his feet. My limit of three
minutes to each pupil was broken for the first time. From this
time on, each pupil wanted more and more time. Each was
eager to stand and give a current event. Then, sometime later,
we started correcting the English of the speaker. One young
man had a beautiful voice. He spoke with eloquence. "You
have, I believe, a wonderful radio voice," I told him. He tried

out at the local radio station. He was given employment, and for a long, long time worked without pay. Now my remedial English pupil is one of the good radio commentators in the country. He has advanced rapidly.

On Tuesdays we had memory work. I let the pupils select their favorite poems to memorize. I did *recommend* certain brief classical poems of the English language, but I didn't *require* them to memorize any of the poems I recommended. The memory work they gave was of a wide variety. I was amazed at some of their ambitious undertakings. One pupil memorized "Cotter's Saturday Night." One memorized "Twinkle, Twinkle, Little Star." After she had said this simple little child's poem, the pupils laughed and laughed. I never had to tell this young lady to select better memory work. From this time on, she gave better selections.

Once I took members of my remedial English class before the pupils of a regular English class. My pupils gave a recital. One boy gave seven hundred lines of poetry from memory. "Not one of us can do that," said a pupil in the class we were entertaining. Any number of my pupils could recite three hundred lines or more. I often asked them to recite the poems they had given the week before. In this way, they retained the poems they had memorized. These poems stayed with them, and they could recite them at any moment. I thought this was good mental training. They memorized many poems that were beautiful and good. Not one was a poem by Shakespeare.

On Wednesdays we had written work. I gave them the freedom to write about any subject they chose. I let them choose any literary forms to express themselves. At first, these pupils told me they couldn't write themes, but after I told them to write about anything they chose, they started writing. Many wrote poems. Many attempted songs. They attempted short stories. One was ambitious enough to attempt a novel. I let them feel their way with their written work. If they didn't have something written on theme day, I didn't lower their grades. Not at first. And here is what happened.

One of my pupils wrote a theme about "The Old Opera House." It was something about the background of this old house, now a theatre in Dartmouth. He told about the plays that had once been given there and the people that attended. Then another pupil wrote a theme about a character who attended the Old Opera House. Soon everybody was writing about the characters that went to the Old Opera House. One pupil, Bill Hockenheimer, told about a pickpocket. If a person ever stepped on the pickpocket's toes in the Old Opera House, and he didn't have enough manners to beg the pickpocket's pardon, the pickpocket always relieved this man of his wallet. They even went so far as to write the play that was given at the Old Opera House. They wrote the song that preceded the play. They worked it out. I didn't.

One of the characters who went to the Old Opera House was a woman from a part of Dartmouth that was so ugly that she first had a beer to help her forget her surroundings. Not many of the well-dressed operagoers paid any attention to her. But there was a rat that did. This rat had grown tired of eating the plush from the decaying opera seats so he, being very tired, crawled upon this lady's lap and went to sleep. Since she did not have many friends in the world, she was very sympathetic toward the rat. I had never heard anything funnier written by a high-school pupil. After he read this theme, many of us wiped tears from our eyes.

Then came a loud knock on the door. I opened the door. It was Mr. Arnold, Superintendent of Dartmouth City Schools.

"Mr. Stuart," he said, with a trembling voice, "your class is making so much noise you are disturbing my office, which is halfway down the corridor of this long building. We," he affirmed, pointing a trembling finger at me, "have never had anything like this in Dartmouth High School. You must either discipline your class or stringent disciplinary measures will be taken immediately! What is the reason for all this?"

Mr. Arnold was an excellent schoolman. He was a Latin and Greek scholar. He was already beyond the retiring age but he wouldn't retire. He had been connected with the Dartmouth City Schools for a half-century.

"Mr. Arnold, one of my pupils read a funny theme," I said. "That's why everybody is laughing!"

"How could anything be so funny?" he asked. "Where is that theme? Let me read it!"

I had to think quickly. He must not see the theme the pupil had just read. Not about the lady who escaped her ugly environment by drinking a beer first, then going to the Old Opera House where she let a rat sleep on her lap. It would never do to let him read this theme. I gave Mr. Arnold another theme, while the pupils tried to suppress their laughter. He read the theme. "Not a bit funny to me," he said. My pupils let out a roar of laughter they couldn't hold back. Mr. Arnold couldn't understand their sense of humor. He went out and shut the door behind him. The four thick walls and the closed door could not confine our laughter.

That very afternoon there was another knock on my door. I opened it, thinking it was Mr. Arnold again. There was a little gray-bearded man with a cane, standing at the door.

"You Mr. Stuart?" he asked.

"Yes, I am."

"My name's Elroy Snoddie," he said. "You have my granddaughter, Gracie Snoddie, in your class. And she tells me," he said, his voice rising, "that your scholars have been writing a lot of fun-making things about my theatre. Now, is or isn't this true? Rats, women, pickpockets, and all sorts of things. Listen!" he shouted, before I could answer him. "Young man, I will sue you! I will sue the Dartmouth City Board of Education! I went to school with old Ben Arnold, and I'll talk to him first."

"But Mr. Snoddie," I said, "Mr. Arnold was in here this morning. It has been stopped. No use to go see him now. He bawled us out properly and plans to take stringent disciplinary action."

"That's enough to satisfy me," he smiled. "When Ben takes that kind of disciplinary action, woe be unto all of you! I won't bother to see him."

On Thursdays and Fridays we had grammar. We didn't use a book. We diagrammed sentences from the editorials in the *Dartmouth Times*. At first, we took short sentences. As time went on, our sentences became longer. We talked about a sentence as if it were a house and parts of speech were the materials we used to build that house. We tore the house down. We put it back together, using all the parts. My pupils were cold to grammar when the term was mentioned, but after we started work they warmed up to it.

4

DARTMOUTH HIGH SCHOOL was one of the best high schools in the United States. For the state of Ohio was rated by many educators to be the "top" state, educationally. Among all of the schools of Ohio—public, church, and private —pupils in the Dartmouth High School had carried away top scholastic honors for three straight years. One high school, in the state of Ohio, where there are many large cities with many fine high schools, cannot carry away top honors three times in a row unless there are excellent teachers in that school system. What made Dartmouth High School an outstanding school in the state—in scholarship, athletics, and music?

They imported their bandmaster from Germany. Their woodworking teacher was born in Norway. One teacher was from England. There were teachers from Tennessee, Kentucky, Indiana, Illinois, Ohio, Pennsylvania, New York, Virginia. The faculty was not only interstate but international. Never have I seen, before or since, a finer high-school faculty working together under one roof. This was the way it should be. Yet not all was perfect. Even in a big school like this, with such a well-qualified faculty, there were drawbacks. There were little faults. There were hindrances.

I had not thought before that a school could be too large. I had not realized before that while the large schools offered so many things the pupils in smaller high schools could not have, the smaller high schools had, in many ways, advantages over the larger schools. For instance, Dartmouth High School had sixty-six men on their first football team. It took eleven men to make the team. Many of these boys only got to play a few minutes during the season. And it took a real man to make this team. Their line averaged over two hundred pounds to the man. They lost one game in two seasons! But look at the young men who wanted to make the Dartmouth Trojans and didn't have a chance! If they had been in smaller schools, they would have been football stars. In the big school only a few could squeeze through to the top, while hundreds could never know the light of glory in achievements that often develops youth.

It was my first time to teach in a school where I didn't know all the pupils; in fact, not all the teachers. A school was a stronger unit, no matter if it were small, where every pupil knew the teachers and every teacher knew all the pupils. I learned this after I started teaching at Dartmouth. To know everybody was more fun, more happiness and enjoyment. There were stronger bonds of unity in a school where everybody could be united in good-fellowship. Never had I thought of the words assembly line or connected them in any way with schools, until I taught at Dartmouth. In this big school teacher and pupil entered the schoolhouse in the morning and they didn't come out until the school day was over. There was not any noon hour. We went in three shifts to the cafeteria, and we had to keep the line moving. We had a thirty-minutes' lunch period. Not so in the little schools, where we had an hour for noon, and a big playground. This broke the day, for we could walk over the school ground and breathe the fresh air, and we could play.

In a large school pupils didn't get that friendliness, love, and warmth from teachers they could get in a small school. Many of the pupils didn't get it from their parents. They needed it in their growing up. In a school as large as Dartmouth, they didn't get the kind word spoken by a friendly teacher, the leisure time to talk to the teacher. Grant Hale once told one of his pupils: "Be brief, young man. I don't have much time. If I spend one minute with each pupil, that's nineteen hundred and thirty-seven minutes. That's thirty-two hours and seventeen minutes. That's more than a day. Think of talking for more than a day!"

This terrific speed, this factory-like coordination and mechanism, baffled me. There was something which the teacher and the pupil were missing. They were not getting to know each

other as they should. They were missing good life—happiness
that would not come again.

Each of us—teacher and pupil—became a little, unknown
part of the vast educational assembly line. Our pupils were
like young crowded trees growing up in a vast forest. They
grew up very much alike. While in a forest where there were
not so many trees, the growth was different. Trees grew up
with originality, because they had not been patterned. This
was the way it should be with young lives. They should be given
a chance when they are young, to grow up individually and
originally.

5

IN MY classes I had the lost and frustrated youth. I had
approximately a third of the sixty-six men on the first-string
football squad. I had many of the second- and third-stringers.
I had pupils whose parents had moved from the South. These
pupils had bright minds, but they never had an early training
comparable to that received by the youth fortunate enough, for
educational reasons, to have been born in Ohio. I had those
not interested in the subject of English. I had those that had
found the subject of English difficult and terrifying. I had
every sort of pupil. I even had pupils put in my classes for
disciplinary reasons. With this group I worked, laughed, and
talked. I tried to be a stabilizing influence. I tried to let them
take the responsibility. They accepted responsibility. They
loved it too. Not any cut-and-dried education for me, worked
out in strict academic coldness, and measured in buckets and
baskets.

Our room was on the first floor in the southwest corner of
this large building. This little room became a place of warmth,
friendliness, and happiness. We were as relaxed as a lazy
cotton-field wind, while a wind of cyclonic speed whirled
around us. In my teaching, there was always work piled ahead
of us that we had never done. I took time out to talk to these

youth about the art of living. About each pupil's ambitions. I worked on the theory that I had always held. Each life was important; each life was "the kingdom of God within you." Human life was the dearest, the most precious, the most valuable possession in the world. It must be helped. It must not be hurt. It certainly must never be mentally and morally destroyed.

The discipline in Dartmouth High School was mechanical. How could it be otherwise? There was a detention room where pupils often spent an hour after the long day in the schoolrooms. How long the pupil remained after school depended upon the misdemeanor. It all depended upon the reports of the classroom teachers to the Principal. Never did one of my pupils reach this detention room. It was not because I didn't have discipline problems, for I did; but I tried to work them out myself.

Since I was exceedingly friendly with my pupils, they started calling me by my first name. In all my teaching experience, this was the first time it had ever happened. I couldn't talk to each pupil and tell them not to do it. I didn't want to make announcements to each class. They would think I was priggish and setting myself apart from them. Here is the way I broke the news to them. Never had one of my eleven colored pupils called me by my first name. Their manners and sense of humor were delightful to any teacher. One of my colored pupils always gave a current event about someone stealing something, about his getting caught. Then he would laugh loudly. One day I announced to each of my classes: "This is the first time in my life I have ever taught colored pupils. I must say their sense of humor, their laughter, is wonderful. Something else, too," I added, "no other race of people on earth excel them in manners. Never has one of my colored pupils ever called me by my first name."

I was never familiarly called "Jesse" again by one of my pupils.

There was another problem that perplexed me at first. A few of my pupils weren't getting enough sleep. They tried sleeping in my classes. Once or twice two boys slept so soundly that they snored. I didn't want to send them to the detention room. So I would figure out a way to stop it.

There was always a copy of the *Dartmouth Times* left on every desk each morning. During the day my pupils had access to these papers. Since many of the pupils had been, and still were, delivering newspapers in Dartmouth, they were experts on folding a newspaper to throw from their bicycles onto a front porch. I gave these experts a chance to throw their papers when we had a sleeper. They folded their papers, rose to their feet, and I gave the signal for them all to cut down on him at once.

"Oh, heaven help me!" Bill Howard shouted once when forty-five newspapers hit him.

Bill jumped to his feet. He rubbed the sleep from his eyes. There was a great roar of laughter in the room. "I dreamed," Bill said, as he looked strangely at us, "that I was floating through the skies on a fluffy cloud, and that I floated into a flock of wild geese. I thought they were hitting me in the face." The pupils laughed louder than ever. Mr. Arnold came to the door again. From this time on, pupils in my class took care of the sleepers. They watched eagerly for them. It was great fun to wake one.

What was the scholastic achievement of the Remedial English pupils? We did something only those in the music classes did. We did something the regular English classes, taught by the finest English teachers in the state of Ohio, didn't do. We got ourselves a radio program. One of the pupils announced. We read themes and poetry of our own creation to the listeners in radio land. We gave an interesting enough program to receive fan mail.

We continued to entertain the pupils in the regular English classes with recitations of poetry written by the English masters and poems written by our own pupils. We read themes to pupils in the regular English classes. These themes were excellent entertainment. We read them with the grammatical errors, just as the pupils had written them. We competed with them in achievement tests. The pupils in the regular English classes won, but not by a safe margin. My pupils had confidence that they could do most anything. And they could. During my year at Dartmouth High School, I failed one pupil. The following year one of my Remedial English pupils won the coveted Founders Award. In five subjects he made an average of ninety-seven.

6

ONE day in Dartmouth I was surprised to see Mom and James. They came to warn me not to return to Greenwood County. I was still running my paper. My editorials were having repercussions among the Greenwood County citizens.

"Jesse, stay here," Mom warned. "You know we'd like to have you visit us often. But don't come back. It's dangerous."

"Stay here, Jesse," James said. "You are better off in Ohio. You won't be bothered here."

But that Saturday I had a date with Naomi Deane in Landsburgh. We had planned to go to the roof garden of a hotel in Auckland and dance to Hal Meyer's "Dixie Bluebirds." I couldn't break this date. I couldn't be cowardly enough to "phone her" that I was afraid to come. Anyway, I had competition for the love of Naomi Deane. Mom could be wrong! James could be wrong! Danger or no danger, I was going to see her. Who was there to keep me from returning to my home town to see her?

When the bus stopped in front of Langdon's Drugstore in Landsburgh, I got off and went inside. There were a few Saturday customers—people I knew from the town and county. Shortly after I went inside the drugstore, I was followed by Enoch Arvin. I didn't think anything about him. He and I had always been friendly. I ordered a milk shake. When I reached for my pocketbook, something came down upon my head that caused me to bite my pipestem in two. I was hit twice more before I could turn around. Enoch Arvin was behind me. In an addled state of mind, I grappled with this man. Blood was streaming down my face into my eyes. With one arm around him, I pinned down his arms. I thought he might be reaching for a pistol. My other hand went to his throat, where I was gradually cutting away his breath. Two men pulled me from Enoch Arvin.

Enoch Arvin had erred in his judgment. I had been able to stand the licks. Why had this man hit me? I had never had a quarrel with him. Up until this time he had never been the subject of an editorial in my paper. What was behind this? Who was behind it? Why hadn't one of those I had scorched in an editorial hit me? Why couldn't we have fought it out in facts on the printed page? Were my editorials getting the better of theirs? Did truth hurt?

The sheriff was called. We were arrested, but the sheriff took a look at the stream of blood that marked the way I was walking on the street, and he changed his mind. He thought I needed to be rushed to the hospital. From this time until a later hour, I remember but little of the story, except that Enoch Arvin was whisked from Landsburgh by a friend for fear there would be an immediate reprisal. Later I learned that the sheriff took me across the bridge to Madden Hospital, Toniron, Ohio, in such a hurry he didn't pay bridge toll. At the hospital I remember vaguely that when I took off my shoes I poured blood from the heels.

Dr. Madden didn't find any skull fracture. He clamped the skin back in place. He closed the three ugly gashes where the skull showed through. Naomi Deane was the first person at the hospital when she heard what had happened. When she came into the hospital I couldn't remember her first name. It was very embarrassing. For days, weeks, and months later, my memory kept coming back to me, until I was all right. At first, I could see a tree, barn, or house, and I couldn't think of their names. The hearing I lost in one ear, caused by one of those licks, never came back.

Enoch Arvin was finally indicted by a Greenwood County Grand Jury. He could have been indicted on a charge of "striking and wounding another with intent to kill," which was a felony and subject to serious punishment. A Greenwood County Grand Jury indicted him for "assault and battery," which was a misdemeanor and subject only to a small fine and a few days in jail.

A date was set for the trial. It was a cold winter day. Gene Raymond, one of my Remedial English pupils, drove me from Dartmouth to Landsburgh. When we arrived at the courthouse for the trial, there were over a hundred men milling silently around the courthouse. Soon as I stepped out of the car, Walter Burton was beside me. He was the small man who followed me outside the Maxwell High School auditorium to help me the night I had to fight Bascom Reffitt.

"No one will hit you with a blackjack here," he said seriously. "I'll see that you are protected. This is my duty."

I had not sent for Walter Burton. I didn't know that he would be at the trial. He was armed with two loaded revolvers. There were beardy-faced men with grim faces, who walked silently about. I didn't know half of these men. One man, who weighed more than 250 pounds, and who had shoulders broad as a corncrib door, and legs like churns that filled his briar-scratched boots, was walking around with a pistol stuck in one boot, and there were prints of pistol handles on each hip beneath his tight-fitting coat.

"I don't like the looks of that man," I whispered to Walter. "Who is he?"

"Never mind about him," Walter said. "He's your friend!"

This man, Buster Sandless, had come in from the hills for the trial. I had never met him, but he was on my side. There were grim and daring, beardy-faced men—men who had killed and would kill again—on both sides. But on my side there were many young men I did know. They, too, had come in from the hills. They had once been boys I had taught in high school. Now they were young men, and, for the most part, rural schoolteachers. These young men, perhaps for the first time in their lives, were carrying concealed deadly weapons. There was not a woman in this crowd. Several public officials—the county and district attorneys, the circuit judge, and the lawyers for the defendant—walked through the crowd of milling men. In a few minutes an announcement was made that the trial had been postponed.

The second date for the trial was set during the spring term of court. The jury was finally selected. The courthouse was packed with people. Three lawyers, one of whom had been in one of my editorials, defended Enoch Arvin. Though on the surface there was much good humor, if a firecracker had gone off in that courthouse I wonder how many men would have died! Lyles Lovell, District Attorney who fearlessly prosecuted Enoch Arvin at this trial, later remarked that he heard the click of pistols while he was prosecuting. About the men on the other side, I do not know how well they were armed. My guess is they were not optimistic enough to come to this trial without arms. I knew about the beardy-faced sullen men who had come in from the hills on my behalf. I knew about the thirty-odd young men—the Hampton boys, my brother, and all of the other young men that I had taught in school. If the firecracker had been set off, I know which side would have won in the bloody struggle that would have followed.

Dr. Madden testified before the court that it took a strong man to stand the blackjack blows that had lacerated my scalp. When he had finished his testimony, there was silence in the courtroom. When the trial was finished, the jurors retired to the jury-room. They were not long about making a decision. They found Enoch Arvin guilty. He was fined $200. There was not any jail sentence.

7

THERE had been a time when Kentucky teachers had to take what they could get. If they followed their profession in Kentucky, in the rural schools, they had to take sixty-five dollars a month for seven months per year. And in Greenwood County many teachers had fears of losing this, which was part of their livelihood. Now something was taking place. Something big was in the wind. They would not have to teach in the rural schools of Greenwood County. They could throw overboard the sidelines that supplemented their little salaries.

There were calls for help in the industries of Ohio, Michigan, Maryland, Pennsylvania. New industries were beginning to arise. Europe had burst into flames. Aggressive armies were on the march. Industry in America was beginning to boom. Rural teachers marched away with skilled and unskilled laborers. They went to Willow Run. They went to Dayton, Akron, Youngstown. They went to Pittsburgh and Baltimore. There was a great exodus North. Many went North to teach school. Positions for teachers were opening in the North as never before. Qualifications were not as rigid as they had been. The northern teachers, too, were going into industrial work. James married Betsy Sutton, whose hair he used to pull in Landsburgh High School. They went to Michigan to teach. Don Conway, Guy Hawkins, Olive Binion, Lucinda Sprouse, Ann Bush, and Budge Waters went North. Thalia and Charles Meyers went to West Virginia. Kentuckians were moving in all directions. Teachers left until the schools were almost depleted of their first-rate teachers.

The teachers I had worked with when I had first started teaching were all gone. I had held out longer than any of them, for I had held better positions and had received better pay. The youth I had taught, including the seventy-one rural teachers in Greenwood County, moved to better-paying teaching positions in the North, or they went to work in factories. I saw a generation of young, vigorous, excellent teachers that I had helped to make, disappear like ripe autumn leaves with a strong November wind.

And at a later date, these teachers were replaced by poorer-qualified teachers to whom emergency certificates were granted. The salaries were too low to hold the teachers with emergency certificates. In one year Greenwood County had four rural schools that never even started. Sixteen more rural schools had to close shortly after they had started, because the teachers quit and they could not find replacements among emergency certificate holders. Kentucky youth were without any schooling whatsoever! Kentucky youth were forced to grow up like uncultivated plants.

. . . O hypocritical, shortsighted, ignorant politicians, living in the middle of this twentieth century, allowing schools to remain closed for lack of financial appropriations, perpetuators of continued ignorance and future crime, I at least shall go on record to rebuke you! Tax us. Tax us to death to pay our teachers. Let them work upon immortal minds to brighten them to all eternity. We educate our people or we perish. . . .

8

I HAD not let Naomi Deane know what I had done. But on this Sunday evening I would tell her. While teachers were leaving their positions in Greenwood County for better pay in factories and mills in the North and East, I returned to the land they were leaving. I returned to my father's house in W-Hollow. My salary at Dartmouth High School had been the best I had received since I had been a member of the teaching profession. I had made $200 per month. But school salaries didn't matter now. I had other ideas.

I dressed in a dark, summer suit for it was better to wear dark on this June night when there was a bright moon in the sky. Because I had returned to my homeland and the land of my enemies. I put my derringer in my coat pocket and my .38 Special Smith and Wesson in the holster on my hip. My father, brother, and I never went any place unless we were armed. We didn't know where or when one of us would be attacked. My fight had been their fight; my quarrels had been their quarrels, and they would stick by me to the last.

There were four paths that led from my father's house to Landsburgh. I always went one path and returned on another. This evening I walked the Seaton Ridge and looked at the deep valley in the head of Tanyard Hollow. I'd never seen the country more beautiful. Little clouds of mist ascended from the valley toward the bright moon. The whippoorwills called to each other from the jutted hilltops. Twice, before I reached Academy Branch, I heard nightingales singing. The air was cool, fresh, and good to breathe. The land was filled with the freshness of spring. It was filled with insects' and night birds' singing. It was a night of music in a land that was poetry.

Maybe this was because I was more in love than I had ever been in my life. This was the time to live. It was great to be in love with the girl whose books I had carried down the street to school when she was in the seventh grade and I was in the ninth. I knew that I was going to marry her if I could. No money in my pocket but I had love in my heart. I had possessions too. I couldn't wait to tell Naomi Deane.

When I walked to the end of the ridge, I walked down a steep path that zigzagged back and forth down into the valley of rising mists. I hurried down Academy Branch and down the back road west of Landsburgh. This way I didn't meet too many people. On this evening I never met a person. Not even when I walked through a back alley to the railroad tracks. I crossed the railroad tracks and was soon on Main Street, where I hurried to the Norris' residence. I walked upon the porch and rang the doorbell.

"You've made it all right?" Naomi Deane said.

"Never met a person on my way here," I said, as I took the derringer from my pocket and unfastened the holster and gave her my .38.

"How lucky," she said. She took my pistols to put in a safe place so her young brother wouldn't get hold of one. Once he did get them and ran through the house among other members of the Norris family, screaming and pulling on the triggers. It was fortunate for everybody in the house the safety was locked on each pistol. This incident did cause some excitement among the members of this quiet-living and highly respected family.

"Plenty has happened in the last few days, Naomi Deane," I said. "I've got a lot to tell you."

"What is it, Jesse? Come sit down and tell me."

"I've come home to stay," I said, as I sat down beside her on the divan.

"But you will go back to Dartmouth High School to teach next September, won't you?" she asked. "You'll just be home for the summer?"

"I will not be back at Dartmouth next September," I answered. "My special work of teaching Remedial English is over. No more Remedial English in Dartmouth High School.

Not any other positions open there. Not that I know of. I just didn't reapply!"

"But, Jesse, what will you do now?"

"I'm going to raise sheep."

She was stunned when I told her this.

"I've bought three hundred acres of rough land," I said. "I've bought two hundred of the prettiest ewes you ever saw."

"How did you do it?" she asked. "I thought you were in debt."

"I was just about out of debt," I said. "But I've borrowed thirty-eight hundred dollars more."

"Oh, Jesse, you've never raised sheep before!" she said. "I wonder if you know what you're doing? You can teach school. You've been educated for that profession. But what if you fail raising sheep? Then what? You'll have a big debt to pay back, teaching school. It will take you at least four years to pay it back. That is," she continued, "if you get as good pay as you did at Dartmouth High School. We may not make much teaching school, but it is sure pay."

"Naomi Deane, why haven't we married before now?" I asked. "It's not because I haven't asked you to marry me. It's not because we don't love each other. How long have we known each other?"

Naomi Deane didn't answer. She looked at me but didn't speak.

"Six years ago I asked you to marry me," I said. "That was when I was Superintendent of Greenwood County Schools. You know the reason you didn't. Four years I was Principal of the second-largest high school in this county. One year I was in Europe on a Guggenheim Fellowship with my expenses paid. While this past year I did special teaching in one of the best high schools in Ohio. Yet we can't get enough ahead to get married. Isn't it time I try something else?"

"Maybe you're right," she said thoughtfully, "but you're taking a big chance when you leave the profession you know."

"You said once that we were intelligent people, and we had to face the facts," I reminded her. "That was on the evening I brought the poems here for you to read. That was six years ago. Now I have some facts."

Naomi Deane sat in silence watching me as I took an envelope from my inside coat pocket.

"In the nine years I've been employed in my profession," I said, "I've made an approximate total of ten thousand, eight hundred and thirty-two dollars. This makes an annual wage of a thousand, two hundred, three dollars and fifty-five cents. On a twelve months' basis, I have averaged one hundred dollars and thirty cents a month. Yet," I continued, as I turned from the paper to Naomi Deane, "I have an A.B. degree and I've done approximately two years of graduate work. I've spent approximately six years of my life preparing myself for my profession. I've been Principal of two large high schools and Superintendent of a large county school system in Kentucky. I've held one of the better-paying teaching positions in one of Ohio's highest-rating high schools. Yet you and I have not been able to get married, because we both could not live from my salary. Isn't that the truth?"

"That's the truth," she admitted.

"Then how intelligent are we?" I asked. "Teaching is not charitable work. It is a profession. It is the greatest profession under the sun. I don't know of any profession that is more important to the people upon this earth. I've loved it. I still love it. But I'm leaving it because it's left me. I'm goin' to raise sheep and farm and write a novel! Then," I added in a softer tone of voice, "I want to marry you. You're a city girl but I want you to come soon as you can to see my farm and sheep."

9

WHEN Naomi Deane drove her father's car up Academy Branch the following Saturday morning, I was waiting for her at Benton Campbell's garage. Benton lived where the passable road for an automobile ended. He lived where the north fork and west fork of Academy Branch united. Up either north fork or west fork of this small valley, there was a path that followed the small streams. Naomi Deane finally found a place in this narrow-gauged valley where she could park her car. Then she came from the car with a picnic basket.

"Good morning, Jesse." She greeted me with a smile. "Which way do we go from here?"

"This way," I said, as I took the picnic basket and we walked side by side along the winding path up the north fork of Academy Branch.

For the rugged acres that I had bought extended from midway of W-Hollow across a high divide into the headwaters of this valley.

"This is wild-looking country," Naomi Deane said, as we walked up the sunlit path between the towering hills, where multicolored butterflies we disturbed on the warm water-soaked sand made bright clouds on the morning wind.

In ten minutes more we came to a new sheep fence my father, uncle, and I had built from ridge to ridge across the valley.

"Over there is my land," I said.

"But how am I goin' to get across to see it," Naomi Deane asked, as she stood behind the fence looking over.

I put the picnic basket down. Then I lifted her gently over the fence. I picked up the basket and reached it over to her. Then I climbed over.

Here she looked at the stream of cool clear water that trickled down the little valley on whose steep banks grew tall gray-barked poplars, the ash, beech, oak, and maple. From the soft loamy soil beneath these trees grew blue and pink Ageratum, whippoorwill flowers, May apple, and blue beggar's-lice.

"Oh, Jesse!" she exclaimed, as she saw the clumps of wild flowers growing everywhere. Then she followed a little sheep path to the closest cluster of Ageratum.

"But we don't have too much time to spend in this valley," I warned her. "Not if we're goin' to get over this farm. We've got a lot of walkin' to do."

When the slow-moving June wind molested the canopy of leaves above us, leaf-sized blotches and pencil-sized stripes of sunlight filtered down to reflect shifting silver on the tumbling mountain water. Naomi Deane stood for a minute and looked at this. Then we slowly walked up a sheep path toward the high hill slope of pasture grass. In one hand, I carried the picnic basket. With my other hand, I held hers. When we emerged from the wooded valley to the pasture's edge, Naomi Deane saw something it will take her a long time to forget.

On the high grassy slope before us, she saw the flock of ewes with little lambs scampering among them. The lambs were playing like little children and crying for their mothers. Above the flock, where the high ridge shouldered to the sky, there was a great cloud of mist, beautiful and white as clean-washed sheep's-wool, that had risen from the deep valley where we had just been. This cloud of mist obscured part of the flock. We watched this cloud, sparkling in the morning sun, as it slowly ascended and floated out to space.

"Jesse, if you can only pay for all of this . . ." Naomi Deane said. "Honestly, this is beautiful."

"You've not seen it all," I said.

"You don't have to carry guns here to protect yourself, either?"

"Only to protect the sheep," I said, "if wild dogs make an attack or if a fox tries to carry away a lamb. That's the only reason I carry my pistols here."

Slowly we climbed the high steep hill. Every few minutes we would stop and look back at the timbered valley below where the stream of cool mountain water, where the sheep went to drink, was hidden under the tall trees. There were little clouds of mist still rising from the valley below us toward the sun.

"How can the lambs find their mothers?" Naomi Deane asked, for she was puzzled as she watched the lost lambs searching for their mothers.

"Don't you worry about that," I said. "If there were a thousand ewes in this flock and a thousand lambs, each lamb would find the right mother."

We climbed to the flock and we stood among them. Naomi Deane picked up a lost lamb and held it in her arms while many of the ewes gathered around us.

When we reached the divide we stood for a minute and looked over the part of the farm that lay in the headwaters of

Academy Branch. There it was, spread beyond us, along the ridge that shouldered to the sky and down in the deep valley where mists were still rising to the sun. It looked like acres that God didn't have time to finish with His great palette when He shaped the surface of the earth. But when He made the laws for His natural paintings to come with each season, He perfected His shades of soft green on these jutted hills for the month of June to contrast with the light-blue wind and the deep overturned blue bowl of sky.

"Are there any old houses on this place?" Naomi Deane asked.

"Only one," I said.

"I'd like to see it."

"That's where we are goin' now," I said, as I lifted her over another fence. "We are in the headwaters of W-Hollow now."

We walked slowly down the path, hand in hand, while the wild birds flitted from tree to tree above us singing their songs of spring. They had nests hidden in the leafy trees and they were carrying worms and insects to their young. Sunlight filtered through the canopy of leaves above us again and the waters of W-Branch looked like a white ribbon winding peacefully under the tall trees. Soon we came to the broader valley below where there were meadows and fields of young corn.

"This is the prettiest of all the valleys I've seen!" Naomi Deane exclaimed, as she stood facing the June wind that blew up the valley from the corn and hayfields. "Where is the house from here?"

"Just beyond that little point yonder," I explained, pointing toward the spot. "The house stands where Shinglemill Hollow comes into this valley."

When we walked a short distance down to the valley, Naomi Deane stood before the old house where we had kept hay, corn, and cows all winter. It was a house my father had rented and we had lived in when I was a child.

"This house is over a hundred years old," I said.

"But it's beautiful," Naomi Deane replied. "Look at those broad logs in it. Let's go inside and see how it looks."

When we went inside, where hay was still heaped in a

corner of the big living-room, Naomi Deane stopped suddenly to admire the big beams directly overhead, the stone fireplace, and the little stairway.

"This house could be fixed up," she said.

"But look over on this side," I said, pointing to the lean-to, where four cows had spent the winter.

"That could all be cleared away," she said. "Look at the well over there with a sweep! Look at these old flagstone walks and the hollyhocks still around this house. What do you plan to do with it?"

"Tear it down," I said.

"Oh, no!" she answered quickly.

"This is the place to live on this farm," she said, spreading our picnic lunch on an old table in the back yard.

"Not any modern conveniences here," I said, taking a bite of home-baked ham. "Four months out of the year one has to ride horseback or walk to Landsburgh."

"That doesn't matter," she laughed, pouring coffee from a thermos into two red cups. "Two generations of your people before you lived in this valley. You grew up here, Jesse. This is your valley."

"Would you like to live here?"

"Yes," she answered firmly.

10

ON THE night of October 12th, Naomi Deane and I started to Auckland to see a movie. I had just sold a poem, "Eternal Destiny," to the *American Mercury*, for which I received thirty-five dollars. I had something more to say to Naomi Deane.

"Let's forget the movie tonight," I said, just before we reached Auckland.

"Why have you changed your mind, Jesse?" she said.

"Look at the autumn leaves on the highway," I said. "Another year has passed. You're thirty-one and I'm thirty-two. Let's get married tonight."

"We've talked about getting married next spring," she reminded me.

"We've been having dates for seventeen years," I said. "Let's not wait until spring. I'm not teaching any more. My lambs made a substantial payment on my land. I'm in the sheep business now, and I've about finished my first novel."

"But I am teaching school, Jesse," Naomi Deane said. "I've signed a contract with the Landsburgh City Board of Education to teach this year. I won't break that contract."

"Don't break it. But let's get married tonight."

"If we get married," she said, "we'll have to keep it a secret. I can't let my people . . ."

"That's all right," I interrupted her.

After we got our marriage license it was past twelve midnight, and the new day was Friday, October 13th. After waiting all these years to get married, we were superstitious about this date. We drove back to Landsburgh with our marriage license.

The following evening I had another date with Naomi Deane. Before midnight we had made all the arrangements for our marriage. With two couples, our closest friends, as witnesses, we were secretly married a few minutes past midnight on the morning of October 14th. Then we drove back to Landsburgh, where she went to her home and I went to mine. I worked to finish my novel while she continued to teach her tenth and last year in the Landsburgh City Schools. Then her dream of remodeling the old loghouse became a reality.